Tapworthy

DESIGNING GREAT iPHONE APPS

JOSH CLARK

O'REILLY®

Beijing · Boston · Farnham · Sebastopol · Tokyo

Tapworthy: Designing Great iPhone Apps
by Josh Clark

Published by O'Reilly Media, Inc. 1005 Gravenstein Highway North, Sebastapol, CA 95472.

O'Reilly books may be purchased for educational, business, or sales promotional use. Online editions are also available for most titles (*http://safaribooksonline.com*). For more information, contact our corporate/institutional sales department: 800-998-9938 or *corporate@oreilly.com*.

Editor: Joe Wikert
Production Editor: Nellie McKesson
Interior Design: Josh Clark and Edie Freedman

Indexer: Ron Strauss
Cover Design: Monica Kamsvaag

Printing History:
    June 2010: First Edition.

ISBN: 978-1-449-38165-3

[LSI]   [2015-10-30]

CONTENTS

Josh Clark is a designer, developer, and author who helps creative people clear technical hassles to share their ideas with the world. As both speaker and consultant, he's helped scores of companies build tapworthy iPhone apps and effective websites. When he's not writing or speaking about clever design and humane software, he builds it. Josh is the creator of Big Medium, friendly software that makes it easy for regular folks to manage a website.

Before the interwebs swallowed him up, Josh worked on a slew of national PBS programs at Boston's WGBH. He shared his three words of Russian with Mikhail Gorbachev, strolled the ranch with Nancy Reagan, hobnobbed with Rockefellers, and wrote trivia questions for a primetime game show. In 1996, he created the uberpopular "Couch-to-5K"(C25K) running program, which has helped millions of skeptical would-be exercisers take up jogging.

Josh makes words, dishes advice, and spins code in his hypertext laboratory at *www.globalmoxie.com*. Follow him on Twitter at *www.twitter.com/globalmoxie*. Josh is also the author of *Best iPhone Apps* and *iWork '09: The Missing Manual*, both published by O'Reilly Media.

In many cases, all it takes is one person to make an iPhone app, but it takes lots more to write a *book* about iPhone apps. Many thanks to all the breathtakingly bright folks who gave so much time to share their design process with me, among them: Facebook's Joe Hewitt, Iconfactory's Craig Hockenberry and Gedeon Maheux, Gowalla's Josh Williams, Cultured Code's Jürgen Schweizer, Mercury Intermedia's Rusty Mitchell, TLA Systems' James Thomson, and ShadiRadio's Shadi Muklashy.

A whole bevy of editors saved me from myself time and again by pointing out technical errors, half-baked ideas, and far too many lame jokes. Thanks to Karen Shaner, the ringleader for this editorial effort, and to technical reviewers Louis Rawlins, Rob Rhyne, James Thomson, and Shawn Wallace who were generous with their advice and cheerfully unsparing in their criticism. Thanks to my friends Peter Meyers, Jonathan Stark, and David VanEsselstyn for their thoughtful feedback and encouragement throughout.

I'm indebted to Edie Freedman whose sharp eye and gentle guidance immeasurably proved the interior design of this book. Thanks, too, to Chris Nelson for shepherding these pages through the marketing and business labyrinth to get this book into your hands.

And finally, very special thanks to Ellen, who endured more than anyone deserves during the writing of this book and responded with nothing but care and support.

—Josh

Introduction

DESIGNING APPS FOR DELIGHT AND USABILITY

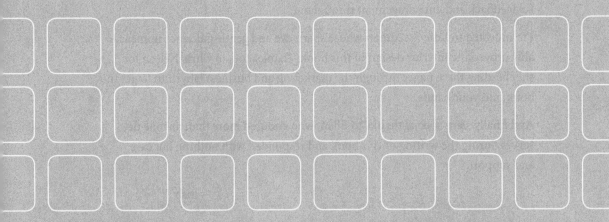

"WE NEED AN IPHONE APP." You've almost certainly heard that one at the office. Or in a conversation with chums. Maybe even around your own kitchen table. Since you're reading this book, you've probably even said it yourself.

You're right: you *do* need an iPhone app. Apple's glossy gadget touched off a whole new kind of computing—personal, intimate, and convenient—that has become both passion and habit for millions of regular folks. That's not going away; looking ahead, we're not going to spend *less* time with our phones, our tablets, our on-the-go internet devices. More and more, getting in front of people means getting on mobile devices, starting with the iPhone. It's a device with the following and technology to get your stuff out there with a rare combination of volume and style.

But First . . . Breathe

An iPhone app isn't an end in itself. It's not something to be hustled through, just so you can check it off your list. There's a whiff in the air of the go-go website panic of the 1990s, when everyone rushed to cobble together some HTML just to have a website, any website, with little consideration of either usefulness or usability. It was at once a period of heady innovation and herd-following mediocrity. The same holds for iPhone apps today. There are mind-bending creations to be found in the App Store, but the store is also chockablock with time-wasting duds. You can do better.

Set your app apart with elegant design. This means something more than pretty pixels. Design is what your app does, how it works, how it presents itself to your audience. Tapworthy apps draw people in with both efficiency and charm. They cope with small screens and fleeting user attention to make every pixel count, every tap rewarding. That means great app design has to embrace a carefully honed concept, a restrained feature set, efficient usability, and a healthy dollop of personality. All of this takes time, thought, and talent, but perhaps most of all, it takes a little common sense. This book distills observation of real people using real apps into plain-spoken principles for designing exceptional interfaces for the iPhone and iPod Touch. (Most of the advice in this book applies equally to iPhone and iPod Touch—and often to other smart phones, too. To keep things simple, though, I refer to iPhone throughout. It's okay with me if you mentally add "and iPhone Touch" after each mention. The iPad gets passing attention, too, but the size and context of its use make the iPad a whole different animal. This book focuses on designing for the small screen, leaving iPad design for another day.)

No Geek Credentials Required

This book teaches you how to "think iPhone." It isn't a programming book. It's not a marketing book. It's about the design and psychology and culture and usability and ergonomics of the iPhone and its apps. From idea to polished pixel, this book explains how to create something awesome: an iPhone app that delights. You'll learn how to conceive and refine your app's design in tune with the needs of a mobile audience—and their fingers and thumbs. Designing a handheld device that works by touch is entirely different from designing any other kind of software interface. Experienced designers and newcomers alike will uncover the shifts in mindset and technique required to craft a great app.

You'll still dive deep into the nitty-gritty of iPhone interface elements. This book explains the hows and whys of every button, toolbar, and gee-whiz gizmo. But it does so from the human perspective of what people want, expect, and need from your app. Throughout, you'll find design concepts explained in the context of familiar physical objects and real-world examples. Humane explanations for creating humane software.

All of this means that this book isn't (only) for geeks. It's for everyone involved in the app design process—designers, programmers, managers, marketers, clients—as well as smitten iPhone enthusiasts who are just curious about what makes this thing tick. Equip yourself to ask the right questions (and find the right answers) to make aesthetic, technical, and usability decisions that will make your app a pleasure to use. The book's aim is to establish a common vocabulary that helps geeks and civilians speak in the same tongue about the goals and mechanics of great apps. This mission is simple enough: when everyone around the table understands the ingredients of tapworthy apps, more apps will be tapworthy.

Advice from the Real World

Great apps seem effortless, and the best make it seem as if the design process came fast and easy. That's rarely true. No matter how sensational the designer or developer, designing a great app takes hard work and careful consideration. Throughout this book, you'll find interviews with iPhone superstars who each share their process, breakthroughs, and misfires. You'll get a behind-the-scenes look at the making of popular apps including Facebook, Twitterrific, USA Today, Things, and others. Early sketches and design mockups show how these apps evolved from concept to polished design—and not always in a straight line.

Looking over the shoulders of the best in the industry cemented the principles described in this book. These apps show how careful attention to both style and substance yields interfaces that are functional and easy to use, sure, but also creates user experiences that are in some way intimately personal. When did anyone ever say that about software? We are in a new era of the oh-so-personal computer, and that means we all have to think about software differently.

"We need an iPhone app." Yes, you do, but more specifically, you need a *tapworthy* app. Designing one begins with understanding exactly how and why people use their iPhones in the first place. That's where this book begins, too.

1

Touch and Go

HOW WE USE IPHONE APPS

AH, THE DAYDREAMS of the gentle iPhone app designer. His reveries roam a sun-dappled land where we users give his app our full and adoring attention. Our fingers swipe, tap, pinch, twist, and flick across the screen with the grace of ballerinas. We instantly understand every icon, tap effortlessly through every screen, take note of every button, and have easy command of all iPhone conventions and gestures. We understand the app because we study it and luxuriate in it just as much as the app designer does.

This, alas, is hooey. The cold reality is that most people don't give much thought to app designs at all, nor should they. The best app designs become almost invisible, and the controls seem to fade to the background to put the user's task or entertainment front and center. Creating this kind of understated but effective design is harder than it looks, but the habits of a mobile audience make it essential.

People often spend only moments at a time with an app, tap quickly through screens without exploring details, then move on to another app. They use iPhone apps on the treadmill, in the car, or in the supermarket. They glance only briefly at the screen so that they can plant their eyes on more urgent surroundings—the road ahead, the date across the table, tonight's reality TV show. They don't know all the standard touchscreen gestures, and they're not particularly interested in learning new ones. The meaning of your carefully crafted icons are lost on them, and, chances are, they find many of your app's features only by accident, if ever.

Don't despair. It's not that people don't care about your app. They may even swoon over it. In the long history of gizmos and gadgets, few devices have inspired as much affection as the iPhone. Along with its big brother, the iPad, the iPhone is in many ways the most personal of personal computers. Our collections of apps are a form of self-expression, where Home-screen icons are as telling as the contents of a handbag or the style of clothes we wear. We ♥ iPhone. And by extension, we ♥ apps. If all goes well, we'll ♥ your app, too.

But just as in matters of the ♥, so go matters of the iPhone. Attention strays, frustration gathers, misunderstandings mount. Even when users love an app, few will give it their full attention or try to understand every nuance. As an app designer, you're embroiled in this dysfunctional romance. You have to forgive and anticipate users' foibles while also crafting an experience that draws them in to explore further. Throughout this book, you'll discover strategies to do just that.

Most of this book explores the nitty-gritty details of specific interface elements and design decisions. Before diving into all that *"how,"* this chapter explores the *why*. In order to organize your screens, choose your features, or even choose your color scheme, you first have to know what you're up against. This chapter introduces you to iPhone users with a quick survey of the habits and know-how that people bring to the mobile environment. The next chapter will help you build on this broad profile to identify the needs of your particular audience and fine-tune your feature set. From there, you'll dive into all the considerations of crafting the interface for those features.

On the Go: One Hand, One Eye, One Big Blur

Go figure, but people use mobile apps when they're *mobile*. We use apps in all kinds of contexts and in a startling range of environments. This take-it-anywhere convenience is what makes iPhone apps at once so great to use and so challenging to design. Your app competes for your audience's attention—a tough battle to win when you pit a 3.5-inch screen against a big bright world full of oncoming traffic, live conversations, and this thing called human contact. Even when your app does have someone's full attention, it's likely to be in a distracting environment that could break the spell at any time—a crowded subway car, a lively restaurant, the family living room.

That means people are manhandling your app in one paw, with just one eye on the screen, paying only partial attention to your carefully crafted interface. They see a completely different app than the one you see as the designer.

This blurry vision of your app calls for careful attention to the organization of information on your screen, with big, juicy, can't-miss visual targets and a merciless spirit of editing—all topics you'll begin to tackle in the next chapter. But more than that, this context of when and where your audience whips out their apps also tells you something about *how* they use them.

Get It Done Quick

The distracted, quick-draw reality of how people use iPhone apps means that sessions get chopped up into quick sprints, wedged between other activities. When a friend suggests going to the roller derby on Saturday, you break from conversation to dash the rendezvous into your calendar, then quickly return to chit-chat. When the wait at the post office gives you a spare minute, you scan your email, Twitter account, and favorite website before it's your turn at the counter. Get in, get out.

The best apps fold neatly into the fabric of a busy schedule. This demands a special degree of efficiency in the interface—get me there in just a tap or two—but

So you're building an app to fly an airplane.

You might build this:

...when users really need this:

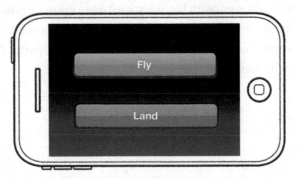

it also demands visual simplicity. In the context of scattered attention and a distracting environment, you can't *expect* people to have the time or patience to study the screen.

As with all things, there are exceptions. Some will spend hours at a time losing themselves in an immersive game. Others will spend long stretches engrossed in an ebook novel or tapping out thoughtful notes. But those very same apps—game, ebook reader, notebook—will just as likely be used for a 30-second sprint in the same person's next session. This means that even apps that encourage longer, more contemplative interactions should anticipate and design for quick hits. (You'll explore more about the specific mindsets that people bring to mobile apps starting on page 32.)

One Tool in a Crowded Toolbox

With all this sprinting, where are your users rushing off to? It's often to another app. When you're engrossed in the design of your own app, it's naturally the center of your attention, and it's easy to imagine that it will be your audience's center of attention, too: for them, it will no longer be an iPhone, it will simply be a device for running Acme SuperNotepad. As an iPhone user yourself, you know better. Every app is just one among many, a character in a big dramatic cast of which you are not the director.

Not only will people hop away to other apps, but those other apps can and will interrupt yours with push notifications. Phone calls will ring in and text messages will saunter through. Users will also expect to share content from your app with other apps and possibly vice versa. For app designers, this means you have to think about your app not in isolation but as part of a community of neighbor apps that will share space, communicate, and occasionally step on each other's toes. (Chapter 11 explores how your app can mingle with the crowd and avoid being the antisocial guy in the corner.)

This noisy throng of apps on your audience's iPhones means that you have to think crisply about your app's role at this party. The best apps have a focused job description. The more tightly you define the idea for your app, the clearer it will be to your audience when and why they should use it. Think of the iPhone as a toolbox with lots and lots of specific tools. The "right tool for the right job" rule applies here. When you assume that people will have lots of other tools in their kit, that means your app doesn't have to do everything. Choose an idea, focus it, figure out the minimum your app has to do to make it happen, and then polish, polish, polish. You'll learn more about focusing your app in the next chapter.

Bored, Fickle, and Disloyal

While your app has to collaborate with other apps, it also has to compete with them. iPhone users churn through a remarkable number of apps, offering up very little loyalty in return. If your app doesn't hold their interest, they have no qualms about moving along, which also means they won't talk it up to friends (sayonara to word-of-mouth marketing). This easy-come-easy-go mindset makes it all the more important, if you weren't already convinced, to craft a great user experience tuned to your audience's wants and needs. If you don't get it right in your first outing, most people won't look back.

App users have a big app appetite, downloading about 10 apps per month on average, but they rarely use these apps frequently or for long. Studies show that the average user never launches an app more than 20 times before abandoning it. Less than 15 percent of downloaded apps get so much as a glance over the course of a week, and two months after purchase, only a third of downloaded apps get used at all. At the bottom of the heap, popular but unsophisticated gimmick apps (fart sounds, gag IQ tests, ringtones) get used only a handful of times before customers give 'em up.

This may not matter to you if your goal is to build one-off novelty apps; in that case, you might even *expect* people to launch your app only a couple of times. Laugh delivered, mission accomplished. If you're trying to grow a following for your app, however, this is uncomfortable news. According to one survey, nearly half of all apps are downloaded based on a friend's recommendation. Loyal users spread the word, but few apps ever manage to create that big fan base.

Double-Tap, Pinch, Twist, What?

If you're an iPhone savant who explores every last obscure feature of your iPhone, here's a headline: Most people aren't like you. Spend a little time with an everyday iPhone user (or for a real surprise, look over the shoulder of an iPhone new-comer) to see just how little they've explored the standard iPhone controls and especially touchscreen gestures—the taps, flicks, and swipes that make the iPhone do its thing.

This disinterest in learning gestures might seem odd since the iPhone's touch-screen is one of the things that was so revolutionary about the device—the inno-vation that makes the iPhone so effortless. And sure, even first-time users get the obvious physical metaphors immediately: swiping screens, tapping buttons, flick-ing number spinners, dragging maps. No problem there; you can count on those interactions because they work just like manipulating objects in the real world. Drag it to move it, tap it to push.

Familiar physical metaphors work well to suggest touchscreen gestures, even for iPhone newcomers. User tests show that first-timers instinctively get how to swipe a picker menu to spin its dials, as in Lose It! (left). In the Air Hockey app (right), newbies immediately understand that they can nudge the mallet with their finger to play.

It's when you get to mildly fancy dance steps beyond taps and swipes that you start to lose people. Even some standard gestures of the built-in apps go unknown and unused for a big swath of people. This is especially true for *multitouch ges-tures,* the ones that require more than one finger. In testing sessions, many iPhone users say multitouch feels awkward, including even the standard pinch gesture for zooming in and out. When possible, most fall back to a single-finger option—double-tapping a map, for example, to zoom in—a reminder that it's best to craft your app for one-handed maneuvers. (You'll learn more about optimizing for one-handed use on page 58.)

Gestures, of course, are especially tricky to get across to users because they aren't a labeled part of the interface, and they're not easily discovered. In the built-in Maps app, for example, even self-described experts often aren't familiar with the two-finger single tap to zoom out. In other cases, custom landscape modes go unseen because users never think to tip the Stocks app on its side, for example, to work with charts. You can't assume that people will figure out your app's gestures no matter how simple, standard, or consistent. Treat gestures as shortcuts for actions that can be accomplished by another (though often slower) route, so that there's always a backup plan. You'll explore gestures more thoroughly in Chapter 8 and device rotation in Chapter 9.

We might forgive users for not instantly grokking gestures which are, after all, invisible, but even labeled icons and buttons go unrecognized, their meaning obscure to your app's newcomers. We're not just talking custom icons either. Even when icons are consistent across all the built-in apps, for example, uptake is slow on what individual icons represent.

Even some of the standard icons of the built-in apps cause confusion for newcomers. After several weeks of use, many users still don't realize the X icon in Safari's location bar can be used to clear the web address. Meanwhile, in user tests, first-timers often expect that the + icon, which is used to bookmark pages, will instead enlarge the page text.

Clumsy Fingers

Fingers are a dazzling engineering invention, capable of a whole slew of remarkable things: A finger can test the direction of the wind, plug a hole in a dike, test the temperature, and even direct an elevator to a specific floor. Fingers, however, are lousy at precision touchscreen interactions. A touchscreen stylus or a mouse pointer can easily hits its target within a pixel or two. In comparison, the finger is all thumbs. It's a blunt instrument that clubs whole swaths of pixels at a time and, to make things worse, obscures the screen so that when you're wielding this clumsy pointer you can't even see what you're pointing at.

Add a rushed and distracted user to the mix, and things get messy. People miss buttons, they tap the wrong target, they "overswipe" by tapping a bottom icon when they mean to scroll the screen. If you put more than a few tappable items on an iPhone screen, users will accidentally tap the wrong one sooner or later. Designing for touch takes careful effort and an attention to ergonomics that's new to many software designers. You'll explore these topics further in Chapter 3.

So, What, Do I Design for Dummies?

Impatient, distracted, clumsy, fickle, incurious, and uneducated. It's not exactly the description of an ideal dinner guest. But iPhone users aren't stupid, and neither are you. Chances are, when you're tapping away at your favorite device, you fit many of these descriptions yourself. We all have better things to do than scratch our heads over an iPhone screen. Our preoccupied iPhone habits flow naturally from the very concept of mobile apps—getting stuff done on the go—

Photo: Adam Frederick

and those behaviors are only reinforced by a device that's so deceptively easy to use that we can allow ourselves to be careless.

So why bother? If most people never pay conscious attention to your design, if they neither notice it nor think about it, then does the design even matter? Why sweat the details for users who routinely stumble past them? If users (like you and me) are so careless, then the answer must be a dumbed-down interface, right?

Here's the thing: careless ≠ dumb.

People don't want dumb from your app; *they want simplicity and ease.* We're all just trying to use our iPhones to work, to play, to learn, to communicate. The best apps get out of our way to let us do that; they become invisible. Great apps don't make us think—at least not about their interfaces. They embrace complicated tasks but shield us from all the complexity under the hood, making it effortless for us to glide through and accomplish our goals. Tap the Fly button to fly the plane, tap the Land button to bring it to earth.

Simple is hard, and effortless takes lots of work. But those adjectives are the hallmarks of great design. While users will, unfortunately, rarely exclaim over your app's elegance, they will *always* gripe about its inelegance. They feel the bumps, and the small screen only magnifies interface missteps. So yes, you really do have to sweat the details. Your mission in designing the user experience is to make sure that every screen and every action delivers delight, efficiency, and results. Every element of your app has to be tapworthy.

Is It Tapworthy?

CRAFTING YOUR APP'S MISSION

IS IT WORTH IT? That's the calculation running in your users' heads with every tap and swipe. Just by launching your app, users have to spend scarce resources—time, attention, thought—that are in especially short supply for mobile apps. What do they get in return? You just saw how mobile users churn through apps at the speed of distraction. Unless you meet their needs and, even better, entice them to slow down and explore, they'll keep on going. Tapworthy design starts with a firm understanding of your audience and their goals.

In the big picture, an app is tapworthy if it makes your users' lives better by helping them get stuff done, make them laugh, stay connected, fill downtime, or do whatever they otherwise need to do to be awesome in that moment. Tapworthy apps might be easy on the eyes, too, but the fundamentals of great design don't hinge on making things pretty. In app design, beauty derives from function, and every interface element has to be focused on helping your users do what they're there to do.

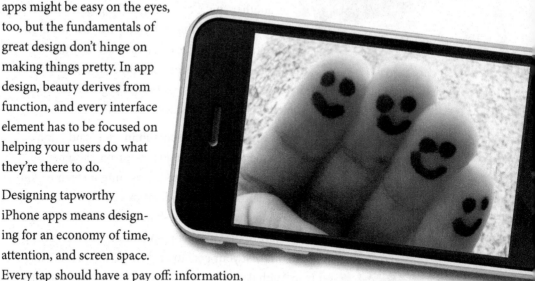

Photo: Peyri Herrera

Designing tapworthy iPhone apps means designing for an economy of time, attention, and screen space. Every tap should have a pay off: information, delight, a completed task, a sense of satisfaction. A great app rewards the user at every turn, from the first glimpse of its app icon through every tap and swipe. This takes both careful editing and definition of purpose. Clearly stating what your app does and how it's unique brings needed focus to the design process. You'll start to dig into the details of designing for the small screen in the next chapter, but before you start slinging pixels and making interface decisions, you have to start with more fundamental choices: *What does your app do . . . and why?*

There's Not an App for That

If only fresh ideas meant automatic success. "Build a better mousetrap," the saying goes, "and the world will beat a path to your door." Lots of would-be mousetrap millionaires have taken that advice to heart: Over 4,000 patents for mousetrap designs are on file in the US, but only about 20 ever turned into successful commercial products. The dense thicket of apps in the App Store is an even more concentrated example, with the vast majority—even worthy ones—languishing in obscurity and indifference. There are lots of reasons for an app to flop, but it doesn't help if the problem was already solved by another app . . . or perhaps the problem never needed solving in the first place. Our friends in the mousetrap industry learned the hard way that it's tough to improve on the no-frills snap trap; better to invest your efforts in something altogether different, something new and needed.

Photo: Angus Stewart

Great design is a worthy pursuit in itself, and I don't mean to suggest that your goal as an app designer must be App Store success, whatever that might mean to you. Marketing and design considerations do align, however, when you meet your audience's needs in an effective and novel way. If Apple's marketing mantra is "There's an app for that," make it your goal to find a case where that's not yet true. With the number of apps in the App Store swiftly approaching the gajillion mark, it's not easy to get a new app noticed, and you won't help matters by mimicking what a few hundred other apps are already doing. If you're building yet another to-do list app, tip calculator, or flashlight, be sure it does something different from (and hopefully better than) the throngs of similar apps that have already found cozy homes in the App Store.

This is Marketing 101, sure, but it leads to a crucial question: *what specific problem does your app uniquely solve for users?* Too often, people start from the other end of the stick, effectively asking, "What does this app do for *me*, the app creator?" Maybe there's an iPhone feature you're itchin' to work with, or your company has specific content it wants to get out there, or you have astounding skills in a particular technology. It makes good sense to build on your passions and strengths, of course, and those considerations are sensible ways to choose the broad domain for your app. But that addresses only what you (or your company) will get out of the app, not users. You have to bend your content, interests, and competencies to meet bonafide user needs.

Features, content, and gee-whiz animations may be crucial building blocks for your app, but they're not the *reason* to use your app. At the broadest level, it's the reason—the *why*—that makes an app tapworthy. People will use your app if it solves a problem, gives them a superpower, or just helps them unwind, but without a clear, persuasive vision of when and why people will use your app, you're just building a technology demonstration, a curiosity.

What's Your Story?

The best apps give users elegant solutions to precise needs—the more focused, the better. As you plan your app, think in terms of actual *use cases* or *scenarios*—brief story lines that cast the user as hero completing specific tasks in specific contexts. Like any good yarn, your app's story should answer "the five W's" that budding news reporters learn to pack into their lead paragraphs: who, what, when, where, and why. "Who" identifies the audience for your app, "what" identifies the actions they'll take, "when" and "where" zero in on context, and "why" describes their motivation and goals. By focusing on these story elements of your use cases—especially the *why*—you'll uncover your app's tapworthy conditions, the moments your users will need your app's superpowers.

Here's the hitch: in order for this to work, your use cases have to be plausible. There has to be an audience of people who not only want to do what you describe (the "who" and the "what") but more important, *they have to want to do it on their iPhone* (the "where" and the "when"). It's all too easy to lose sight of this mobile context. The iPhone is, after all, a full-fledged computer with an Internet connection and a grown-up processor capable of all kinds of complex tasks. For folks used to designing websites or desktop software, it's tempting to think of the iPhone as a "regular," if downsized, computer. While that's true in a technical sense, it doesn't translate to real-life use.

People behave very differently when using mobile apps on the go than we do when typing away at our desks. Just because you can put sophisticated software or a complete content reference on an iPhone doesn't mean anyone will actually want to use it there. The iPhone's form factor and relatively underpowered processor mean that the device is better for some uses than others. That means the "why" of your use cases has to embrace not only why users would use your app's features or content but why they'd use it on an itty-bitty handheld device.

What Makes Your App Mobile?

As extraordinary as your app might be in features, content, and technical razzle dazzle, it's only tapworthy if your users find it convenient, necessary, and easy to use in a mobile context. "Mobile" means on the go, of course, but in the iPhone context it's helpful to think of its meaning more flexibly as "away from my desk." Whether you're on the peak of Kilimanjaro or just curled up on your couch, both are mobile contexts—each with their own opportunities and potential distractions. What mobile context are you designing for? Why would you use this app when you're away from your desk or computer? Why is it especially convenient to have anytime-anywhere access to this app in your pocket?

Sometimes this is a no-brainer; some apps are naturally mobile because their whole purpose is to be used in the field. Take a gander at iBird Explorer Plus, a sprawling field-guide encyclopedia of birds and bird calls. It's an app for bird watchers (*who*) to look up info and birdsongs (*what*) when peeping at their fine-feathered friends in the wild (*when* and *where*) to identify a bird or attract one with a bird call (*why*). This is a niche audience, to be sure, but it's also a natural mobile app whose value is undeniably tapworthy if you happen to be a birdwatcher in the brush. By wrapping your five W's tightly around a mobile context, you've got the makings of a must-have app for your audience.

iBird Explorer Plus, like any field guide, is intended for the field. Its utility as a mobile app is naturally baked into its essential concept.

iBird is an example of an *accessory,* an app that augments an activity—a bird-watching expedition in this case—but accessories don't have to be so *explicitly* mobile. Other iPhone accessories like a calculator, guitar tuner, or recipe collection are just as useful on your couch or in your kitchen. These, too, are mobile contexts—nontraditional computing environments— where you can craft a convincing set of five W's for an app to extend and enhance another activity. No matter what the specific setting, consider how your app can take advantage of the size and portability of the iPhone to do something that desktop computers cannot.

First Person: Josh Williams and Gowalla

Gowalla is a location-based social network that lets you and your entourage check in when you arrive at a new place, a way to share activities, discover new places, and find out what's happening nearby. The app gives you a passport to fill with stylish stamps as you roam your city (or anywhere in the world). The app stamps your "passport" with a sleek icon for each new location you visit, and if you're lucky, you'll also find a virtual item (guitars, koi fish, cutoff shorts, you name it) hidden at the new spot. Pick up or swap these collect-em-all icons to build a pixel-perfect collection of virtual swag, a goal that turns the app into a global scavenger hunt.

Gowalla built on the demonstrated strengths of Alamofire, the company behind the app (and since renamed Gowalla). The inspiration for the app began with Alamofire's talent for building playful, collectible icons for Web and software interfaces. In 2005, the company created IconBuffet, a website for designers to collect, trade, and buy sets of icons for use in their own projects. This pixel swap meet led the company in 2008 to create PackRat, a Facebook game for collecting and stealing virtual cards sporting the company's signature icon stylings.

IconBuffet was the Gowalla team's first experiment with icon collecting. The website was aimed at software and Web designers, offering colorful collections of stylized icons. Although the icons were intended for practical use in interface design, the site's users instead treated them as collectibles and social markers.

Alamofire's PackRat game for Facebook capitalized on the IconBuffet discovery that a substantial audience enjoyed collecting icons. Soon, hundreds of thousands of users were playing the game to collect, steal, and buy icons through their Facebook accounts.

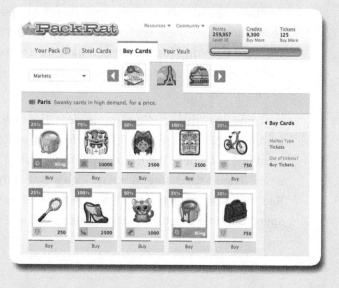

The success of the Facebook game and the company's unique skill for icon design led them to start thinking about what an icon-collecting game might look like on the iPhone—an idea that evolved into Gowalla.

Josh Williams is CEO of Gowalla and lead designer for the app. He shared the story behind the app's inspiration and evolution.

Big Talent for Little Icons

Josh Williams: People are drawn to the personality of these icons, and we learned that for the people who play our games, the icons are more than just game pieces; they're a fun representation of their social status. We learned a lot from the original IconBuffet experiment. We built that site thinking that people would come and collect these icons and use them for practical purposes in website designs. Ultimately, we found that 90 percent actually never used them for anything at all. They were just there to collect the icons for kicks. And then with PackRat, we learned that people would spend four, five, even ten hours a day flipping cards on

Facebook just to collect these icons. There's a big draw in this strong urge to collect and share these pretty little things. We started thinking about how we could develop a location-based game to use that social aspect and those game mechanics to encourage people to get out and explore their world around them.

We came up with a couple of game ideas, but they weren't really mobile at all, and nothing was really sticking. I decided just to get away for a week and went out to Tahoe in the fall of 2008, and I worked up some pencil sketches in a tiny, iPhone-sized notebook. The idea was that there would be these collectible icons layered on top of a map. We decided that this is what we needed to spend our time on, and we gave ourselves a three-month deadline.

Get to Pixels Fast

Josh: We have two giant walls painted in whiteboard paint. When we're trying to design a flow, whether it's on the iPhone or on the Web, the whiteboard marker just comes out. It's all very rough and very raw, and after we have an idea of what's going on, we get to pixels pretty fast.

I do a good bit of the design work, and I'm an Illustrator junkie. You'll find a lot of Web designers who swear by Photoshop, but for me, I do all my design in Illustrator. The vast majority of the artwork you see coming out of here is coming from Illustrator just because it allows a remarkable level of pixel precision. So we develop the broad strokes of the visuals in Illustrator—the colors, the button shapes, the overall style. Once those are set in place, we set design mockups aside and focus instead on the code.

Icons are Gowalla's primary visual building block as well as the app's currency. Icon design moves quickly from sketch to pixel as shown in these Gowalla icons of a GPS device and a tent. To keep the production line moving, the team collaborates with Iconfactory, the company that produces about a third of Gowalla's icons. Icons: David Lanham, Iconfactory.

Making It Work

Josh: The early design was extraordinarily bare-boned. We just wanted to figure out how to specify a location both on the phone and in the database so that you can "pick up" or "drop" an icon at a certain location. So really for about six weeks we were playing around with something that was completely utilitarian just to see if we could make it work.

When we finally got this prototype working, we discovered that it kind of sucked. For anyone who just picked it up, it made no sense whatsoever. We didn't see all the problems while we were designing it, because we knew how it worked and we knew what it was supposed to do. So we'd been looking at it through the goggles of how we *imagined* it would be used. But unless you had one of us there to explain how it worked, you wouldn't get it. The reality was that no one had really done anything like this before—this idea of mixing a virtual scavenger hunt on top of a location-based social network. We made all these assumptions that we thought made perfect logical sense from a design standpoint, but it turns out that a lot of those assumptions were off.

Try, Try Again

Josh: One of the things that drove us back to the drawing board was that the check-in button appeared and disappeared depending on how close you were to a known location. That meant people often didn't even know there was a check-in button, even though checking in was the whole reason for the app. We had thought that as you got close to a location where an item was hidden, it would be really cool to have an indicator tell you you're getting warmer, warmer, now you're hot, now you're there, and then you can check in. But the check-in button didn't actually appear until you were within the given range. It was terrible and really unintuitive, but the thing is that it made sense in the abstract: why display a button if it can't be used yet? It turns out that it's helpful to have something there—a dimmed button—to let people know that their goal is to check in and get an item.

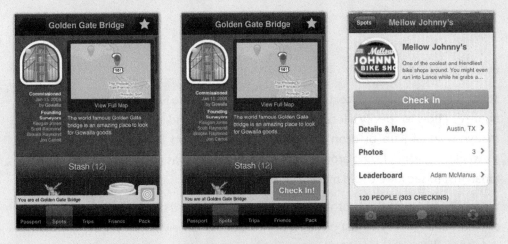

The case of the disappearing check-in button: in the first version of Gowalla, the app's check-in button appeared only when you were standing within 15 meters of a precise coordinate location. If you were just a few paces away (left), the button went away, appearing only when you stepped into place (middle). Later versions (right) made the button permanent and much larger.

On top of that, our original GPS logic for checking into a location was way too strict. So the app says there's an item at Stubb's Bar-B-Q in Austin, but I'm at Stubb's right now, and the stupid thing's telling me that I need to walk 43 meters southwest. So I've got to get up from my lunch and walk down the street? And then, maybe if I'm lucky and I happen to stand in the right 15 meter radius, the check-in button appears and I can tap it and actually get the item. We realized that it sucked.

Finding Focus

Josh: We knew there was potential, but the design was wonky and the GPS logic was off. The special sauce was all wrong. So we had to go back and revisit both from a technical standpoint and a design standpoint to really figure out how people would flow through the app. We took a really deep dive to consider what's most important in the app and, at the same time, pour some eye candy into it to make the best use of the iPhone.

During that time, there was definitely a lightbulb moment: oh man, we're building something really big and meaningful here, something more than just a simple game. We realized that game mechanics could be used to give an incentive to a mass-market audience to share their locations and encourage people to go out and visit more and different places. That really changed our attitude and made us realize that we had to be more aggressive about making design decisions to make something that would appeal to people beyond the gamer crowd.

Optimizing for the Primary Task

Josh: It was important that we make it as stupid-simple as possible to pull out your phone, launch the app, and check in where you are. That's the core experience we had to optimize—to make it as fast as possible. It has to be extraordinarily simple to choose your location and then actually check in. I'm a big fan of the "BFB" [Big F—kin' Button] and I think you always want to make it almost painfully obvious what people are supposed to do next. So on the detail view for a check-in spot, we've got a big orange check-in button. You can't miss it.

But before version 2, every time you launched the app, you got the Passport screen, the dashboard of where you've been instead of a view of what's going on right now. That was a problem. We wanted to put more emphasis on making it easier to help you check in, or to find where your friends are. So we made the Activity screen the first screen.

The Passport screen still has some problems. The screen displays the number of stamps and pins you've earned. If you tap that number, it takes you to a view that shows all those stamps or pins, but the problem is that it's not plainly obvious that you can actually tap that number. I'd like to improve the design so that we keep that data there, but make it more obvious that this is something that you can interact with.

In its original version, Gowalla's main Passport view (left) put an emphasis on stats without even hinting at a check-in option. A later version (middle) replaced those stats with a chunky check-in button and an inviting display of your icon collection. In version 2.0, however, the Passport screen was demoted to the end of the tab bar, and the Activity screen became the first screen (right), emphasizing what's happening right now instead of your past history.

Building for Exploration

Josh: Starting with Gowalla 2.0, we baked in some new features to let users continue to use the app beyond the 10 seconds that it takes to check in. We let people leave comments about their location, upload photos, see where friends are, and find where most people in the neighborhood are going tonight. We wanted to support this almost toy-like interaction where you can just play with it and go in different directions and tangents based on your current location. I like this idea that you can kind of get lost in it, that there's a sense of exploring.

Still, the core activity is the check in, and it has to be optimized for that. The challenge is to do all these other things without adding more cruft to the interface. How do we allow for all of those kinds of angles, but still keep that process super simple? Those are the kinds of things that are a continual boxing match around here. I believe that you can have a dense level of information but still keep the flow extraordinarily simple.

Colorful Personality

Josh: We're obviously big fans of bright, bold, even garish colors. Not everyone likes it. It's not the majority of people, but we definitely hear, "Oh man, green and orange. That's like the worst color combination ever. It feels like I just puked all over my screen and stuff, and what's with all the avocado?"

I get that it's not for everyone, but the flip side is that it's a talking point. It's our brand. Most people love it, but the people who don't are very vocal about it as well. It adds a level of personality, and people talk about it both for the good and the bad.

We've used orange historically in a lot of our products, and so that makes another appearance here. This time it just happened to be coupled with green. And I think that was kind of the outdoor, earthy vibe that we were trying to put across. You've got the green representative of getting out there and exploring, and orange . . . well, because we like orange.

Josh says the Outback wanderlust of the film *Australia* inspired the Gowalla logo (left). The original app icon (middle) was green to conjure a sense of the outdoors but was later replaced by a brighter icon (right).

Less Flash, More Function

Josh: You have to be careful with the eye candy, though, because if you have too much, you distract from the functionality. In some of the earlier design iterations, we used more gradients and more gloss and shine in places. Since then, we've systematically stopped using gradients in the app. We're using flat colors almost everywhere, except for the icons themselves. Part of that no-gradients decision comes from a style standpoint. We wanted to dial it back a bit. Another part of it, though, is that it also reduces our development time. It's less work for our programmers to go in and write code that uses these flat colors.

Our goal with the design is to create the right frame. In the end, we're celebrating these icons. The app needs to be the appropriate setting for those, and it should highlight them, not distract from them. You have to look at everything as a whole from the top down. It's not just about having a great design but a great design that's appropriate for the device or the environment it resides in.

Early on, we thought about making it look more like an actual passport where you're flipping through the pages and, you know, take the metaphor and just beat it to death. In some ways, that would be really cool, but the flip side to doing this rich immersive graphical treatment is that we realize that the iPhone's not the only platform we want to operate on. We have to keep in mind Android and WebOS and Blackberry. Whatever design we come up with has to translate to those platforms. We don't want the Android version to look like a bad hack of the iPhone version. You have to boil down some of your design elements to very basic, sensible things that can be reused from one platform to the next.

The App Doesn't Have to Do It All

Josh: We have a lot of plans for Gowalla, but lots of those features will wind up on the website, not in the app. There are certain things that are power-user enough or deep enough that it's not worth putting them into the iPhone experience. For us, we definitely want Gowalla to go beyond the iPhone even though that's the primary mode of interaction at this point. We want people to get in the habit of coming back to the website. When you show up at a restaurant and you're about to sit down for dinner on a date, that's not exactly the best time for an immersive Gowalla experience. So, when you're out on your iPhone, you just want to check in quickly and get back to real life. But later, when you have more time to explore, we want to invite you to come back to the website where you can dive in and interact in a deeper way with a different set of features.

Mobile Mindsets

As you ponder the features and mission of your app, always return to the mobile use cases where your app might provide a solution. A good way to do that is to step back and think about the reasons we launch apps in the first place. Of course, there are as many individual reasons to use the iPhone as there are iPhone users, but it turns out every mobile impulse typically boils down to one of three mindsets:

- "I'm microtasking."

- "I'm local."

- "I'm bored."

"I'm Microtasking"

As smart phones keep getting smarter, more and more of us are leaving our laptops behind, leaning instead on our trusty phones to keep up when we're away from home or office. Unlike laptops, notebooks, or messy collections of Post-It notes, our iPhones rarely leave our sides, making them handy vessels for bottling brainstorms, managing to-dos and itineraries, or capturing on-the-go information like expenses or billable hours.

Slowly but surely, we're learning to get stuff done on the small screen, but it's important to keep this miniature revolution in perspective: the iPhone can't match a laptop in many respects, and you shouldn't assume people will use it the same way. No matter how blazingly fast your fingers and thumbs might be, for example, delicately pecking away at a touchscreen keyboard won't win any speed records. The iPhone is better tuned for parking quick notes than powering through the Great American Novel. A new style of device encourages a new set of work habits.

The iPhone is a device of convenience and context, ideal for short dashes of activity—*microtasks*. The best iPhone apps emphasize quick access to ideas, contacts, tasks, info, forecasts, or entertainment. These apps thrive on simplicity, offering fewer features than desktop counterparts, but also making it faster and easier to get it down quick. Compared to traditional computer work of long, sustained work sessions, the best *productivity apps* are tuned for short but frequent hits, encouraging users to capture new information and ideas as they happen, typically to be processed and massaged later. The iPhone is likewise ideal for reading and even editing documents in the otherwise lost time of grocery-store lines or subway commutes. (This also happens to be true of the best iPhone games, which are typically designed for quick but tasty bites of gameplay, just a few minutes at a time.) There's room for more leisurely exploration, too, as you'll see on page 37, but in all of the iPhone's contexts, the device's quick-draw convenience lets users make the most of downtime, whether for work, play, or creative contemplation.

Productivity and reference apps in particular should be tuned to make the most of these intrawork interludes, making themselves tapworthy with efficient interfaces that are well-suited to this evolving style of work. As you consider your app's use cases, build the resulting features around microtask sprints of brief activity. Identify the recurring tasks that your users will perform with your app, and then polish, polish, polish. Optimize the design and workflow to make those tasks quick and effortless to accomplish on the go. Tapworthy apps get it done fast.

Tapworthy apps accommodate users in a hurry, optimizing for frequent, recurring jobs. The to-do list app Things (left) makes it fast to add new tasks from any screen: Just tap the + icon that's always parked at the bottom left of every screen. The built-in Calendar app takes a similar approach for new events, placing its + icon at the top right of all screens.

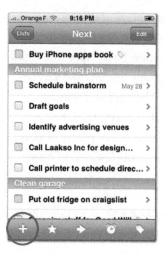 

"I'm Local"

We launch mobile apps to get the skinny on our surroundings: "I'm local, tell me what's happening around me." We've celebrated the personal computer since the days of disco, but the iPhone is the most personal computer yet—a device that knows tons about you and your surroundings. More than just a precocious phone, the iPhone is a personal sensor device tricked out with a camera, microphone, GPS, motion detector, and compass, all backed with Internet know-how. With sight, hearing, and touch, it lacks only smell and taste to round out the five senses (and really, that would just be creepy).

The iPhone is at once hyperlocal weatherman, restaurant radar, source of directions, know-it-all travel guide, and more. Trekkies, eat your heart out. Sensor-savvy apps turn the iPhone into the tricorder of Star Trek yore. Like a pack of pointy-eared science officers, we whip out our phones for a confident read on our personal habitat, using the iPhone's sensors to filter sprawling amounts of information for a local view of our immediate environment. Fascinating.

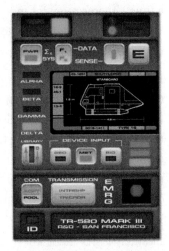

Get your geek on. The Tricorder TR-580 app lets Star Trek devotees fire up an ersatz tricorder. As packed with sensors as the iPhone already is, though, it turns out this novelty app isn't so far from reality.

Tapworthy apps take advantage of iPhone sensors to give personal context to tasks and info where appropriate. For most location-based apps, the whole goal is to put an appealingly nearsighted lens on a vast universe of data. The built-in Maps app is of course the most familiar example of this type of app, and the App Store is full of plenty of novel map-driven apps. A few examples among many:

- Yelp lists nearby businesses and dishes reviews from über-opinionated locals.

- Zillow is a drive-by home shopper's dream reference, mapping nearby homes for sale, along with property values in the neighborhood.

- HearPlanet is an on-the-fly audio guide, speaking descriptions of sites and landmarks around you.

As useful as these what's-nearby apps can be, the genre has quickly grown familiar—perhaps over-familiar—as general-purpose local guides have popped up faster than you can say, "Where's the nearest Starbucks?" With any app, it's important to stake out how it's different from the rest, but if you're playing in this crowded sandbox, it's especially crucial to do something beyond what the other kids are doing. As usual, paying special attention to defining a unique set of five W's helps you stake out your own tapworthy territory on the map. Think hard about how you can craft your location-based app around a very specific audience (*who*), content (*what*), or need (*when* and *why*). The highly personal context provided by the iPhone's location sensors encourages a peculiarly personal niche focus. As more and more geotagged data makes its way into the world, we're surrounded by data ghosts whispering information about our immediate environment. A creatively tuned iPhone app is like a set of special goggles for bringing *some* of these ghosts into view, letting your audience focus on a hobby interest or particular need.

Identify your audience, and help people connect with their passions (or maybe just a restroom at an urgent moment). These apps make themselves unique with narrow content and focused audiences. From left: SitOrSquat finds nearby public restrooms; Trees Near You tells you what type of trees are around you if you happen to be in New York; abikenow serves the public bike-sharing programs of Dublin, Brussels, and Lyon, telling residents where bikes are available for pickup and spaces available for drop-off.

Location-based map mashups are perhaps the most obvious way to put iPhone sensors to work, but it's worth thinking creatively as you plan your app about other ways that personal location can be put to use. The camera and microphone, for example, let you go beyond "what's nearby" to provide info about "what's in front of me." Audio-minded apps can analyze your sound environment for dictation, transcription, making music, or even helping you tune out extra noise.

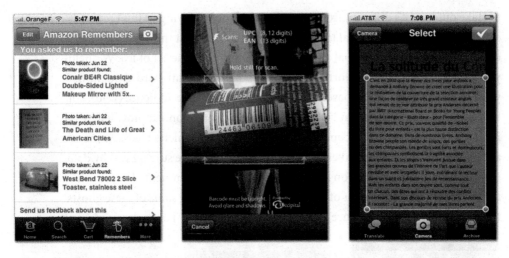

Shutterbug apps use the iPhone's camera to dish info about what users are looking at. Take a photo of just about any product with Amazon Mobile (left), and the app will identify it and provide an Amazon link for more info. RedLaser (middle) does a similar trick, but with bar codes; aim the camera at a bar code, and the app tells you where to find the best price. Babelshot (right) translates photographed text to and from scores of languages, a nifty trick for travel.

Sensor-savvy apps can listen in on the microphone to provide feedback and stow info. SoundCurtain (left) shuts out noise by playing ambient sound through the headphones, adjusting the volume based on the sound around you. Dragon Dictation (middle) listens to your voice to transcribe brief snippets of speech. Midori Soundhound (right) identifies songs playing in the background, even ones that you hum to it.

These examples feature the iPhone sensors as the main event, tied directly to the apps' key features. But there are also opportunities to provide more subtle interventions, providing location-based info, for example, in apps where geography hasn't been a traditional concern. In to-do list manager OmniFocus, for instance, you can use your location to show tasks that are tied to nearby locations, handy for tackling errands while you're out and about. Similarly, Shopper is a grocery list organizer that detects what store you're in and organizes your shopping list according to the order in which you'll encounter the aisles and departments of that store.

When you put a fistful of sensors in users' hands, it opens lots of opportunities to present tasks and information in entirely new ways. Tapworthy apps consider what it means to be local and act on that knowledge to change the app's interaction. Don't force it, though; think practical, not gimmick. Not all apps need to be photo-fantastic, audio-optimized, and geographically generous. But used in the right place, the iPhone's sensors can personalize your app to make its features more helpful and relevant.

"I'm Bored"

Let's not kid ourselves. All this talk of microtasking and local data analysis makes it sound like every iPhone-wielding citizen is a paragon of productivity. The iPhone is swell at getting stuff done, but your glossy gadget is even better at wasting time. For every productivity enhancer in the App Store, there are at least three productivity killers, and that's a good thing. The world shouldn't always rush rush rush, and well-crafted iPhone apps can help us unwind, relax, and find shelter for mindful moments. The iPhone is great for staving off boredom for the same reason it's great for microtasking: it's always with you, at the ready to fill downtime with easy distraction, giddy gaming, or even high-minded escape into the world of literature. What could be more tapworthy than helping you survive a dull-as-paste moment?

Even a quick peek at the App Store's numbers reveals that Apple's online emporium is more arcade than office. Games dominate, accounting for three quarters of the most popular paid downloads since the store opened. And it's no wonder: the iPhone is a fun, quirky, and genuinely delightful gaming device. Its limited but intuitive controls—the touchscreen and motion-detecting accelerometer—make iPhone games accessible to everyone, but fresh enough to grab seasoned gamers. With a huge library of games, most available for less than a pack of Slim Jims, there's no shortage of casual games to enjoy in bites of a few minutes at a time. We're hooked.

 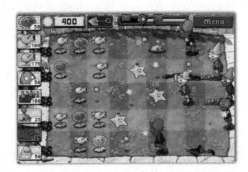

Casual games are ideal boredom busters. As shown here, games let you escape into worlds where cartoon birds fling themselves at an occupying army of pigs (Angry Birds, left) and where lawn plants defend against a horde of invading undead (Plants vs Zombies, right).

The boredom battle doesn't fall only to guns-a-blazin' video games. The antidote for boredom is simple enough: something that's better than what I'm stuck with right now. When we're bored, we want something to occupy us beyond the bleak reality of the Post Office line, the tedious meeting, the eternal wait at the bus stop. *We want something to do.* And, often, we want something to make us laugh—a fact that has, on mobile devices, shifted the whole nature of consumer software. It turns out that *millions* of people think that novelty apps for making fart sounds are a gas. The commercial appeal of toilet humor isn't anything new (just ask Chaucer), but it's the first time that it's become a full-fledged software genre. Until now, most folks bought computer software to do work, period. Now, on the iPhone, users want entertainment, too, even if it's occasionally vacuous or flatulent. On this device, people see software as content, not merely a set of tools.

This doesn't mean your app has to rumble with intestinal distress. But it does mean that you should consider how your app might give your audience some moments of delight and distraction, or even encourage them to slow down and lose themselves for a while. All but the most simple utility apps (like the built-in

Weather and Clock apps, for example), can give users something to explore or play with to pleasantly pass the time.

The common thread to boredom-busting apps is *exploration*. A great app gives you someplace to go, a world to creatively travel or distractedly get lost. That's why video games are such effective crusaders in the war on boredom, and why ebooks, news apps, YouTube, and Twitter clients are so popular on the iPhone, too. They all provide a story, an escape. But what might not be so obvious at first blush is that relatively mundane, workaday apps can provide a similar experience of exploration, too. Even get-it-done-quick apps can afford opportunities to slow down for thoughtful contemplation.

That's especially true for apps that collect personal information. Calorie trackers, fitness logs, and to-do lists, for example, are essentially catalogs of the user's past or future achievement. When presented in the right way, these apps transform themselves into personal-history video games. While these apps are (and should be) focused on micro-tasks for collecting and tracking info, an important use case is to allow users to massage that meticulously gathered data to see their progress and sort out where they're headed.

Health and fitness apps, like all apps that collect user info, gives users boredom-busting opportunities to explore their personal histories. Lose It! (left) lets you browse your calorie intake on weekly, daily, and meal-by-meal basis to review your weight-loss progress; here, a chart lets you explore your daily calories. RunKeeper (right) stores your running stats, letting you revel in minute-by-minute reviews of all of your runs. Here, a bar chart shows your pace for every minute of the run; tap a bar to see its details.

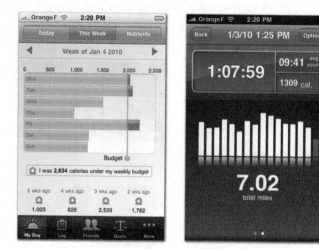

As important as it is to plan your app to accommodate frequent, rapid micro-tasking, don't forget the more occasional but equally important leisurely crawl through the app. Whether it's the user's own content, usage history, fresh news, community, or recommended content, consider what you can give users to explore. That's your boredom buster.

What Makes You So Special Anyway?

So you've got an idea of what you want your app to do, and you've got a pretty good sense of how and why people will use your app on the go when they're multitasking, local, or bored. You're off to a good start. But chances are, someone's already got an app that does something at least vaguely similar to what you've got in mind. How will your app be different? What will make your app stand out from the rest?

With a new angle, even upstart newcomers can get a toehold in territory already staked out by established apps. Consider the category of "check-in" apps that let you share your current location with friends. Loopt was among the first iPhone apps to do this, providing an efficient system for plotting your pals on a map, making it easy to meet up with them wherever they might roam. As more apps joined the category, the best of these fresh faces added a new spin that made check-ins more fun. Foursquare added a point system to the formula, turning the activity into an urban game where everyone in the city is a player: check in

From left, Loopt, Foursquare, and Gowalla all offer similar functionality, but each offers its own spin, providing three very different experiences and incentives for sharing your location with friends.

more than anyone else at your favorite watering hole, and you become its mayor, a competitive incentive for exploring your own city. As you saw earlier in this chapter, Gowalla tweaked the recipe by letting you collect virtual objects, pick up icons, and add "stamps" to the app's passport as you roam your city. Instead of scoring points, Gowalla focuses on serendipity and the surprisingly addictive discovery of unexpected objects when you go to a new spot.

All three of these apps focus on the same activity—announcing your location—but all offer distinctly different rewards for doing it. These different approaches—efficiency, competition, and discovery—give these apps distinct personalities which in turn suggest different audiences and use cases. Despite surface similarity, the three apps are unique.

What makes *your* app special? Some possibilities: a unique set of rewards or incentives; a tight focus on a specific audience; niche content that no one else can provide; a new way to visualize or present information; technology that simply works better; a big network of other users to play with; a solution for saving money over other apps; or a website or real-world component that enhances what you do or see in the app.

All of the advantages in that list are, in a sense, "skills." If you do any of those things better or differently from others, you have a hook. But it also helps to think about apps like we think about human beings. It's not just skills that make us want to spend time with certain people. There's also the slippery but irresistible matter of charisma. Personality and looks matter, too (sometimes more than we care to admit), and the same goes for apps. Much of this book emphasizes efficiency, focus, and substance, but there's no doubt that style matters. Even if your app does exactly the same job as everyone else, you make an impact if it does that job with a flourish.

Just go carefully. Like people, apps with oversized personalities are as likely to distract and disgruntle as they are to seduce. Overdoing it with animations and sound effects will irritate users who don't want to be bothered. If you choose to make your app's graphical style one of its main differentiators, be sure that the style isn't so noisy that it drowns out your app's actual info and features. Adjust the style and design to suit the content and audience, and be careful not to

Tapbots is an iPhone development shop whose apps push hard on personality. The company's apps do tasks that are mundane to the point of blandness—a weight log, a unit-conversion calculator, and a clipboard manager—but their clever interfaces are frankly adorable. Shown here from left to right, Weightbot, Convertbot, and Pastebot all feature retro-robotic designs complete with whooshing hydraulic sounds that make it, yes, *fun* to convert miles to kilometers. Design and whimsy are features, too.

become so smitten with your app's good looks that you begin to confuse form with function. Great design isn't just about aesthetics.

Wait, Wait, Come Back!

Your app's shelf life on a user's Home screen is exactly as long as it can hold that user's attention. iPhone owners chew through apps, gulping down their content, then tossing them out and moving on. Apps with a fixed amount of content or data are particularly vulnerable to getting jilted; once your users read your ebook, play all the levels of your game, or flip through all the flash cards of your vocabulary builder, there's nothing left to keep them around. If that's your intent, that's fine; some apps simply have a limited lifespan, and once the content is exhausted, that's the end. But if you're trying to create a long-term relationship with your audience, your app has to keep giving. It has to have a heartbeat to stay alive and remain tapworthy.

Certain kinds of apps have a built-in heartbeat thanks to the fundamental nature of their key features. Tools that organize personal info (to-do lists, calendars, expense trackers, contacts) keep people coming back as often as they need to check an appointment time or add a reminder to pick up the milk. Likewise, utilities that perform a common task (Skype calls, instant messaging, barcode scanning, weather forecasts, notebooks) continue to be useful as long as the underlying task itself is in demand.

For most of us, tools and utilities still account for the majority of our desktop software. Most folks use computers to work . . . to *do*. That doesn't hold so true for iPhone apps. Instead of tools, the majority of apps in the App Store are some flavor of *content app*—games, entertainment, books, references, novelty apps. When we use this category of apps, we're consumers, not doers. When there's nothing left to consume, we move along to a new app. For these apps, it takes more work to keep the heartbeat thumping. Sometimes that simply means fresh content. News apps, of course, have a bottomless and constantly refreshing reservoir of news, drawing users back regularly for more about the latest political brouhaha or Brangelina update. For these apps, as long as the content continues to appeal, users keep coming back.

Non-news content apps have to be a bit more creative, but the challenge is the same: to continue to provide fresh content. Games can offer additional levels through in-app purchases, which also has the happy side effect of steering additional cash into the company checking account. But new game levels are about more than just an opportunity to keep playing; they're markers of achievement.

In-app purchases and add-ons let users keep the good times rolling . . . literally, in the case of the Skee-Ball-themed game Ramp Champ (left), which lets you download new ramp themes for free or fee. Skies of Glory, an aerial combat game (above), lets players upgrade the game's gear for a fee. Here, a Zero plane will run you three bucks.

You've beaten the game and you're ready for more, even ready to *pay* for more. There's a collect-em-all mindset, and the game grows as you get better. That approach might seem unique to games, but other types of apps can offer a similar sense of expansion as achievement, letting you unlock new content as you master various chapters, challenges, or lessons.

Travel apps are especially road-ready examples of apps that benefit from content that expands and adapts to mirror users' activities. Lonely Planet Travel Guide, for example, comes with a single city guide to San Francisco, but offers scores of other travel guides and phrase books for purchase inside the app—buy a new guide when you're headed to a new city. The app's content collection expands according to your needs (and pocketbook), so it stays as fresh as your arrival in a new city. This collection of destination guides meanwhile memorializes your globe-trotting meanderings as readily as stamps in your passport—or vanquished levels in a game. Similarly, OffMaps lets you download maps and guides for offline use anywhere in the world, handy for dodging international roaming fees that otherwise make it ruinously expensive to use the built-in Maps app abroad.

Travel apps can expand their content as you expand your travel horizons. OffMaps (left) lets you download maps as you need them. Lonely Planet Travel Guide (right) offers new guides for sale inside the app, ready when you arrive in a new city.

This steady unlocking of content is also a staple of fitness apps. CrunchFu, for example, is an app for acolytes of the six-pack ab, a training program to help transform bellies from wishy-washy to washboard. The app gives you a daily training program to do a recommended number of crunches. As you complete each day, you unlock the next day's program, each one gradually more difficult until you finally gut through 200 crunches at a single go. These steady, game-like accomplishments keep users coming back while also encouraging a safe fitness ramp-up, an effective way to give the app a healthy heartbeat.

CrunchFu keeps users coming back with its progression of gut-busting training programs. Even when the program is done, though, the app's head-to-head "crunch battles" maintain interest.

Even so, CrunchFu's content is limited by the fact that its training program has a finish line. After you hit 200 crunches, you're done. Normally, when users finish an app's content, they'd amble off into the sunset, never to look back at the app again. Once again, though, gameplay saves the day. Even when the training program peters out, CrunchFu provides a game to hang on to some portion of its users. The app offers "battles," head-to-head crunch competitions with other CrunchFu users. No matter where you are in the training program—beginning, finished, or somewhere in between—the app lets you find someone else at your fitness level and challenge them to see who can do the most crunches, earning points as you go. Human contact for the win!

It might not look like it as we tap away at our iPhones, off to ourselves and oblivious to the world, but we are irresistibly social creatures. iPhone or not, we're drawn to activities that let us communicate, compete, or contribute. Like a physical place, apps that bustle with the activities of other people feel alive. Community features give an app life beyond its fixed set of content. Even after you've mastered a game, the chance to test your skills against other players gives you an incentive to keep playing. For other apps, sharing content with friends and seeing what others are saying lets your users provide an ever-replenishing supply

of fresh content. Among its many other features, for example, the Movies app by Flixster pools reviews by regular-Joe moviegoers. You can follow the advice of the grand mass of public reviews, or just listen in on what your friends have to say. Yelp adds similar value by encouraging customer reviews for local businesses, and Amazon, of course, does the same with reviews of its products. In all of these cases, community-driven reviews give extended life to the basic content provided by the app developers.

You don't have to build this stuff yourself; you don't even need your own community. Just plug your app into the established social networks, where millions of people are already talking. Facebook and Twitter both provide easy platforms for sharing content from iPhone apps. For games, social networks like OpenFeint or Apple's Game Center let developers plug high-score leader boards and head-to-head challenges into their apps.

The idea is to wrap secondary features around your app's main content to enhance and extend its value. The apps described so far have done this by growing or sharing that primary content. But another effective, if less elegant, approach is simply to bolt on complementary tools. The Typography Manual, for example, is an app for budding graphic designers. It's essentially an ebook spelling out the history of typography, tracing its letterforms and laying out its technique. While the app does a fine job of dotting the i's and crossing the t's of its subject, it remains like any book, a fixed set of words and images. But the app also throws in a handful of tools that are useful to folks who sling type for a living. There's a font ruler, some font-size calculators, and a comprehensive reference for easy-to-forget HTML codes for special characters. Even after users finish reading the book, these add-on utilities keep them coming back by continuing to provide some modest value.

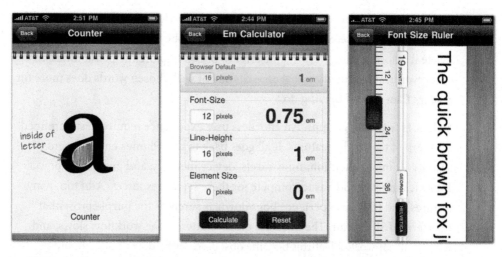

In addition to its reference content—a visual typography glossary (left), an ebook, and an HTML reference—The Typography Manual includes a font-size calculator (middle) and a font ruler (right) to provide lasting utility even after you've consumed the app's content.

As with all things iPhone, however, use restraint. Think hard about the features that can give your app extended longevity, but don't just pad the app with features willy-nilly. It's often a useful service to your audience to design your app for a steady, long-lasting heartbeat. But as you do this, it's even more important to keep the app simple and focused.

Throw Out the Babies, Too

The initial planning for your app should be big and bold. Be expansive in how you think about its features, the audience it should address, the opportunities to set the app apart from the rest. We're still in the early days of exploring the possibilities of devices like the iPhone, and invention is important. Let the crazy ideas roll. Fill the drawing board with rainbows and unicorns, and drum up any feature you can think of that will make your app do things no app has ever done before.

And then, take the features on your lovingly crafted wish list and throw most of them out.

"Murder your darlings," advises the favorite writers' adage, counseling flowery wordsmiths to be ruthless about trimming flabby text. "Whenever you feel an impulse to perpetrate a piece of exceptionally fine writing," said the wag behind the homicidal phrase, Sir Arthur Quiller-Couch, "obey it—wholeheartedly—and delete it before sending your manuscript to press." Explore the possibilities, in other words, but remember that an economy of well-chosen words does more for readers than literary derring do.

So it goes with mobile apps. An effortless user experience requires a streamlined selection of tapworthy features. It all goes back to the iPhone's environment of scarcity—limited attention, time, pixels, device memory, and processing power. Every feature you add has to compete for these scarce resources. Add too many features, and the app experience bogs down as surely as the purple prose that exasperated Sir Arthur. The interface grows cluttered, the workflow slows, and potentially tapworthy features become obscured. Instead, your app should be tightly focused on a unique task and a handful of use cases. While you don't have to throw out all of your rainbows and unicorns, you should spare only the small handful your users will need to get the job done. *Think big but build small.*

To start, identify the single task that's most important to your app. Go back to the most important use case you've crafted for your app—the who, what, when, where, and why—and identify the recurring task your users will most frequently need to tackle to knock out that use case. If your app is a to-do list, the key task might be adding a new to-do item. If it's a calendar, it might be scanning the day's events. All of the design work you do from here will flow from this decision. Once you've identified the key activity, think hard about what your app can do to help your users microtask that activity in a hurry.

Secondary tasks will naturally emerge from that primary activity. Once you can add items to your to-do list app, for example, you need to be able to review, edit, and check them off, too. Keep it simple, though. Figure out the bare minimum required to bring your idea to life, then optimize the experience with delight, efficiency, and polish.

The app doesn't have to be crammed with features and functions to be the best in its category. In fact, a lean diet of features often delivers a better user experience that's more carefully tailored to specific needs and use cases. You might even pare the entire app down to answer a single important question for your audience.

"Umbrella: The Simplest Weather Forecast" is a disarmingly simple app approaches weather forecasts by answering the question, "Do I need an umbrella today?"

The less-is-more approach probably doesn't fit your gut instinct about how to build a great app. Developers of websites and traditional desktop software are accustomed to waging a features–arms race with competitors. Enterprise software outfits evangelize the idea that the more features you have, the better the software. Marketing for new versions trumpets all the new-fangled gizmos that have been tacked onto the update. The benefits of feature pile-on are dubious on the desktop—the result is often bloated software—but the effects of an overstuffed iPhone app are downright hobbling. Don't assume that your app has to do *everything* related to your content domain. Pick your slice of targeted work to do and let other apps pick up other slices. (In Chapter 11, you'll learn how you can make your app fit into this larger iPhone ecosystem.)

Of course, the trick is picking the *right* slice, the appropriate mix of features for your selected audience. As you winnow features, merrily murdering darlings along the way, stay tuned to the needs of the majority of your users. Choose the features that *most* of your users will need most often, and don't fret over the esoteric needs of a minority fringe. That's common sense, sure, but the fringe is often the noisiest, the power users who gripe in iTunes reviews that your alarm-clock app is a bust if it doesn't display seconds in atomic clock units. *No caesium-133 radiation cycles? FAIL. I want my 99 cents back!* Simmer down, Marie Curie. There's nothing wrong with caesium-133 radiation cycles, but of course they have no meaning to a general audience. That said, the fringe can sometimes tip you off to a potential niche app. Who knows, there may very well be a tidy market for an atomic alarm clock app—in which case, the fringe *is* your audience, and mainstream users become the fringe. Form a clear picture of your audience and tailor your app's features to the majority of those users.

At the same time, in all this paring down, be sure that you're still giving people at least a minimum feature set to accomplish what they expect of your app.

When the first version of the Facebook app launched with a limited feature set, Facebook users were vocally disappointed, even angry, that essential features were missing like browsing friends' photos, writing on their walls, or commenting on status updates. Later versions added these features, but the app maintained its keep-it-simple focus by dividing the Facebook app into "sub-apps," a concept explored in the Facebook case study on page 236. As always, the lesson is: know your audience and their needs. Give them *just enough* to do what they need to do with your app.

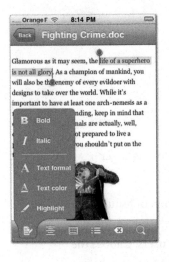

Quickoffice Mobile Office Suite is an example of careful feature pruning. By iPhone standards, it's a complex and ambitious app. Quickoffice lets you read, create, and edit Microsoft Word and Excel files. The desktop versions of Word and Excel are packed with a jillion features and functions, and it would be unwieldy—and probably impossible technically—to pack all of them into an iPhone app. The gang at Quickoffice had to do iPhone triage, supporting only features that would be most frequently used in a mobile context. They made the safe assumption that when you're thumb-tapping the text of a word-processing document, for example, you probably won't futz with formatting complex table layouts, which is work you'd more likely fine-tune later on the desktop. So, while Quickoffice can display tables and images in a document you receive, it doesn't let you edit them—a fair trade-off. Meanwhile, more common formatting options, like bold and italic text, bullet lists, and text alignment are always just a tap away. The result is a useful, compact app that provides all the basics of document editing while gracefully sidestepping more advanced (and unlikely) use cases.

Can't I Get That on the Web?

If you're creating a companion app for your website, chew over how the app might improve on the original site. How is the app better than using Safari, the built-in browser, to view the content online? From your perspective, sure, there are distinct *marketing* advantages to creating a separate app. Repackaging your website as an app gives you another outlet, a spot in the much-trafficked App Store. And homesteading an icon on a user's phone keeps the content front and center in a way that a Safari bookmark does not. But that's all about *you,* not your audience. If you're a website publisher designing a companion app, think hard about how you can make the app improve on the mobile Web experience, not just duplicate it. Here are a few tips:

Efficiency is a feature. One of the most important user needs in the mobile context is efficient access. The best website redux apps improve on the interfaces of their Web counterparts. This is especially the case for apps whose companion sites don't yet have a mobile version. Authoritative movie website IMDb, for example, launched an elegant iPhone app for navigating its sprawling film database before ever launching a mobile Web version. The full-sized website at *www.imdb. com* is a hassle to navigate on the small screen, but the IMDb app is a pleasure to use—compact, speedy, and ready to settle pop-culture bets at a moment's notice.

Like most websites, *www.imdb.com* (left) is accessible via Safari, but with a constant dance of pinching and zooming to read each page. Meanwhile, the IMDb app (right) formats the vast site for the small screen, making it a cinch to resolve forehead-slapping "who *is* that?" movie moments.

Native polish makes content shine. A polished interface can set apps apart even from websites especially designed for mobile use. Although the newspaper *USA Today* already had an iPhone-optimized website, for example, the USA Today app provides an even better experience for speeding through news, photos, sports scores, and weather. (See page 90 for a case study of the app's interface development.) While the content for both app and website are essentially identical, the app is custom fit to the iPhone screen with elegant, responsive controls that only a native app can deliver. (Standard web technologies can come mighty close, though. Website owners interested in developing an iPhone app might start by developing an iPhone-targeted website, where most of this book's design principles also apply. *Building iPhone Apps with HTML, CSS, and JavaScript* by Jonathan Stark is a recommended resource on the subject.)

A well-designed app can improve on even a savvy mobile website. The *www.usatoday.com* mobile site (left) is cell phone-sized and built for quick loading over mobile networks. But the USA Today iPhone app (right) provides a much more efficient experience for scanning content and images, packing lots of content into each screen and delivering a strongly branded interface that never distracts.

Save it for later. Collecting a stockpile of offline content is an especially tap-worthy feature for mobile content apps. A common difference between a great app and its website counterpart is that the app *caches* content, stashing it on the device for offline browsing. Many news apps, like USA Today, grab all the latest articles when online, saving them so that you can read the news later when you're on a plane, in the subway, or otherwise Internet indisposed. Other apps cache individual pages on demand, adding an interesting new wrinkle to web browsing. Wikipanion Plus, for example, is an app for browsing Wikipedia. Turn on the app's "queue" feature and instead of jumping straight to a new article when you tap a link, Wikipanion adds it to a wanna-read list, the Queue screen. The app downloads these articles in the background, so they're ready when you are—useful over slow network connections or for later, when you have no connection at all. (The feature is also especially well-suited to Wikipedia articles, which are so densely sprinkled with tantalizing links that it requires real discipline to read an article to the end without leaping away. The queue feature lets you line up links to follow later.)

Wikipanion Plus improves on regular web browsing with its clever caching and queuing features. When you tap and hold a link (left), Wikipanion saves the page for later reading instead of opening it immediately. You can review any of these saved pages from the app's Queue screen (right), where downloaded pages are displayed for offline reading.

The upshot: well-considered features and presentation, carefully crafted for mobile scenarios, can turn even content that's freely available online into a tapworthy app for your chosen audience.

Touchpoints

✓ Focus on "the five W's" to uncover your app's tapworthy conditions.

✓ Focus your app's features for away-from-the-desk contexts. Consider the mobile mindsets: microtasking, local, and bored.

✓ Identify what makes your app different from similar apps. "Skills" and "charisma" set apps apart.

✓ Give your app a long shelf life by replenishing content or building community.

✓ Think big, but build small. Give users *just enough* to do what they need.

✓ When building a website companion app, consider how to improve on a mobile website, not just duplicate it.

3

Tiny
Touchscreen

DESIGNING FOR SIZE AND TOUCH

AT FIRST BLUSH, the iPhone's tiny size might seem its biggest design challenge. When you're accustomed to creating websites or desktop software for monitors at least a foot across, 3.5 inches is mighty stingy. Yet while designing with a limited supply of pixels is a demanding part of the job, leaving it at that would suggest that your role is only to create efficient screens. The challenge turns out to be more subtle than that, because the iPhone isn't just small: it's handheld and works by touch. That means you're doing something more sophisticated than organizing pixels.

You're designing a physical interface that will be explored by human hands, directly manipulated in a way that desktop software never is. Of course, there's nothing *literally* physical about your app. Your interface is just a virtual representation drawn by so many flickering liquid crystals. But the way it's *used* is physical. Unlike phones or desktop computers, the iPhone has practically no physical interface of its own—no keyboard or mouse, just the single Home button. The device is a blank slate, a palm-sized slab of glass onto which you, the app designer, impose whatever interface you might dream up. You define the physical experience of the device. Your app's buttons may be virtual, but they nevertheless require direct touch and define the device in a very physical way.

Photo: Oscar Alonso

This means your project is not only a challenge of visual and graphic design but of industrial design, too. Just as surely as if you were soldering circuit boards, molding plastic, or shuffling die-cast buttons, you're designing an app to be man-handled—or at least hand-handled. There are honest-to-god ergonomic issues to account for. Considerations of size and touch combine in iPhone design to present new challenges for interaction designers.

You've already seen how manner and mind-set shape the broad environment for your app and the features you should pursue. The rest of this book deals with a much more immediate set of constraints: the form and conventions of the device itself. This chapter kicks off the process by reviewing the big picture of designing for a tiny touchscreen. You'll explore how fingers and thumbs roam the screen, discover some ergonomic guidelines for comfortable tapping, and wrap up with some good practices for tap-friendly screen layouts.

A Physical Feel

More than simply how the app looks, you have to consider how it *feels*. How well does your interface work when used one-handed? Are the most common tap targets within easy thumb range—and what about lefties? Are buttons chunky enough for easy tapping, or does it take surgical precision to hit them?

The tactile nature of iPhone apps is reinforced by the powerful illusion of real-world physics conjured by the iPhone operating system. The iPhone's interactive metaphors are all about tapping, sliding, and flicking—direct manipulation of onscreen objects that respond with lifelike realism. Flick a scrolling list and watch it slow as "friction" takes hold. Fling it even harder against the top or bottom of the screen and the thing actually bounces. Tug the screen down and watch it snap back into place with rubber-band realism. Everything on the iPhone responds to the familiar rules that apply to the everyday physical world: inertia, momentum, friction, elasticity, follow through. The result is an irresistible impression that you're working with real-world objects.

Don't break that spell. More than just tending to appearances—*wow, it looks so real!*—creating an interface that "feels" like an actual device matches expectations created by the iPhone operating system as well as the concrete reality of tapping away at the hardware itself. (Chapter 8 has more on phone physics and visual feedback, starting on page 257.) Some apps even go all the way with the physical-device metaphor by mimicking the look of familiar gadgets. There are undeniable usability benefits to cribbing a real-world interface that's been used for decades or even centuries, especially when your app performs a similar role to that of the original gizmo. Few will scratch their heads to figure out how to make a call with the built-in Phone app. Its push-button interface conveys its meaning immediately (even three-year olds, for better or worse, know how to dial a phone), and the keypad layout also has the benefit of proven ergonomic success in a handheld device.

Interfaces that mimic physical devices benefit from intuitive familiarity and proven ergonomics. Here, Phone and Rowmote, respectively, crib the telephone keypad and Apple's physical remote control.

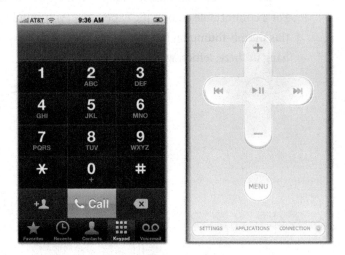

You'll find more discussion of interface metaphors in Chapter 6, but whether or not your app actually apes the look of a mechanical device, that's exactly what it is in practice. Your app's screen design is the sole interface for the iPhone, a gizmo that works by hand, and you have to address the demands of a physical device. When fingers do the walking, designers have to clear the way for them.

Organizing the layout of an iPhone interface means organizing for fingers. More precisely, it means organizing for *the thumb*, since that's the digit that gets the workout when you work the iPhone one-handed. The iPhone is sized perfectly for use in a single hand, allowing your thumb to sweep easily from one corner to the other with only a modest stretch. And because you *can* use the iPhone with one hand, most of us very often do. Whether you're hoisting a coffee, hauling a baby, or eating your lunch with that other hand, you can still keep tapping away with one thumb to answer email, make calls, or browse the web. Your design should optimize for this one-thumbed tapping.

Rule of Thumb

Thumbs are marvelous. It's our thumbs, along with our affection for celebrity gossip, that separate us from the beasts, but they do have limited range and flexibility. While a thumb can manage to sweep the entire screen, only about a third of the screen is in truly effortless territory—at the side of the screen *opposite* the thumb. For a comfortable ergonomic experience, you should place primary tap targets in this thumb-thumping hot zone. (We'll focus for now on right-handed users, but hang in there, lefties, we'll get to you in a sec.)

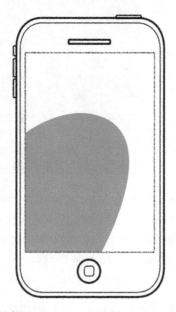

The comfort zone for the right thumb falls on the opposite side of the screen, at the left edge and bottom of the screen. (The top right and bottom right corners are the toughest thumb zones for right-handed users.)

That's an important reason why toolbars and tab bars always go at the bottom edge of the iPhone screen—the opposite of what we're accustomed to for traditional screen interfaces. Desktop software conventions put menus at the top of the screen or window, and websites typically position primary navigation at the top of pages. Our limited thumbspan, however, flips that convention on its head. Navigation and primary tap targets sink to the bottom on the iPhone. This tap zone gives you hints about how to organize the visual hierarchy of tap targets. Frequently used buttons and navigation tabs should occupy the bottom left of the screen, while lesser used buttons and those that make changes to data can be tucked safely away at top right. The Edit button for changing, deleting, or reordering list items, for example, is conventionally placed at top right, putting it in easy view but also in an isolated and relatively difficult spot to tap, making accidental changes less likely.

The standard iPhone toolbar (left) and tab bar (right) always go at the bottom edge of the iPhone screen in convenient thumb-tapping range. To-do list app Things (left) puts the Edit button at top right safely out of accidental tap range. At right, YouTube's left-edge video thumbnails are chunky tap targets in the hot zone of right-handed users.

Let your thumb point the way in laying out your screens according to the most common use cases for your app. Twitterrific, an app for Twitter users, organizes its buttons according to this thumb-thinking hierarchy. The two left toolbar icons respectively refresh and post tweets, reflecting the two most common Twitter-related activities, reading and posting. When you want to do something with an individual tweet, tapping the toolbar's asterisk icon summons a set of buttons whose thumb convenience likewise reflect their importance—commonly tapped buttons at left, less common at right. "We think a lot about where things get placed based upon ergonomics," explains Craig Hockenberry, Twitterrific's lead developer. "The Delete button is off to the right, the hardest location to tap for right-handed users, and we put other options where your thumb has to work less in order to get to more commonly used actions." (For more about Twitterrific's design, see the developer close-up on page 205.)

Twitterrific orders its toolbar icons so that the most frequently tapped buttons appear in the right thumb's hot zone, highlighted here in red.

Happily, this organization happens to coincide with the way we read—our eyes naturally scan onscreen menus from left to right, just like the written word. So, for right-handed use at least, physical and visual considerations align. But what about lefties? The hot zone for the left thumb is, naturally, the mirror image of that of the right, which means left-to-right organization makes for awkward tapping for southpaws. When you optimize for right-handed people—about 85 to 90 percent of users—you're actively inconveniencing left-handed folks (as well as righties who switch to the left hand while they scribble a note).

Some conscientious apps, including Twitterrific, go so far as to include a setting for lefties to flip the layout, putting common controls back in the thumb's hot zone. For very tap-intensive apps, this may be a worthwhile strategy. Consider a calculator, for example, which is all about constant tapping. Like Twitterrific, the scientific calculator app PCalc includes an option to flip the keypad layout to accommodate lefties (see page 69). There are downsides to this approach, though. Ordering the most important tap targets from right to left reverses the way we visually process information, asking lefties to burn a little extra brain power to take in your interface. (This effort is repaid with improved ergonomics for frequent taps once they grok the layout, of course.) Perhaps more important, a left-handed option adds an additional preference to your app's settings, which as you'll see starting on page 176, should be pared to a minimum. Finally, there's the addition of a modest amount of code to do the visual switcheroo on your app's controls. Whether it's worth the extra work to ease the thumbstrain of 10 percent of your

Twitterrific offers a setting for left-handed controls, flipping the normal button layout (left) to a mirror layout (right) better suited to lefties.

users depends, as always, on the app. A complex, button-heavy, tap-intensive interface might suggest more mercy for lefties than apps that require less manual manipulation.

In interface design as in politics, sometimes it's better just to meet in the middle. Many standard iPhone controls, including buttons and list items, span the entire width of the screen, an equal-opportunity layout for both left and right thumbs. When space allows, full-width controls are the way to go—an important reason, for example, that wide buttons are cooked into the layout of *action sheets,* the

Full-width buttons, like the ones in the standard action sheet (left) or the WordCrasher and Epicurious apps, make for easy tap targets no matter what hand you're using.

iPhone's standard multiple-choice button views (page 167). Big chunky buttons not only give clear guidance to users, they also provide can't-miss tap targets no matter what hand you're using.

Size always matters in interface design. Big text, small text, giant buttons, or tiny ones—they all provide visual cues to what's important on the screen, gently guiding the eye to the next appropriate action. On touchscreen devices, though, fixing the right size for each tappable element is even more important, since every button and control has to be fitted to the finger. Make the buttons too small and you create an exercise in tap-and-miss frustration. The more important or frequent the action, the larger the associated target should be. Big buttons win.

The Magic Number Is 44

But just how big is big enough when it comes to iPhone tap targets? Well, what's the size of a fingertip? Apple pegs it precisely at 44 pixels and this measure appears reliably throughout the standard iPhone controls. In portrait orientation, 44 pixels is the height of buttons in the Calculator app, of the keys of the iPhone's virtual keyboard, of items in a standard list display, of the screen-topping navigation bar, and the list goes on. (With the iPhone's 163 ppi screen resolution, 44 pixels is about 7mm, or just a hair over ¼ inch.)

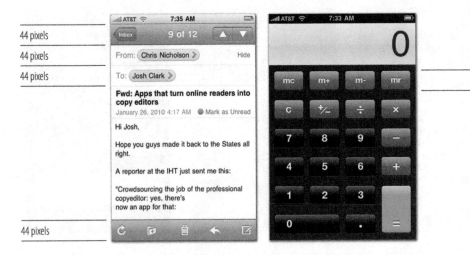

The 44-pixel block is, in many ways, the basic unit of measurement for the iPhone interface, establishing the visual rhythm of many iPhone apps. That metric is significant as the recommended minimum size to make a tap target (like a button or list item) easily and reliably tappable. Put another way, it's the spread of a fingertip pressed to the screen. By building its standard controls in proportion to that measure, Apple created a device that's not only built *for* the hand, but *of* the hand—measured out in finger-sized units. (In fact, it's wise to craft your overall design to a 44-pixel rhythm, a topic you'll explore on page 75.)

Ideally, any button or other tap target should be at least 44 × 44 pixels. That doesn't necessarily mean that what you see—the outline of the button itself—has to spread over that entire area. Buttons inside the standard navigation bar, for example, are only 29 pixels high, but their *tap area* extends to the full 44-pixel height of the navigation bar. Even if you tap just above or below the button, it still catches the tap as long as you're still inside the navigation bar. Likewise, taps immediately to the left or right are treated as taps on the button itself. Even though the button is *visually* smaller, its tappable footprint honors the 44-pixel minimum, making the button effectively larger than its outline suggests.

Buttons in screen-topping navigation bars (left) have tap areas much larger than their visual footprint. The active tap areas are outlined in red here and span the entire height of the navigation bar, reaching horizontally to the title text. Similarly, icons in screen-bottom tab bars (right) have tap areas that extend several pixels above the tab bar's visible outline.

Apple helps you get this right by providing a whole stable of standard controls that stick to this standard height (you'll explore these built-in views and controls in the next two chapters). When you use Apple's prefab navigation bar, toolbar, or keyboard in your app, its controls automatically use these finger-friendly dimensions. It's only when you start working with custom button sizes and other home-brew controls that you'll need to start counting pixels to make sure you hit the 44-pixel threshold.

As in most things, compromise is sometimes necessary. Even the iPhone's standard controls fudge the 44-pixel rule from time to time. In the keyboard, for example, keys are 44 pixels tall but only 30 pixels wide—similarly, in landscape view, the buttons are 44 pixels wide but 38 pixels high. Apple doesn't have much choice here; it's crucial to include the full QWERTY keyboard in this view, but all the keys just won't fit as 44 × 44 buttons. Something's gotta give. When limited space puts the squeeze on tap targets, here's the rule I've found works best: as long as a tap target is at least 44 pixels high or wide, you can squeeze the other dimension as small as 30 pixels if you really must (these are the same dimensions as a keyboard key). That means, *the practical minimum size for any tap target is 44 × 30.*

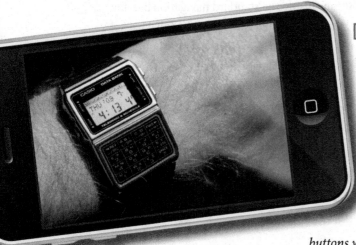

Photo: jonrawlinson.com

Don't Crowd Me

Your faithful author spent many years of his misspent youth with a svelte Casio calculator watch strapped to his wrist before finally retiring it in 1985. The problem wasn't just its tiny controls or its dampening effect on my prom king prospects. *The buttons were too close together.* Forget factorials or logarithms, the hardest thing about doing math on this thing was just hitting the right button. You'd aim for a five, but come up with a two or an eight, who knows—it was more wheel of fortune than calculator. Button size, in other words, isn't the only determining factor of tap accuracy; you have to consider spacing, too.

The iPhone's 320 × 480 pixels make for cozy quarters, and you'll inevitably be tempted to deal with that challenge by crowding the interface. "I'll just nudge these a little closer. I'll just add one more button to this toolbar." To quote a popular phrase of the calculator-watch heyday: "Just say no."

The iPhone's standard tab bar ensures comfortable spacing by limiting app designers to five tabs—no crowding allowed. If you add more than five, the tab bar displays only four of them, adding the More icon which takes you to a screen with additional options, as shown at left in the New York Times app. Apple's guidelines suggest limiting toolbars to just five icons, as shown at right in Safari.

Once again, Apple's standard controls help you do the right thing. For example, when your app uses a standard tab bar at screen bottom to switch between modes or views, the operating system automatically spaces them out for you and limits you to a maximum of five tabs. Toolbars don't impose the same automatic limit, but Apple nevertheless recommends that you limit toolbar icons to five, too. (You'll learn all about tab bars and toolbars on page 106 and page 143 respectively.) In both cases, the screen's 320-pixel width is technically large enough to cram up to seven 44-pixel icons, but they'd bump right up next to each other, introducing the calculator-watch problem for your audience.

It's especially important to give fingers some breathing room at the bottom of the screen. Usability testing reveals this to be a clumsy area prone to mistaps when targets are placed too close to an app's tab-bar navigation. The frustration is

Call Global App and Skype both include phone keypads with buttons that press right up against the tab bar. Call Global (left) makes things especially difficult by making the adjacent buttons narrow and tough to hit, with frequent missed taps. When you want to see your balance, a mistaken tap sweeps you away to the app's World Call screen. In Skype (right), the problem is less pronounced because the big buttons are tough to miss.

compounded by the fact that accidentally tapping a tab bar icon often takes you to an entirely new screen. If you must place targets near the tab bar or toolbar, make sure they're large enough to hit easily. (See how USA Today worked around this problem on page 94.)

First Person: James Thomson and PCalc

Since its introduction in the 1970s as the first mobile computer, the pocket calculator hasn't changed its essential form. The calculator's familiar key layout remains a remarkably stable handheld interface, one that Apple faithfully reproduced in the built-in Calculator app for iPhone. In fact, the reliable ergonomics of handheld calculators would seem to make it a no-brainer for developing an iPhone version. Just clone the key layout as-is on the iPhone screen, and you've got a proven, intuitive, and well-proportioned interface, right? Turns out it's not quite so simple, especially if your calculator happens to offer a complex collection of features.

PCalc, a calculator with functions aimed at programmers, began as a desktop application for Macintosh in 1992. Over the years, PCalc for Mac blossomed into a full-featured scientific calculator to manage all the math you can muster including hexadecimal, octal, and binary functions; programmable functions; unit conversions; and a library of scientific constants. It's a brainy calculator for math mavens.

The PCalc desktop application for Mac OS X.

When the iPhone arrived, PCalc developer **James Thomson** thought his application and its familiar interface would translate easily to the handheld device. He soon ran headlong, however, into the limitations of the iPhone's tiny screen, wrestling with button sizes and working out creative ways to preserve features in limited screen space. James shared his experiences exploring the constraints and

opportunities of a virtual keypad and what it means to design a tap-intensive app for fingertips instead of a mouse and keyboard.

Designing for Touch

James Thomson: On the Mac, PCalc has always been an onscreen simulation of an imaginary physical calculator. My initial thought was just to port that directly to the phone, but it didn't really work very well in practice. The iPhone screen is too small to have all the buttons visible and usable at once, and the desktop layout just wasn't ideal for holding in your hands. With the Mac version, people typically use the keyboard shortcuts rather than clicking on virtual keys with their mouse, so the actual key layout isn't crucial. With the mobile version, however, it became one of the most important things to get right. There's

Early, basic prototypes for PCalc provided a way to test the button sizes and spacing, making sure that PCalc "felt right."

limited screen space, and you can only make buttons so small and packed together before they become unusable.

When I first started to design the key layouts, I sketched them all on paper. Doing that was much closer to the feel of a real device than designing on a desktop screen. I'd actually hold the paper mockup in my hand to see how it felt to "push" the buttons. From there, I did a lot of my early development in the iPhone simulator on the Mac, but I learned that when you do it that way, you miss out on how an application actually feels when you hold it in your hands. The iPhone screen has a much higher pixel density than my desktop screen, so apps are much larger in the iPhone simulator than on the device, making it hard to judge whether a button is the right size for your fingers. By far the most important thing was to try my early designs on a physical device as soon as possible.

In version 1.0 of PCalc for iPhone, the buttons were on the left because that's how they'd been in the Mac version for 18 years. It was only after the first version was released that it became clear it wasn't the best layout for a handheld device. In fact, lots of people assumed I was left-handed from the 1.0 layout. So I changed that, but introduced a mirror of the horizontal layout for left-handed people who liked the number buttons on the left.

In landscape orientation, the original version of PCalc for iPhone (left) placed numbers at left, but this placement was awkward for right-handed users. Later versions changed this layout (right), but added an option to let lefties use the original layout.

Give Me Feedback

James: When I first started writing PCalc, I wasn't yet very accurate with the iPhone touchscreen keyboard and the visual feedback of popping up each key as you type was a great help. It seemed obvious that you would want some similar system for entering numbers into a calculator, so I spent quite a while studying and emulating the Apple keyboard so that PCalc would give similar feedback when you tap a button.

On the desktop version, if the calculator wants to tell you you've done something wrong it beeps at you. If you have the volume turned all the way down, it flashes the whole screen. The first-generation iPod Touch, which was what I was developing on, didn't even have a speaker or vibration, so I couldn't use those. And it's a bit obnoxious to have something beeping at you on a portable device, as you are more likely to be out in a social situation. So I tried to cover all the bases, making the LCD screen flash as well as vibrate, if possible.

Tap-intensive activities require visual feedback to confirm that you're tapping what you expect. PCalc's keypad (left) borrows the keystroke feedback of the iPhone's built-in keyboard (right).

Pimp My Calculator: Virtual Keypads

Old-school scientific calculators have always had a space problem, packing in more features than they have available buttons. They've traditionally solved the problem by adding a "2nd" button which, like Shift or Control keys on a keyboard, lets each calculator button have a second function. On the iPhone, virtual key-pads improve on this tradition, letting you change the keypad's physical look and layout on demand. PCalc's virtual keypad offers different layouts tuned to different needs (engineering, programming, common scientific functions, and so on). PCalc's savvy use of virtual keypads means the app can offer its full range of features without crowding the keypad. Theme settings, meanwhile, let you choose your own color scheme.

James: Given limited screen space, a complex application can't present everything on a single screen. For PCalc, I chose to focus some of the layouts on one task and some on others. I can imagine adding new layouts for financial tasks, for example, where you wouldn't need the scientific features. Ultimately, since the layouts are just built from simple XML files, I hope to add an editing feature so that users can customize the layouts themselves.

PCalc offers several keypad layouts, each tailored to specific calculation categories. PCalc's Basic and Engineering layouts are shown here.

I think my typical users are happy to explore a user interface to see what it can do, but that doesn't work for all kinds of apps or people. On the whole, I don't think PCalc is that much more obscure than some of the classic calculators that inspired it, so it perhaps helps that my audience is used to somewhat cryptic key markings on calculators.

The style customizations offered by themes are perhaps less easy to justify than the keypad layouts. One argument against themes is that they are proof that you couldn't come up with one single good visual design and would rather have ten average ones. But I think people like the choices, and it lets them make PCalc "theirs." The themes are popular, too, judging by the number of people who buy the additional theme pack via in-app purchase in the free app.

Originally, all the button graphics were pre-rendered bitmaps. But, when I was making the additional layouts, I found I was constantly creating new graphics to cover all the different button sizes. It made sense to draw the buttons live, rather than rely on bitmaps, so I wrote some code, a theme engine based on XML files, to create looks and draw all the buttons that I previously had to make in Photoshop. So, the choice of using a theme engine was originally made to support the functional layouts, but once it was in there, the temptation was to use it to create different looks, too.

PCalc's themes let number-crunching aesthetes adjust the color scheme and button style.

Pointed Design

So far, this chapter has emphasized the physical more than the visual, pushing the ergonomic angle of app design. As always, though, form follows function, and all this talk of tap targets and thumb-friendly layouts influences more than just button sizes. When you plan the placement of your app's touch controls based on comfort and ease of use, other aspects of your design naturally fall into place. The best iPhone apps also share a common visual hierarchy broadly following these tap-friendly guidelines:

- Place important info at the top and sink controls to the bottom.

- Design to a 44-pixel rhythm.

- Where appropriate, create at-a-glance displays that avoid scrolling.

- Whittle onscreen elements to the bare minimum.

- Push advanced tools and controls to the background.

Like any set of guidelines, these aren't ironclad laws, just useful practices that can help you quickly block out your design in an appealing, efficient, and accessible layout. The next few sections give you the gist.

Take It From the Top

The most important or frequently used info should float to the top of the screen above the app's primary buttons and controls. This meets our expectations not only of graphic design—headlines at the top—but also the way we hoist and handle just about any physical device. The screen bottom is the most comfortable thumb zone for a handheld gadget, but that's also where the screen is most likely to be obscured by hovering hands. To keep info in clear view, position it above your app's controls. This is a familiar, common-sense layout that applies to most physical devices—iPods, calculators, cell phones, bathroom scales, you name it. Here again, though, it's the opposite of what we'd expect from Web and desktop software where toolbars and menus stake out the top of document windows with primary content below.

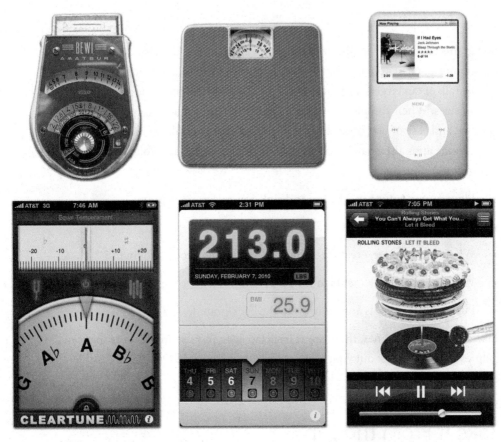

Tapworthy apps follow an interface convention familiar with all kinds of mechanical devices. Even when they don't directly mimic real-world gadgets, they organize controls at the bottom and content on top. From left, Cleartune, Weightbot, and iPod.

For primary app navigation, Apple helps you do the right thing by cautioning designers to place tab bars and toolbars at screen bottom (see page 106 and page 143). Likewise, when you summon a keyboard by tapping a standard text field, the built-in keyboard automatically slides in at screen bottom, nudging the typed results to the top of the screen. Follow Apple's lead here: everywhere it makes sense, let the primary controls sink to the bottom and main content float to the top.

This guideline is easy to follow when content and controls are separate, but not all iPhone apps make such a ready distinction. In many apps, the primary display info doubles as a view's main controls. That's especially true for list content;

In Gowalla's Passport view (left) every display element doubles as a touch control, but the Check In and New Spot buttons anchor the screen as the most frequent tap targets. Similarly, while the stats at the top of RunKeeper Pro (right) are tappable, the main Stop and Pause buttons remain at bottom, leaving the stats display prominently visible at all times.

whether you're scrolling through contacts, to-dos, songs, or email, you tap list items to see their detail views. In those cases—as well as examples like Home-screen icons or photo album thumbnails—the entire display turns content into tap target from top to bottom. This double duty encourages you to directly tap anything you want to know about, a natural interaction and a good design. Even in these cases, though, it's a good practice to place *the most frequent* tap targets at the bottom, as discussed earlier.

Design to a 44-Pixel Rhythm

The iPhone looks good, sure, but it *feels* good, too. The industrial design gurus at Apple carefully designed the iPhone hardware to feel right in your hand, with weight and proportions that are as appealing as the device's glossy sheen. The same should go for your app design, with screens that are not only pretty but are constructed in proportion to the hand, with a sense of balance in each element's visual weight.

Part of that, as you've seen, is a matter of using finger-sized tap targets placed in easy reach. But the size of a fingertip can do more than just determine button sizes: as a unit of measure lifted from the hand itself, fingerspan provides a visual building block for giving your interface design a consistent rhythm in natural proportion to your paw and its pointer. By loosely blocking out your design in a

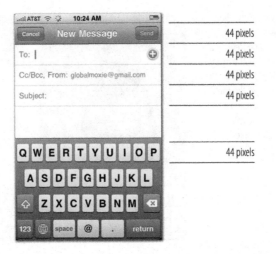

	44 pixels
	44 pixels
	44 pixels
	44 pixels
	44 pixels

44-pixel grid, you ensure that interface elements are sized in harmony with one another as well as the fingers that work the device. As you saw earlier, several standard iPhone elements—navigation bars, toolbars, list items, keyboard keys— are sized to 44 pixels, establishing the vertical rhythm of many screens.

Go with that flow, at least loosely. You don't have to rigidly stick to aligning every single element to a 44-pixel grid. In fact, you *can't,* since the iPhone's 320 × 480 dimensions don't round neatly to 44, and some of the built-in controls like the tab bar at screen bottom veer into slightly different sizes. Instead, the point is that the

	88 pixels
	88 pixels
	88 pixels
	88 pixels

The iPhone Home screen builds on the 44-pixel visual rhythm by organizing icons into 88-pixel rows.

44-pixel measure provides a natural size to build with, one that rhymes with the size of several standard controls. Creating interface elements based on that proportion gives your designs visual balance and stability.

Be a Scroll Skeptic

Another way to reinforce an impression of sturdiness and weight is to build screens that stay put—no scrolling required. When it's possible to comfortably fit a screen's content into a single no-scroll view, you should go for it. The "out of sight, out of mind" effect is especially strong on the iPhone, where distracted mobile users speed through apps. When info isn't front and center, chances are good they won't see it at all. It's a matter of both brain and strain: scrolling requires extra thought as well as extra swipes, and one of your jobs as app designer is to reduce both.

This might seem subtle, but just asking users to *figure out* that they need to scroll requires them to fire up brain cells: "Wait, what's missing, and how do I get to it?" By contrast, taking in a screen's complete content at a single glance lets users focus exclusively on the content without making their gray matter do any background processing about what's offscreen. This might seem like coddling—seriously, it'll break their brains to scroll?—but the best apps bend over backward to reduce the overhead required to work the app itself. No-scroll screens require less brainwork while also reinforcing the illusion of your app as a physical, not virtual, device. A fixed screen gives a sense of solidity.

The point here is not to avoid scrolling at all costs (this section is titled "Be a Scroll *Skeptic*"—not a zealot, reactionary, or dogmatist). Eliminating the scroll is just one tactic for designing a display that's easy to absorb, not a goal in itself, but when it suits your app's content, it's a design tactic that encourages healthy restraint.

There's a whole category of apps devoted to the single-screen display. Apple dubs them *utility apps*, narrowly focused tools that provide quick summaries or perform a simple task, almost always in simple no-scroll screens. The built-in Weather app is the quintessential utility app. It provides streamlined forecasts for up to 20 cities, each tidily presented in a get-it-quick, no-scroll view—you flip

The Weather app offers a compact weather forecast, summarizing a week's weather in a single screen. The border around the info creates a solid container to signal that there's no additional scrolling content below. The page indicator dots at screen bottom indicate that more screens await (see page 103 for more info about page indicators).

through them like cards. The app's presentation lets you absorb the week's forecast for each city with just a glimpse. The carefully contained layout makes it instantly clear that there's no additional info below the fold, no "Is there more?" thinking required.

The Weather app pulls off its single-screen layout by stripping content down to the bare minimum. A few icons and high/low temperatures hardly tell the whole story of your local weather, a topic that occupies entire websites and 24-hour weather channels. Instead of indulging in complex detail, the app focuses on giving the quick gist in a simple and efficient display. This just-the-basics approach is a good strategy for utility apps, the simplest class of iPhone software. Like Weather, the best of these apps rely on graphically rich displays to telegraph simple info quickly, with big can't-miss text and images that sink in with just a quick peek. Contrary to what you might expect, the success of compact interfaces often relies on big text and chunky images cushioned with generous surrounding space. Apps pass *the glance test* when you can hold them at arm's length and still soak up their info effortlessly.

The glance test reinforces an essential principle of tapworthy app design: *clarity trumps density*. A crowded screen creates more work and confusion for your audience. This doesn't mean you're obliged to chuck your app's detailed info in order to have a beautiful and intuitive interface. It's not an either-or bargain. Complexity itself isn't bad; the trick is making complexity seem uncomplicated.

From left, apps like Surf Report, Delivery Status Touch, and Tea Round pass the glance test with high-impact text and graphics that are easy to read even from several feet away. Surf Report shows water conditions, Delivery Status Touch shows package whereabouts, and Tea Round shows whose turn it is to brew the tea.

Even within the iPhone's tiny screen, it's possible for apps to reveal complex information in a simple display—and yes, without scrolling.

The AccuWeather.com app, for example, is a sophisticated alternative to the Weather app that steps beyond the utility category by providing several screens of detailed weather info. Each of these screens (see page 80) is self-contained in a no-scroll display, providing dense information layered in multiple but uncomplicated views. Want to find out what the humidity will be in a few hours? Tap the desired hour in the app's 15-hour forecast and the details pop up immediately. The main screen shows the big-picture overview, and the app tucks additional details behind tabs or icons instead of piling it all into the same screen at once. It's at once intuitive and information-rich, no scrolling or crowded layout required.

Healthy scroll skepticism means recognizing that you don't have to reveal all your information in one shot. It's a bit like the art of conversation: don't be that guy who drones on and on without pausing to check if he's saying something that actually interests his suffering listeners. Especially when there's lots to be said or explored, the best conversations are interactive, with listeners allowed to ask questions instead of passively receiving info. In an app, a tap is effectively a question in the conversation. The best apps provide top-level, need-to-know information

AccuWeather.com's simple tab control lets you flip between current, hourly, and daily weather forecasts. On the hourly and daily views, you can tap the day or hour to get more info—an intuitive way to make data available without crowding too much into the display at once.

at a glance and, from there, let users tap something to "ask" for more information about it. Chances are, you don't need to know what the local wind speed will be at 3 p.m. every time you launch AccuWeather.com, but when you need it, the answer is just a tap away. In the meantime, the main view still gives you the basic at-a-glance info that you'd get from the built-in Weather app.

Are all these extra taps really better than scrolling? Just on the basis of physical comfort, a tap is an easier gesture than the swiping scroll. A more important consideration than tap quantity is tap *quality*. As long as there's an appropriate reward waiting on the other side of every tap, extra taps are okay—and usually less of an imposition than a long scrolling screen. If you focus the main screen on the most important tools and info, you can safely tuck secondary content into another view. If done right, tapping through fixed screens requires you to do less visual scanning than it takes to locate content on a scrolling page. Content and controls on a fixed screen remain reliably in the same place visit after visit, so it's easy to duck in and out of an app to get the info you want without pausing to get your bearings.

Even long-form content allows creative alternatives to scrolling. Most apps for reading books, for example, use a page-turning metaphor instead of scrolling to advance the text. This lets you tap the screen just once to flip the virtual page to a fresh screen of prose, sparing you constant swiping while also reinforcing the illusion of handling a physical object—convenient and familiar. Instapaper Pro, an app for saving and reading lengthy online articles, likewise offers an option to page through screens a tap at a time. The app also offers scrolling but with a clever ergonomic gimmick to spare you swipe-swipe-swipe tedium: you can scroll just by tilting the phone back and forth to advance the text.

Stanza and Instapaper Pro offer thumb-sparing alternatives to swiping through long text. Like most ebook readers, Stanza (left) lets you tap the screen to flip to a new page of text. Instapaper (right) offers a tilt-scrolling feature to advance text by physically tipping the device.

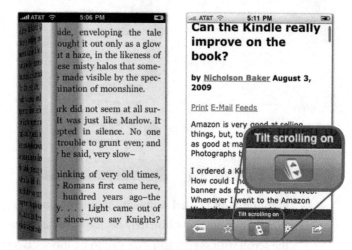

But let's not be strident anti-scrollers. While it's good to avoid scrolling where appropriate, it's not like it's inherently evil. It's part of the fun of the iPhone's physics, and it's obviously essential to some apps. To-do lists, news feeds, articles, and emails inevitably run long, and scrolling is (usually) the best way to handle those kinds of long-form content. List-based interfaces that try to wriggle out of a scrolling screen often just feel awkward (see the interfaces the USA Today designers experimented with on page 91).

When your app does require scrolling, just be sure to keep the primary app controls anchored in one place. In early versions of the Facebook app, for example, the tab control for flipping through a friend's profile content was itself part of the content area, which meant it scrolled out of view with the rest of the page. When you finished reading through a pal's status updates, for example, you had to scroll back up to the top of the screen to switch over to your friend's photos—assuming that you could even remember where you last saw those tab controls. Facebook 3.0

remedied this where'd-it-go problem by anchoring the wayward tabs to the bottom of the screen, saving both time and head scratching. The lesson: scrolling or no, a view's primary controls should never skitter offscreen. Anchored elements create a sense of stability and consistency.

In Facebook 2.0 (left), the control for switching between wall posts, profile info, and photos was part of the scrolling content area and could disappear offscreen. In Facebook 3.0 (right), the tab control is always anchored to screen bottom.

Ergonomic and visual simplicity should be important goals for your app design. Whether or not you ultimately decide to include scrolling screens, approaching the scroll with skepticism asks you to be more discerning about what you include. Committing to the iPhone's 320 x 480 footprint puts limitations on your design as firm as if you were designing a real-world device. When there's only so much room for your tools, controls, and content, you have to ask yourself a useful question: "Do I really need all this stuff?"

Edit, ~~Edit, Edit~~

The Guinness world record for "most multifunctional" pocket knife belongs to Wenger, the company behind the storied Swiss Army knife. The company says the knife's 87 gadgets (including a laser pointer, cigar cutter, and golf reamer) can be used for no fewer than 141 functions. The $1400 gadget is a nifty feat of Swiss ingenuity and—who knew!—Swiss humor, too. Alas, weighed down by its three pounds of gizmos, this "most multifunctional" knife has no practical function at all, a pocket knife that doesn't fit in your pocket. This slice-n-dice Goliath

was, of course, never really designed to be used. It was a novelty created for the company's 100th anniversary, a whimsical project to bring together every gadget the company ever included in its knives. At a certain point, as Wenger's craftsmen added more and more tools, the knife suddenly stopped being a knife, and it just became a doorstop.

In geekspeak, you might call this a crowded interface. While the knife is obviously (and intentionally) ridiculous, it's a winking reminder that somewhere in the reptile part of our brains, a misguided instinct tells us that more is always better. More features, more preferences, more flexibility—the gizmo that does the *most* is always the best. In the end, of course, the best gizmo is the thing that lets us do what we need to do with the greatest ease. In mobile devices—whether it's a Swiss Army knife or an iPhone—that almost always means removing features and *chrome*, the buttons, icons, and other controls that often crowd an interface.

The last chapter encouraged you to trim your app's functions in the planning stage, whittling the app to a sharp focus on the most important features. Apply the same tapworthy filter to every onscreen element, too. Include controls only if they're likely to be used most of the time by most of your audience. Be ruthless when you consider every button and icon: Does this element invite attention? Is it clear what it does? Does it deliver something meaningful? Every tool should be tightly related to the primary task at hand, and auxiliary tools and content should be dispatched to a secondary screen or sliced out altogether. Text labels should be terse and words shouldn't be repeated.

It might seem harmless to add just one more icon, but every onscreen element comes with a cognitive cost for your users. It takes longer to scan the screen, longer to absorb the possible options, longer to figure out what you're supposed to do. Don't make 'em think. When every pixel is precious, your app doesn't have room for question marks that will snag users as they hustle through. It's like the pocket knife: it's easy to choose a blade to use when there's only one of them, but it takes forever when there are 87.

Just as you saw in the AccuWeather.com app, you don't have to show every last scrap of information all at once. Consider whether second-tier content and controls might be dumped entirely and, if not, nudge them over to a separate view in your app. The built-in Contacts app does this, for example, when you add or edit a contact. The main screen is a no-scroll view of the most common contact info; the app doesn't pester you about less frequent fields and instead provides an "add field" button at the bottom of the screen. From there, you can choose from among 12 additional fields to round out your contact info when the standard fields don't do the trick.

When you add a new contact, the Contacts app displays only a few primary fields (left). Tap the "add fields" button at screen bottom to go to a secondary screen (right), which offers 12 less common fields.

Apple is particularly clever about doing more with less. The company's software has a well-deserved reputation for both elegance and ease of use. It looks great, works intuitively, and drips with good taste. Like all good editors, Apple's designers do this in part by removing distractions and plucking out features that aren't relevant to mainstream users in order to focus more screen real estate and polish on the features that matter to the most people. What's not included in Apple's built-in iPhone apps is as important as what is.

Secret Panels and Hidden Doors

Here's the thing: leaving stuff out inevitably drives some people nuts. Power users will, in particular, pine for all the tools and flexibility that mainstream users don't miss. For many, the basic Weather and Stocks apps just don't cut it. If your app addresses an audience with more advanced needs, then you'll almost certainly have to add more features, tools, and content than your app's mainstream counterpart. That doesn't give you a pass to create mind-numbingly crowded interfaces. The same rules apply, and the pocket knife still has to fit in the pocket. If your app really does have to include those extra features and controls, you've still got to prevent the extra interface chrome from elbowing aside the main content.

This is a challenge that the many iPhone Twitter apps wrestle with. On the surface, Twitter couldn't be simpler: post terse updates and read those posted by others. Yet an enormously complex infrastructure of tools, social customs, and third-party services has emerged around this basic concept. Your tweets can link to photos or videos, point to your physical location, mention other Twitter users, "retweet" someone else's post, embed #hashtag metadata, and more. The dilemma for Twitter apps is how to make a dead-simple interface for firing off a quick tweet while also surfacing the many power features that make Twitter megausers tingle. The brute-force approach is to pile a bunch of icons and controls into the tweet-posting screen. Trouble is, when you add a keyboard to the mix, all that extra chrome quickly squeezes out the most important thing: the text you're typing. It's a sign of trouble when controls leave little room for the content.

The Twitter app (formerly known as Tweetie) solves this problem by hiding all those add-on controls behind the keyboard. The button that displays the

In the Twitter app, tapping the character-count button (left) slides away the keyboard to reveal a control panel (right), a compact means to put advanced features within reach without crowding the screen.

remaining character count for your tweet doubles as a toggle switch that slides the keyboard out of the way to reveal all the options you can apply to your tweet—a secret control panel for power users. When you're done, the keyboard slides back into view, and you're back to typing, no extra chrome in sight.

Other apps use similar tricks to move interface elements out of the way. Ebook apps Stanza, Kindle, and Eucalyptus all hide their main controls completely to allow book text to fill the screen when you're reading. Ditto for the Photos app when flipping through full-screen pictures. Hiding primary controls like this admittedly brings a risk of disorienting people, leaving them uncertain about how to escape the current view. In all of these examples, though, tapping the screen summons the controls again, a tactic that even panicked users will try soon enough. It's a legit approach, but one that should be used sparingly and only by apps that get a big benefit from an unsullied full-screen view.

Advertisements also count as interface chrome, and unlike primary controls, most users wouldn't mind seeing them slide away for good. Ads present a business and usability dilemma: they take up valuable real estate and present content to which many users are actively hostile, yet many free apps rely on them to fund the whole operation. The sliding panel approach provides a useful compromise. In the USA Today app, for example, a 50-pixel ad banner slides up from the bottom of the screen when you first arrive at an article screen. It holds its place for a

Kindle banishes its controls to turn over the full screen (left) to your book. Tapping the screen brings the controls back (right).

marketed plaster target balls for marksmen and invented a plaster laying nest for chickens that was infused with an anti-lice powder.

But even Woodward's firm, the Genesee Pure Food Company, struggled to find a market for powdered gelatin. It was a new product category with an unknown brand name in an era where general stores sold almost all products from behind the counter and customers had to ask for them by name. The Jell-O was manufactured in a nearby factory run by Andrew Samuel

plaster laying nest for chickens that was infused with an anti-lice powder.

But even Woodward's firm, the Genesee Pure Food Company, struggled to find a market for powdered gelatin. It was a new product category with an unknown brand name in an era where general stores sold almost all products from behind the counter and customers had to ask for them by name. The Jell-O was manufactured in a near

Location 206-209

few seconds before sliding out of view—a reasonable compromise for both advertiser and reader.

The point here is that for all of this chapter's talk about designing your app to feel like a real-world device, it's okay to bend the rules to take advantage of your app's virtual environment. Virtual keyboards and sliding panels let your app do things no physical gadget could do by swapping out the interface for a new set of tools or content. These "cheats" let you layer secondary tools and content into your app without crowding the main screen. Turns out it's not all that different from the Swiss Army knife after all, a handy gadget that can constantly become something new. While pesky considerations like size and weight prevent the Swiss Army knife from offering too many tools, the iPhone's virtual interface gives you a theoretically unlimited interface surface area. Just keep flipping through secret panels as you need them, right?

Well, yes and no. The trouble with hidden content is, you guessed it—it's hidden. You'll continue to bump against the "out of sight, out of mind" problem. The more secret panels you spirit away, the more overhead you ask people to take on to remember how to find them. You have to take care to provide visual cues to help them find their way. If you decide to use a hidden door, that means you have to put the latch in clear sight to make it easy to open. Ideally, this trigger should be well-labeled or at least in such close proximity to the content you're working

The search bar is hidden offscreen in the Mail app until you tug the screen down to reveal it.

with that it suggests what you'll find on the other side. The latch for your hidden door should look tapworthy and invite action.

A more discoverable approach is to hide interface chrome in plain sight. Most apps that have a search feature position their search bars at the top of the screen, premium real estate. The built-in Mail app, among many others, reclaims this valuable space by scrolling the view so that when you first land on a screen, the search bar is tucked away just out of view. If you want to search, you tug the screen down or tap the screen-topping status bar to zip the search bar into view.

Another strategy for discoverable secondary controls is to offer toolbars that emerge temporarily from the app's main navigation. Quickoffice's iPad-style pop-over menu provides tools for formatting text, for example, and Twitterrific's filter bar lets you choose the type of tweets you'd like to view in your Twitter timeline. As always, the goal is to keep your interface visually uncomplicated, no matter how complex your app may be. Limit interface chrome, but hide only as much as you have to. Give all of your features and controls a hard look before you include them in your design to make sure they're really tapworthy. If they pass muster, be

Quickoffice (left) offers secondary tools in popover menus when you tap an icon in the main toolbar. Twitterrific (right) similarly reveals icons in a second tool-bar when you tap the funnel-shaped Filter icon at far right.

sure to place each element carefully in intuitive, easy-to-find locations, hidden or not.

Touchpoints

✓ Ergonomics matter: consider how your app feels in the hand.

✓ Put primary controls in the thumb's "hot zone."

✓ Forty-four is the magic number. Make tap areas at least 44 pixels, and design to a 44-pixel rhythm.

✓ Be generous with space and don't crowd your design.

✓ Feature primary content at the top, controls at the bottom.

✓ Keep the main controls within easy reach, and avoid scrolling where practical.

✓ Reduce interface chrome by dispatching power tools to secondary views with secret panels and hidden doors.

First Person: Rusty Mitchell and USA Today

National newspaper *USA Today* is known for its compact approach to news and its colorful graphic design. While other news outfits offer more depth, *USA Today* emphasizes efficiency, aiming to be the news source for business travelers and others looking for a quick-scan update about what's happening in the world. The newspaper's iPhone app reflects this priority on get-it-quick news with a design that cleverly packs lots of content into every view while also maintaining the newspaper's brand identity throughout.

USA Today turned to Mercury Intermedia to create the app. As vice president of creative development for Mercury, **Rusty Mitchell** was creative director for the project. Rusty shared his experiences wrestling with the challenge of making a content-rich app compact yet easy to explore.

Rusty Mitchell: *USA Today* is known for being more bold and colorful than traditional newspapers. Large color photos, graphics, and diagrams along with shorter news articles define the *USA Today* news experience. Its summarized approach to news delivery works especially well in a mobile context where people often only have a few minutes broken up throughout the day to skim and quickly find out what's going on in the world. We view mobile users as information snackers who often use their iPhones and other mobile devices to fill small gaps in their day—waiting in line at the grocery store, waiting for a friend at lunch. When we were developing the app, it was very important to us that its information load quickly and efficiently and be easily accessible with as few actions as possible.

USA Today pioneered the use of colorful infographics in the news industry, and the newspaper's brand is as much about graphics as text. As a result, the app puts graphical content like photos, infographics, and weather on the same footing as more traditional news. The app's primary tab-bar navigation organizes content into five sections: Headlines (news), Scores (sports), Weather, Pictures, and Snapshots (infographics and polls).

All the News That Fits

The app's main section screens divide content into several topic categories. The Headlines section, for example, organizes articles into News, Money, Sports, Life, Tech, and Travel sections. The Photos section similarly organizes its images by topic. The design challenge was how to create compact controls that offered all these content categories without crowding out the content. Early on, the designers arrived at an "accordion" display, a collection of stacked, sliding category headings (see page 92). Tap a category to reveal its content; the category slides open and other categories slide shut, a variation on the secret-panel approach. The accordion approach embraces scroll skepticism and works well for some types of content. However, when the team ran into trouble using the accordion for news headlines, they appropriately embraced a scrolling list.

Rusty: In the Weather and Pictures sections, each of the categories hold similar weight, so we didn't want to place too much emphasis on one of the section categories over the others. It was important that all categories remain onscreen. It was an instance where "out of sight, out of mind" was really true. All of the categories in these sections were too compelling to allow them to be overlooked because they were hidden offscreen. The accordion approach worked well and let us fit everything into the same screen.

We thought we'd try the accordion for the Headlines section for news articles, too. Our original mockups used an accordion section selector like the Weather and Pictures sections. You could flip through headlines by swiping left and right the same way that you can page through cities in Weather. We quickly discovered that paging through ten headlines one at a time was just never going to be as quick or efficient as a traditional list view. It's important to

USA Today's accordion view displays photos by category in a single screen. Tap a topic heading to slide open the thumbnails for that category, and then tap a thumbnail to see the full-sized photos.

The USA Today team experimented with several designs using an accordion view to browse news articles, but all the interface chrome left room for only one headline at a time. Here, mockups tested ways to change that one visible headline with arrow buttons (left) or with swiping, with your progress shown on page-indicator dots (right).

recognize early on if doing something unique or cool is actually slowing down access to information. We settled on the need to return to a standard list view.

Psst . . . Hints for Working Custom Controls

Because the accordion view didn't allow enough room to display content, the team instead decided to use a horizontal slider at the top of the screen, a compact solution that left plenty of space for headlines. You swipe the slider left or right like a dial to see more content categories, tapping the topic you'd like to browse. The original Facebook app introduced this style of slider navigation and, although later versions of that app no longer use a slider, Facebook had already helped make the control familiar, if not quite a convention. For those who don't find the control immediately obvious, USA Today provides a subtle animation that hints at the control's use by showing its intended movement, a live demonstration that's repeated until people pick it up themselves.

Rusty: I get really excited about the small things, especially when we can find a way to demonstrate a new or non-standard user interaction without interfering or slowing down the users ability to use the app. With the horizontal section slider, we found that some users didn't understand that they could slide the bar to reveal additional sections. We originally thought that breaking the "Life" section so that it is partially obscured on the right edge of the screen would be enough to indicate to the user that more information would be revealed by sliding, but that wasn't always enough.

To help, we added an animation so that when a user launches the Headlines section of the app, the categories in the slider navigation bar slide into place from the left of the screen. It keeps doing this every time you visit that section

Until users slide the navigation bar themselves for the first time, the app animates it at launch, sliding the bar in from the left to hint that it can move and nudging users to give it a try.

until the user slides the bar for themselves. Once the user slides the bar for the first time, we stop doing the animation. We felt this was a good way to train users who were having trouble recognizing the control without having to add an annoying message or interfere with those users who already understood how the slider control worked.

We do something similar when you first arrive at the Weather or Pictures screen. The section bars in the accordion view drop into place from the top of the screen. The movement suggests that you can do something with them, re-inforcing that you can tap the accordion bars to reveal additional information.

Big Problem with Tiny Buttons

Just above the tab-bar buttons at the bottom of the screen, the app offers a narrow utility bar with a button to refresh content and the standard "i" settings button. Locations near the tab bar always make for troublesome tap targets, a problem compounded by the need to save space and make the buttons small.

Rusty: We knew that if we were going to fit these controls on the screen, they were going to have to remain small and unobtrusive. They needed to hold the correct hierarchical weight and if they were going to have their own bar in the interface, it needed to take up as little vertical space as possible. The main problem presented itself early on: because of the small size of the info and refresh status bar and its proximity to the tab bar, we found that it was much too easy to inadvertently switch sections in the application when attempting to tap "i" or refresh. We had the idea that, instead of making the buttons them-selves larger, we could make their invisible tap area larger instead. They would still take up the same amount of space, but they would be easier to hit.

Unfortunately, Apple had the same idea. When we tried to add a larger tap area to our buttons, we discovered that the tap area for buttons in the stan-dard tab bar extends several pixels above the tab bar, right into our info and refresh bar. That not only blocked our attempt to use those pixels for our info and refresh buttons, but it actually made our problem worse than we originally knew. Since Apple doesn't give developers control to adjust the tap area of the standard tab bar, we had to build our own custom tab bar control so that we could control the tap area and make this idea work.

Either/Or: You Can't Fit It All

Early designs of the app's article view included buttons to jump to the next or previous article directly from the navigation bar at the top of the screen. When the team wanted to add an option to share articles with friends, something else had to go, and it forced them to take a hard look at the next/previous buttons.

Rusty: We had a lot of back and forth discussion about losing those arrows. Several other news apps use the next/previous arrows to move through articles, and I assume that's because it works so well in the built-in Mail app. However, unlike the Mail app where I usually want to read all of my emails, I'm normally not nearly as invested in reading all articles in a given news section. Unless you plan to read all articles, it really isn't any more convenient or efficient to blindly move past three or four articles you're not interested in than it is to return to the list view and find an article you want to read. When we needed to find room for the "Share Article" button in the navigation bar, it was an easy decision on my part to sacrifice the next/previous article arrows.

Early designs included next/previous arrows at the right side of the top navigation bar (left). The feature was dropped to make room for the Share Article button (right).

4

Get Organized

STRUCTURING YOUR APP THE APPLE WAY

AS YOU BEGIN PLANNING your app's design, set aside the pixel-by-pixel nitty-gritty of your app's buttons and colors and icons. Let go of the *look* of your app, and consider how it *works*—its big-picture organizational design. When you pull way back to look at your app from a high level, you'll see that its essential operation depends on easy movement from screen to screen. All but the most simple iPhone apps are collections of multiple screens, each one dedicated to an individual task or to specific content. How you choose to string those screens together determines how people will steer their way through your app, and it's one of the most fundamental choices you'll make when planning your design.

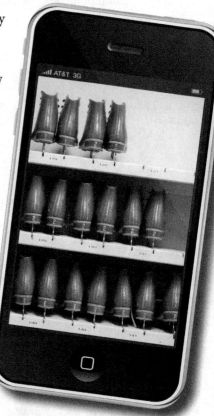

This chapter tours the iPhone's navigation styles to explore the options for arranging your app's content and tools. Specifically, you'll get an overview of the several prefab organizational approaches that are baked into the iPhone SDK, the coding toolkit developers use to build apps. You're not obliged to use any of these methods to build your app—you'll explore custom alternatives in Chapter 6—but leaning on the built-in navigation models gives your audience a structure that's instantly familiar. It helps your app blend both visually and organizationally with other apps. *Blend in?* Of course you want your app to bloom like a unique flower, and it will, but you're not operating in a vacuum. Designing for the iPhone, like designing for any platform, means respecting the norms and conventions of its operating system. An iPhone app

Photo: Paul Goyette

should look like an iPhone app. Adopting one of the stock organizational structures (and choosing the right one) is a fundamental way to do that.

The best apps have a design that fits in as if designed by Apple itself. That familiar feel is helped along by savvy use of the standard navigation methods and interface controls. This chapter begins to explore these standard presentation methods, starting with navigation and organization, and the next chapter surveys individual controls. The goal of these two chapters is to help you design apps the Apple way. Before we get started, here's one recipe for doing that—at every interface decision point, ask yourself this question:

WWJD: What Would Jobs Do?

Illustration: Dale Stephanos

Apple co-founder Steve Jobs built an entire brand around impeccable taste, quality, and ease of use. There's much to be learned by carefully studying Apple's own app designs and following the company's example. At the simplest level, Apple makes pretty things; if you're going to ape an aesthetic, Apple's a good choice. (That's true not only for what Apple puts into its built-in iPhone apps, but for what the company leaves out, too. As you've seen in previous chapters, tapworthy apps winnow features and limit controls for efficiency and ease; Apple's apps are refined examples of disciplined moderation.)

But this is about more than just style and looks. Apple's design decisions set the standard for the device, the frame in which all apps are considered and understood. The iPhone is like a celebrity red carpet: there's plenty of room for individuality, but ultimately you still have to wear an evening gown. Don't let your app wear a hobo costume to a formal ball. Following the dress code makes your app consistent with other apps, which in turn makes it easy for your audience to make sense of your app and understand how to make the thing go.

The remarkable consistency of third-party interfaces on the iPhone is a significant reason for its ease of use. This level of app affinity is unusual for any software platform, especially one that's so new, and it didn't happen accidentally. As a company, Apple is famously opinionated in matters of design. Rather than leave developers' interface choices to chance, the company created detailed rules for designing iPhone apps and codified them into a document called the *iPhone Human Interface Guidelines,* commonly known as *the HIG.* The HIG delivers Apple's design commandments, the company's definition of what it means to be a good iPhone citizen. Most operating systems, including Windows and Mac OS X, have a similar HIG to outline software best practices and behaviors. Like the device itself, however, the iPhone HIG feels different than that of other operating systems. It's an accessible read for regular folks, not just developers and is an essential document for everyone involved in your app's design. Download the HIG at *http://developer.apple.com/iphone.*

The HIG surveys the iPhone's toy chest of standard controls and views and explains the right way to use them to do what users expect them to do: *use this interface gizmo to do this, use that widget to do that.* This chapter, along with the next, introduces those gizmos and widgets, building on the HIG's basic concepts. These chapters offer examples and best practices, as well as warn you away from problem areas so that you can make smart decisions about when, where, and why to use the various controls and navigation options.

While the HIG focuses on interactive behavior more than visual design, it nevertheless has visual implications. The standard collection of buttons, controls, and views that Apple provides in its code toolkit strongly suggests how things should look on the iPhone, not just behave. The controls come in standard colors, many lodge automatically in certain parts of the screen, and the absence or inclusion of certain types of controls in the SDK implicitly encourages certain design choices. Apple doesn't provide checkbox controls, for example, so the iPhone's checkmark accessories and on/off switches become the norm instead (see page 153 and page 173 respectively).

Pay attention to these guidelines. More than just informed and battle-tested suggestions, Apple's interface guidelines are also criteria for App Store approval. Misuse a toolbar icon or bobble an activity indicator and you risk having your app kicked back to you for a fix before Apple's reviewers will accept it into the App Store. Avoid trouble by favoring standard controls in your app and abide by the guidelines in the HIG and in this chapter. Aside from the threatening stick of App Store rejection, there are also some tasty carrots in it for you when you use standard controls. Apple's guidelines reflect the sensibility of the interaction designers who created the iPhone interface, undeniably a bright bunch of people, and the conventions they've developed are good ones. Let's take a look.

Getting Around: Apple's Navigation Models

There are any number of ways to organize an app, but the iPhone code kit provides three ready-made navigation models that you can drop into your app. They cover the needs of a huge swath of apps and they'll be immediately familiar to any iPhone user. Each one comes with specialized toolbars and controls that your audience will use to hop from screen to screen. The next few sections explore each of these navigation styles in detail, but here's the quick rundown:

- **Flat pages.** This method targets relatively simple apps that have a single main screen—usually a highly graphical, no-scroll display like that of the built-in Weather app. The apps might have multiple versions of that main screen (forecasts for different cities, for example), and you can swipe through these "pages" like a deck of cards, optionally flipping them over to change the app's basic settings.

- **Tab bar.** The tab bar is a set of buttons at screen bottom that lets you switch among the app's main functions. Tap a button to jump to a new screen.

- **Tree structure.** Drill down through a hierarchy of categorized options or content (like folders on a desktop computer) and then easily pull back up to the surface.

There's also the "none of the above" option—what Apple calls an *immersive app.* These are typically full screen, highly graphical apps that dispense with standard controls and navigation schemes to create their own custom environment. Most games fit this category, as do other apps that use their own interface metaphors for users to explore. If you go this route you'll create your app's entire interface from scratch. You'll see some examples of these anything-goes interfaces in

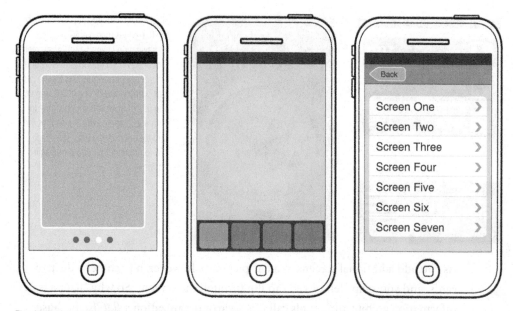

The three navigation models each have signature design silhouettes. From left to right: flat pages, tab bar, and tree structure.

Chapter 6 (page 182). For now, start off by getting a handle on the three common navigation models.

Flat Pages: A Deck of Cards (or Just One)

The *flat pages* navigation method is especially suited to *utility apps*, which provide tidy spoonfuls of simple, focused content in screens presented like cards. The main info appears on the card's "front," and it flips over to show basic settings on the "back." As you saw in the last chapter (page 77), utility apps often feature bold, splashy graphics designed to pass the glance test, an easy read at arm's length. At their simplest, utility apps consist of just a single card, like a Dashboard widget in Mac OS X, and are even sometimes just a one-sided card without any settings offered on the back. There's not much guesswork involved in figuring out how to get around a one-screener like that—no navigation required— and if that's your app, congrats, your navigation work is complete. Move along, nothing more to see here.

Single-screen utility apps demonstrate the flat-pages model at its simplest—no navigation beyond a settings screen. Global SOS (left) informs travelers of the emergency phone numbers for the current country, and the built-in Compass app (right) gives you your bearing. In both apps, tapping the "i" icon flips the card to show setting info. (See page 176 for more details about managing settings.)

As you add additional screens to a flat-page app, however, it becomes a deck of cards, and you swipe left or right to flip through the screens. So why "flat pages"? Information architecture nerds call this style of organization a *flat list*, because there's no hierarchy of information, no organizational scheme at all. The screens aren't grouped into categories, but are instead presented in one big pile that you page through one after another—a "flat" collection of pages.

This method is best suited for *browsing* and *discovery*, ambling through many variations of the same screen. For example, the built-in Weather app uses flat pages to show a forecast for a different city on each screen; the layout is the same for each page, but the forecast for each is city-specific. ESPN ScoreCenter similarly uses flat pages to show sports scores for specific teams or leagues on each screen; different colors provide visual cues, but the fundamental role of each screen remains the same. Both of these apps allow you to configure the screens and content to show in the app—cities in Weather, or leagues and teams in ESPN ScoreCenter—and you tap a settings button to flip the screen and choose the pages to include. Not only do flat-page apps work like a deck of cards, but they often let you choose and shuffle those cards, too, adding or removing from the deck as you like. In this scenario, where the number and content of screens is always changing, the flat-pages method is a better choice than the tab-bar navigation model, which you'll explore in the next section. There, the navigation options are offered as a fixed set of categories in a set order. If your app features a changeable number

Screens in ESPN ScoreCenter show a roundup of sports scores, with each "page" targeted to a different team or league. Tap the gear icon to see the app's settings.

of screens, particularly variations on the same relatively simple display, the flat-pages navigation model is a better solution.

To help people keep their bearings while browsing through the stack of screens, include the standard *page control,* the collection of dots at the bottom of flat-page apps. The dots represent the number of pages in the collection, with the highlighted dot showing your current position in the deck. The presence of a page control gives your audience a visual hint that this is just one of several screens, and it's also interactive. Tap on the left or right half of the control to sashay to the previous or next screen—an alternative to swiping. You might expect that tapping a specific dot would let you jump directly to the corresponding page, but alas no, the page control lets you step through only one page at a time. (Even if you could jump to a specific page, tapping just the right dot would take mighty fine finger precision; don't forget the 44-pixel rule from page 62.)

The presence of a page control signals that you're browsing a collection of flat pages, with the highlighted dot showing your current place in the stack. Usability testing reveals that many folks, even relatively experienced iPhone hands, think that the individual dots are themselves tappable controls, but they're not. Under the hood, the page control consists of just two tap areas, shown here at bottom. Tap the left half to go to the previous screen, tap the right to go to the next.

This adds up to a thumb-throbbing downside to the flat-pages model: you can't jump directly from the first screen to the last. You have to swipe or tap through each and every page—quite a workout with a big stack of screens—and a good reason to keep the page collection relatively small in this type of app. Screen dimensions encourage moderation, too. A page control can display only about 20 dots before those dots start spilling offscreen, clipped from view. The Weather app manages this problem by limiting its collection of forecasts to only 20 cities; try to add more and the app gently suggests that you remove another city first. Twenty screens already make for a lot of swiping, though; do the world's thumbs a favor and use flat pages for primary navigation only in apps with about ten pages or less. (It's no accident that the iPhone's main display of app icons—the *springboard*—is limited to 11 screens, even if your phone contains many more apps.)

The inability to jump to a specific screen means flat pages aren't ideal for apps whose screens offer very different functions or perspectives on the app's content. For example, Phases is a gorgeous little app for tracking the phase of the moon, with each of its four screens offering a different angle on lunar activity. Phases uses flat-page navigation, but because it has a fixed set of screens aimed at providing very different information, the app's navigation would be eased by using a tab bar instead. Rather than asking you to wax and wane through all the screens to get at specific aspects of the moon's phases, a tab bar would let you jump directly

Phases uses flat pages to display different aspects of the lunar cycle. A tab bar would provide a more natural navigation model for this type and amount of content.

to the screen of interest. This saves on more than extra swipes; it also saves brain cells. When a tab bar advertises each screen with a labeled button, you don't have to remember the content and order of the cards in the deck. In Phases, the variety of subject matter and the small, fixed number of screens suggests that tab-bar navigation would make for easier navigation.

As usual in app design, however, there are competing considerations. Shoehorning a tab bar into Phases would put a tight squeeze on the displayed info. A tab bar soaks up nearly 50 pixels of screen height, while a page control takes only a sliver, with dots that are just 6 pixels tall. The app's designers no doubt decided that asking users to flip back and forth through a modest number of screens was better than sacrificing some combination of content, readability, or the app's tidy no-scroll display. Using flat pages here is a compromise—a tab bar makes the most sense for navigating this content collection—but it's only a modest compromise given the small number of screens involved. The designers decided it was better to sacrifice on that point than to risk sacrificing real estate (and the principle of scroll skepticism) on the individual screens.

Striving for a no-scroll layout is always a good idea (page 77), but it's especially important in collections of flat pages. Because the page control anchors the bottom of the screen, it abruptly and awkwardly lops off scrolling content. Compare the clean finish of the screens in Phases, for example, to the clipped screens in ESPN ScoreCenter. The deck-of-cards metaphor in flat-page apps is most successful when each page *looks* like a card, complete and self-contained. Even more important, adding vertical scrolling to a flat-page screen introduces an ergonomic challenge, too: you're navigating in two directions—horizontally and vertically. It's all too easy to swipe a few degrees askew and land on the next page when you mean to scroll, or vice versa. People are most successful at navigating the touchscreen when moving in just one dimension; adding a second requires more precision and thus, more effort, from your audience. Avoid it when you can.

Flat Pages

Pros	Cons
• Ideal for quick, focused content; suited for casual browsing of screens	• Must swipe through the stack one page at a time; can't jump to any screen other than immediate neighbors
• Adapts to variable number of screens with customized content	• Doesn't scale well to large number of screens; page indicator limited to 20 dots
• Easy to use; navigation relies on familiar swipe gesture	• Doesn't handle scrolling well, not good for lengthy content
• Limited interface chrome; page control requires very little space, leaving lots of room for the content itself	• Users may overlook the small page indicator and miss app's additional screens

Tab Bar: What's on the Menu?

The *tab bar* is a dock of buttons anchored at screen bottom, giving your audience a menu of options to choose from. The result is a tidily categorized app, with its primary features explicitly listed and labeled. Unlike the undifferentiated pile of cards in flat-page apps, the tab bar's categories divvy an app into neat silos. Tap a *tab*—one of the tab-bar buttons—to jump directly to the associated screen, and the tab lights up to reflect where you are in the app.

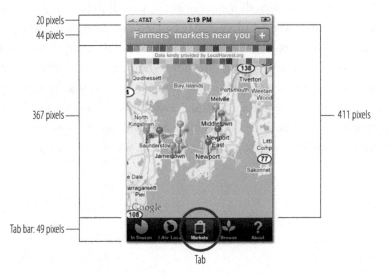

Urbanspoon uses a tab bar to offer five different ways to approach a restaurant search. The screens for the Shake, Browse, and Scope tabs are shown here from left to right.

You can display anything you like behind each tab, but it's most helpful to plan tab-bar organization around the different types of activities or information your app offers. The screens associated with each tab can (and often should) have their own independent interface style, each one tailored to fit the specific content or tools at hand. The built-in Clock app, for example, features four very different ways to work with time, each behind a dedicated tab: World Clock, Alarm, Stopwatch, and Timer. These screen designs vary widely; all of them are tuned to the specific needs of the current activity. The effect is that each of the features behind the tabs behaves almost like an independent app, a useful way to think about planning tab-bar categories.

Rather than focusing on tools and functions, as Clock does, tab bars can also be used to offer different perspectives on the app's information. Restaurant finder Urbanspoon, for example, organizes its tab bar around five different ways to browse and discover local tables. Each of these five tabs will eventually lead you to the same type of content—where to go for dinner tonight—but in very different ways. "Shake" spins the app's slot machine to find a nearby place at random; "Browse" lets you burrow through restaurants by various criteria; "Scope" visualizes nearby eateries; and so on. Likewise, news apps frequently use tab bars to offer options for filtering articles according to various characteristics (latest, popular, saved, topics, search, and the like).

As these examples illustrate, tab-bar navigation is ideal for letting the user choose among *modes of operation* tailored to specific features, information, or even states of mind ("I can't think of a restaurant, pick one for me"). A tab bar summarizes what your app does; it's a series of miniature advertisements for how the app can help. Tab bars make for efficient navigation, since they take people directly to specific screens to perform specific actions, but they require careful planning by the designer. The tab bar should offer a set of options that match up neatly to specific and common missions your audience has in mind when they launch your app.

At its simplest, tab-bar navigation can lead to a collection of simple single-screen displays, like the Phases screens you saw in the last section. More commonly, though, tabs lead to screens that in turn lead to additional screens, which means there's an additional layer of subnavigation nested within each tab. Urbanspoon's Browse tab, for example, uses a scrolling list to drill down into a directory of restaurant listings—that's tree-structure navigation within a tab. The stock navigation models aren't mutually exclusive, in other words, and you can mix and match, even in the same screen to provide subnavigation. You'll explore these mashup possibilities further, starting on page 114.

The standard code Apple provides to create tab bars comes with certain rules. The tab bar always appears at the bottom of the screen, 49 pixels high. Each button includes a text label and an icon. Design your own icon (page 194), or use one of the several stock versions that come with the operating system (page 145). The buttons vary in width depending on the number of buttons you include, expanding or compressing to fit the available space. Just don't expect to squeeze lots of buttons in there; tab bars have a five-button limit. If you try to add six or more, the tab bar automatically sprouts a More tab in the fifth position, leaving room only for your first four tabs and bumping any additional tabs to a separate screen. Tap the More button to see the remaining buttons. This overflow screen of extras automatically comes with an Edit button, and tapping it lets you customize the first four icons shown in the tab bar. Drag an icon down to your preferred slot in the tab bar, and poof, it settles into its new home, replacing the previous icon.

The More screen lists the tabs that don't fit on the tab bar. Here, the New York Times app offers section-specific content from its More screen (left). Tapping a section name in that screen takes you to a list of articles from that section. Customize the tab-bar icons by tapping the Edit button (circled), which reveals an icon view (right) that lets you drag your favorite sections to the tab bar.

Avoid the More button. When you sweep key navigation elements behind the More button's curtain, you add more than just an extra tap. You ask users to remember what options are back there, a brain burden that might seem trivial but will inevitably cause those hidden features to go overlooked and underappreciated. One of the tab bar's big advantages is that it puts your app's key features front and center—easily scanned, clearly labeled, and just a tap away from any screen. The More button undercuts that at-a-glance utility, burning one of the precious five tab slots in the process. The ability to customize the tab bar from the More screen is, in theory, a nifty trick to minimize the five-tab limitation by letting users choose their favorite tabs from the overflow. Unfortunately, testing reveals that most users don't know about that standard feature, rarely trying the Edit button on the More screen.

Stick to the five-tab limit. Not only do you dodge the More button, but the constraint encourages you to sharpen the definition of your app and the key features it offers. Five primary navigation elements make for a manageable structure for your audience to remember and understand. Keep it easy and don't make them think too hard about what your app does. Be frugal with the number of top-level features and screens you offer. If you find that you need more than five navigation categories, then the tree-structure navigation model may be better for your app since it adapts more gracefully to a larger number of categories.

Tab Bar

Pros	Cons
• One-tap access to all of the app's main features	• Only five tabs can be displayed at once
• Clearly labeled menu advertises primary features, shows current location	• Absorbs significant screen space on all (or most) screens of the app

The tab bar is a commitment. Its 49-pixel height takes up over 10 percent of the screen and typically appears on every screen of your app—a chunky piece of interface chrome. You're not absolutely obliged to put the tab bar on every screen of your app, though. It's appropriate to remove the tab bar on screens that need full-screen treatment—ebooks, photo slideshows, or document readers, for example—or that require additional controls that would otherwise crowd out the content, like the media controls in the iPod app's Now Playing screen. But the tab bar's sturdy reliability is one of its virtues, allowing fast leaps across the app's various features, and it's best to keep the tab bar planted on most if not all screens of your app.

The built-in iPod app drops the tab bar (left) from the Now Playing screen (right) to make room for the playback controls.

Tree Structure: Let 1,000 Screens Bloom

From the Dewey Decimal System to the animal kingdom to your Aunt Rhoda's filing system, big collections of information typically get organized into categories—and subcategories, sub-subcategories, sub-sub-subcategories, and so on. This is a *tree structure,* an information hierarchy whose category outline branches into an upside-down tree when you draw it like a flow chart (think corporate org charts or family trees). Tree structures are an efficient way to tuck away vast amounts of stuff and still put your hands on any one item quickly—the same dance step clerks have performed for centuries: go to file cabinet, choose drawer, open drawer of folders, pick folder, pluck out document. This file-and-folder fandango is the durable metaphor that makes desktop computing tick, letting you shuffle electronic documents among neatly nested folders.

The iPhone's tree-structure navigation model borrows directly from this desktop legacy. In fact, the column view of the Mac OS X operating system displays files

Tree-structure apps use the same file/category structure that we use to organize our desktop computers. The column view of Mac OS X (top) matches up conceptually and visually to tree-structure apps. The built-in Mail app lets you drill down to an individual mail message the same way you would drill down through folders on the desktop. Tap an account, then a mailbox, then a message to finally see its details.

and folders in the same way most tree-structure apps list their options on the iPhone. Every screen of a tree-structure app corresponds to a column in the Mac OS X display. Because the iPhone's not large enough to show the entire document tree, you see just one "column" at a time, each one skidding into view from the right as you tap through another level.

Tree-structure apps are ideal for managing big hoards of categorized items—emails, to-dos, expenses, photos, music tracks, contacts—but you can also use them to present large-ish sets of features. If you need to categorize your app into more than the five options you can squeeze into a tab bar, a tree structure allows longer (and more customizable) menus of options.

The main screens of Twitter app Birdfeed, left, and faxing app finarXFax, right, use tree-structure navigation to present their main features, a long-form substitute for the tab bar.

This style of organization and navigation lends itself to lists. An outline-style organization of categories and subcategories is, after all, a list of lists. You tap an item in one list to get to another list of items and then another until you wind up at the detail view of the item you're looking for. So, as you might expect, the most common and efficient way to visually organize tree-structure apps is as basic text-based lists, or *table views* in iPhone geekspeak. The tree-structure examples shown so far have been table views, simple lists whose items you tap to move along to the next level. You'll learn more about working with table views on page 152, but there are other, more graphical ways to display options in tree-structure apps, too.

Facebook, for example, introduces its many features with a set of icons, a layout that resembles the iPhone Home screen. The approach is not only graphical and familiar but also highlights that Facebook (as both platform and iPhone app) is really a collection of mini-apps comprising news, contacts, messages, calendar events, and more. This main-screen arrangement may look different than the previous list-based examples, but it's the same underlying organizational structure. A list of primary features leads to lists of content, and you keep tapping to drill down through these structured layers. (For more about Facebook's design

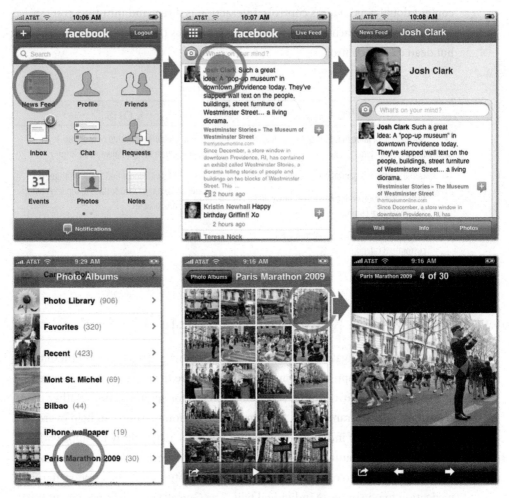

Facebook (top) uses icons in its main screen to represent the app's primary features. The built-in Photos app (bottom) uses thumbnail images to represent individual photos in the album view.

process, see page 236.) The built-in Photos app uses a similarly graphical presentation when you browse an album of photos. Instead of a list of photo titles—not very helpful on their own—the app gives you a pleasingly dense screen of thumbnail miniatures to choose from and then view full screen.

Whether you use lists, icons, or images for your presentation, all of these tree structure navigation examples offer similar advantages. In particular, they require very little interface chrome; the content itself is the control. This saves you space as a designer, but more important, it saves your users extra thought. When the content doubles as an app's controls, interaction is direct and intuitive: you tap what you want to learn about, allowing for interfaces that are information-rich but dead easy to control.

Tree Structure

Pros	Cons
• Scales well for large numbers of categories, features, and items	• Primary features are listed only on top-level screen, unlike tab bar's always-on display
• Familiar outline organization is easily understood	• Inefficient switching among main features or categories; you have to surface to top level before drilling down again
• Direct interaction with content is intuitive and limits interface chrome	
• List-based display adapts well for user-customized categories	

Combining Navigation Models

The three stock navigation models aren't all or nothing. You can blend them together in the same app, using one model to organize the app's primary features and the others to move around secondary screens for subnavigation. Rather than creating a hideous frankenapp, this kind of navigation mashup can help overcome the shortcomings of individual navigation methods, particularly for apps with lots of content or features to explore. An especially common design pattern uses tab-bar navigation to organize the app's primary features but adds tree-structure navigation to one or more individual tabs. The Gowalla app, for example, uses tabs to organize its four primary app categories, with three of those tabs presenting standard table-view lists of options on their main screens. Within each tab, you drill down through a tree structure to find the information you want for that particular category.

Gowalla uses tab-bar navigation for moving among its primary features but offers list-based tree navigation from three of those main screens as subnavigation. Here, the top-level Spots and Trips screens let you browse local places and scavenger hunts. Tap a category to drill down into the app's collection of content.

This approach files the sharp edges off a tree structure's big drawback, the inability to hop easily from one primary feature category to another. By lodging your app's main features in a tab bar, people don't have to climb all the way back to the app's surface to switch features; just tap the feature on the tab bar instead. If you go this route, your app can and should remember the state of affairs for each tab as users move around the tab bar. In developer lingo, this is called *restoring state,* and the principle is simple: when someone leaves one of your app's "rooms," don't redecorate while they're away. Returning to a tab should restore its screen to the same tree-structure position, or search results, or detail view, or whatever they were last looking at. Whatever you do, don't dump them at the top of the tab's tree structure and make them drill their way down to find their place again. This keep-my-place politesse is important throughout the iPhone experience, and it's a topic you'll revisit in Chapter 7 (page 226).

Gowalla also shows how flat-page navigation can likewise be embedded inside an app at a secondary level. The app's Passport screen shows your collected icons, and tapping one reveals its details and history, letting you flip through your collection as a set of flat-page cards by swiping left and right. The effect is like firing up a separate mini-app inside Gowalla. The view slides up from the bottom,

Both Gowalla and Safari put flat pages to work for secondary navigation inside the app. In Gowalla (top), tapping an item on the Passport screen conjures a slideshow-style view for flipping through your icon collection. In Safari (bottom), tapping the toolbar's window button lets you flip through the various pages you have open.

covering the previous screen, including the app's tab bar, so that the screen is dedicated entirely to browsing your collection. When you're finished browsing your treasures, tap Done to dispatch the items and return to the main Passport view.

This deck-of-cards display is well-suited to layouts with few or no buttons or controls, so using flat pages for just a portion of an app's content works best inside a dedicated view like those used by Gowalla and Safari. Extra controls tend to fight the card-flipping metaphor and muddy otherwise simple navigation from screen to screen. Better to let flat-page views temporarily take over the full screen while users swipe through the cards, save for any controls you need to dismiss the screen. (While Safari keeps its toolbar when you're flipping through open pages, for example, the app's typical icons are replaced by New Page and Done buttons.)

This treatment, where a screen temporarily takes over the entire app's display, is called a *modal view*, a brief detour from the app's normal operation. The important role of modal views is worth a detour of its own.

Modal Views and Navigational Cul-de-Sacs

If you think of an app's navigation model as the road your app travels, modal views are its cul-de-sacs—single-screen pull-offs for editing, viewing, or manipulating a screen's content. In computerese, a *mode* is a special circumstance where the app behaves differently than it usually does, often changing its interface in the process. Modal views are how you handle modes on the iPhone: a modal view is a screen that briefly hijacks your app's normal operation, swooping in to cover the current screen to let you perform some task related to that screen's content.

You just saw a pair of examples from Gowalla and Safari, which use modal views to browse content. Modal views are also commonly used to add or edit content. For example, the built-in Mail app uses modal views to move messages to a mailbox folder or compose new messages. These actions both summon a separate screen—the modal view—that lives outside Mail's normal tree-structure path of accounts, mailboxes, and messages. In both cases, those screens shoot up from the bottom of the screen—standard behavior for a modal view—and cover the previous screen while you take care of business. When you're finished, the screen retracts, letting you continue to browse and read your mail.

These task-focused, single-screen detours are full-screen examples of the hidden-door approach introduced in the last chapter for reducing interface chrome (page 85). Modal views neatly tuck away controls and interface elements that you need only occasionally for handling secondary tasks. By zooming up from the bottom to cover the current screen, modal views subtly reinforce their role as a temporary detour from the app's normal browsing, where screens typically swap out left and right, not up and down. Make sure you make it easy for people to get back to business as usual; in addition to including all the necessary buttons and

Mail uses a modal view to let you move a message to a mailbox folder. Tap the Move button in the toolbar of a message screen (left), and the Mailboxes screen shoots up from the bottom to cover the message until you file the message in a mailbox folder or tap Cancel. Like all modal views, the screen briefly interrupts the app's regular interface to complete a task. Tapping the Compose icon in the toolbar (left) likewise triggers its own modal view, this time with a screen for writing a new email message.

other controls to complete the task, add a Done or Cancel button to let people bail out if they change their mind.

These cul-de-sac pages hang off of individual screens, which means they sit outside the flow of the navigation models you've explored so far. They're not the main cards in a stack of flat pages, and they don't rest on the main branches of a tree structure. Instead, modal views are accessories to those primary screens; you conjure a modal view to perform some related task and then dismiss it. While that means modal views are not the main screens of a standard navigation model, it's also true that for some apps, modal views are all the navigation you need.

Safari, for example, is essentially a collection of modal views dangling from the main browser screen. There's no tab bar, no app categories to browse. The entire app is about the main screen of web content, with various tools popping up in modal views to change or share the content in the browser. The iPhone's virtual keyboard springs up to help you type a Web address or search term; the Mail Link screen slides up to send an email; the Bookmark screen zips in to help navigate to a saved page; and the Windows screen lets you switch among your open web pages. The app has no formal app navigation where you flow from screen to

Safari's operation relies on a collection of modal views instead of navigating a flowing series of screens. The keyboard as well as the email and bookmark screens are all modal views that you use to change or share the content of the main screen. They all briefly replace the browser window until you complete the task. (With the keyboard at left, the main browser window is visible underneath, but dimmed and inaccessible, peeking through the modal view that covers it.)

screen. Instead, you pop in and out of these single-purpose spurs jutting off the main view.

From elaborate tree-structure cascades to Safari's one-main-screen approach, you've seen lots of ways to organize the screens of your app using Apple's standard navigation models. When planning apps that have to juggle lots of content or tools, it's all too easy to get lost among these several options. When planning your app's navigation flow (and its occasional side-road detours), it helps to draw a roadmap to stay on course. Before you dive into the details of the standard iPhone controls, first sketch out how you'll put Apple's standard navigation models to use in your app. As you do this, think of your app as a story.

A Tangled Web

Remember *Choose Your Own Adventure* books? These popular kids' books of the 1980s had pre-teens weaving their way through ghost stories, westerns, and galactic expeditions, making a decision at the end of every page to choose what happened next. *To search for clues in the pantry, turn to page 31. To question the*

gardener, turn to page 48. The outcome of every adventure depended on how you moved through the book's pages, with scores of possible endings. I loved these books as a kid, but with every one of them, I eventually developed the nagging feeling that I'd missed a storyline, that some combination of pages had eluded me. The real fun became finding the missing endings—it was less about the story than about figuring out how the game worked, trying to find every path and conclusion. The book was a riddle.

That's *not* how you want people to experience your app. You don't want it to have hidden corners and undiscovered territory. It should be clear and evident how to navigate to every desired conclusion—more adventure, less mystery. The way you organize your app's screens makes all the difference.

Like the books, your app has a set of pages with fixed rules for how to navigate among them. What made the books tough for nine-year olds to explore with confidence is that the narratives got tangled. Stories didn't simply branch out, with each decision creating its own unique yarn. The plots crisscrossed and tangled with each other. You could make several different decisions but still land on the same ending ("buried alive!"). Instead of a tidy tree structure, the books were shaped more like a web, creating ambiguity and uncertainty. When you actually map the various paths of one of these books, the web reveals itself.

Don't organize your app like a web. People should be able to flip through its screens in a straight line (flat pages), a simple set of categories (tab bar), or a neatly categorized collection (tree structure). Paths through your app should be predictable and, ideally, unique: aim to build your app according to a "one room, one door" principle so that every screen has just one approach. While you might reasonably think that adding more doors makes it easier to get around, it instead adds more complexity, challenging your audience to create twisting mental maps

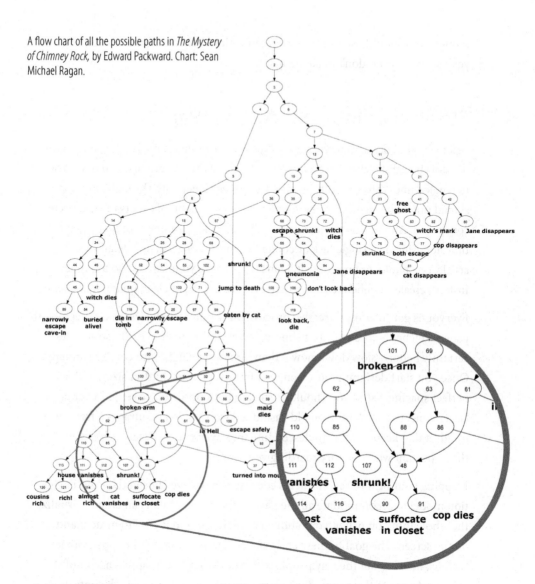

A flow chart of all the possible paths in *The Mystery of Chimney Rock,* by Edward Packward. Chart: Sean Michael Ragan.

of the app's layout. You want to build an app that people can explore, but you don't want them getting lost along the way. It's easier to remember just one path to a screen. (There are apps, of course, where the whole point is to present a web to untangle. The mission of many games, for example, is to solve puzzles, and an app that maps molecules might let you wander through a maze of atoms. In those cases, the goal is to present a riddle or a web of information—purposely creating the sense of getting lost and finding your way. If that's not what you're up to, though, you should use more strict organization. When it comes to figuring out your app's features, don't make people guess.)

Storyboarding Your App on Paper

Before you build, diagram your app's flow of screens, like a movie director preparing storyboard sketches for every scene of a shoot. Make sure that you have clean, untangled lines through your hierarchy of pages. Every path through your app should unfold like a quick story, following a logical chain of events to an expected conclusion. Along the way, each screen should tackle just one plot element at a time, focusing on a single task or content element—one list, one detail view, one article, one photo, or one contact. Don't try to make your screens do too much. Instead, create a deliberate pace where every screen has a clear, unambiguous role.

Everyone's got their own creative process, but it's almost always best to begin with paper sketches before you start slinging pixels in Photoshop or Illustrator. It's certainly better—slow down now—than jumping straight into coding your app. Once you start designing onscreen, you fret over colors, button sizes, and pixel-perfect spacing—stuff you shouldn't worry about until you've settled your app's larger concerns. Sketching on old-fashioned wood pulp encourages a free-form mindset that keeps you from descending into overly fussy details while you do the important work of storyboarding your app.

Mapping your flow of screens helps confirm that you've chosen the right navigation model to accommodate all the pages of your site. If you can crisply visualize the whole thing on paper, your audience will likely find it easy to understand on the screen. The goal in these early stages is to rough out your app's primary screens, figuring out the way people will flow through your app to accomplish primary tasks. At this point, don't worry over the specifics of which controls to use—you'll explore the standard iPhone controls in the next chapter. For now, your sketches should simply address the broad strokes: the screens you'll need, the actions to take on each one, and the general visual proportions of the tools and content to include. You're organizing your screens and prioritizing tasks at this stage—sketching, not designing.

If you're working in a team, this is a good stage to get all the decision makers involved. Sharing sketches, or drawing them together on a whiteboard instead of paper, is a cozy way to make sure everyone has the same basic vision of the app and its goals. When your group works with sketches—basic wireframe storyboards—you're able to talk about the bones of the app without getting distracted (or lulled) by considerations of style, color, and personality. Now's the time to make the big decisions about how the app interface should work. Changes that

The design team behind the Things to-do app created a *paper prototype* of every screen before starting to code, sketching the flow through every screen of the app. For more about the Things design process, see page 127. (Sketches by Cultured Code designer Christian Krämer.)

you make at this stage are easy—grab the eraser—but they become harder and harder as the design and development process proceeds. Don't wait to get sign-off until after you've already started applying your gorgeous graphics. Work it out on paper first.

Even though you're just thrashing through rough concepts at this stage, it's useful to make sure you're working in consistent proportions and a realistic size. Sketching iPhone-sized screens on graph paper is a perfectly good homegrown approach that helps keep your screens in balance with one another. As your sketches become more refined and you start to zero in on the precise layout you plan to use, the graph paper will help to size specific elements in the right neighborhood (think 44 pixels).

If you're doing lots of these screen sketches, you might consider splashing out with a more formal iPhone sketchpad. App Sketchbook (*www.appsketchbook. com*) sells spiral-bound notebooks with three life-sized iPhone templates per page, each with 20-pixel rules and title bar markings. Notepod (*www.notepod.net*) sells a pad of iPhone shaped pages, with correctly sized blank screens that let you sketch and tear off screens as quick as you please. There are also several download-and-print templates that fill the same role, like this PDF from the excellent "First & 20" website: *www.firstand20.com/articles/iphone-graph-paper.*

Put Something Ugly on Your iPhone

Congratulations, you've just built an iPhone app out of paper. Now it's time to shuffle those pages to get your stick figures off the page and onto an actual iPhone. As you learned in the last chapter, it's as important to make the app feel right as it is to make it look good. As soon as possible, before you start sprinkling your magic design dust on your sketches to turn them into a sparkling iPhone app, you should test how your sketches feel on an actual physical device. Don't worry about making it pretty; get an ugly prototype onto an iPhone just to see whether your design will work. This step helps you test that your layout makes sense and the ergonomics seem right before you invest in the careful work of style and color.

This pixel prototype doesn't have to be fancy, and it certainly doesn't have to be a working iPhone app. Since you really just want to see how the layout looks and feels on the phone, keep it low-tech: scan or photograph your sketches and, using a graphics program, size them to the iPhone's 320 x 480 screen. Add these images to your computer's photo collection (iPhoto on the Mac, for example) and sync them to your iPhone, where you can flip through the sketches full screen in the Photos app. Again, nothing fancy here; this just gives you a sense to check that your design's sizes and proportions work.

If you're feeling more ambitious, create a simple dummy iPhone app to try out your bare-bones layout. If you've got an iPhone developer handy—or if you're one yourself—you can build a quick-and-dirty app using standard buttons and controls that match up to your sketched layouts. This prototype shouldn't do much more than flip through screens. Use fake content just to show text placement, and wire up your buttons so you can tap from screen to screen. Or take a hybrid approach: build a working prototype app that uses your screen sketches but adds tappable regions to them that respond like real working buttons to flip to new screens and views. Happily enough, developer Rob Rhyne has developed a nifty iPhone code framework called Briefs that does just that—find out more at *www.giveabrief.com.*

Once you're satisfied that your rough sketches are moving in the right direction, you can start designing more polished mockups. Several developers have been kind enough to share their personal comping kits, collections of pixel-perfect iPhone elements that you can download and use in your favorite graphics program to assemble realistic layouts. Here are a few:

- iPhone elements for Photoshop (Teehan+Lax): *www.teehanlax.com/blog/2009/06/18/iphone-gui-psd-30*

- iPhone elements for Illustrator (Mercury Intermedia): *www.mercuryintermedia.com/blog/index.php/2009/03/ iphone-ui-vector-elements*

- iPhone elements for Fireworks (Blog*spark) *http://blog.metaspark.com/2009/02/fireworks-toolkit-for-creating-iphone-ui- mockups*

- iPhone elements for Omnigraffle (Patrick Crowley)
  www.graffletopia.com/stencils/413

But now we're getting ahead of ourselves. Before you start working with true-blue iPhone controls, you'll need to know their details. Working with these tools the Apple way is the topic of the next chapter.

Touchpoints

✓ Following conventions doesn't make your app conventional. Embrace Apple's design sensibility.

✓ Apple's built-in navigation models provide organizational solutions for most apps. Understand the pros and cons of each, and choose the best match for your app: flat pages, tab bar, or tree structure.

✓ Storyboard your screens to plan a clear flow through your app. Do big-picture thinking on paper before jumping to pixels.

✓ Start ugly. Begin with a primitive prototype app before starting to code with your full design.

First Person: Jürgen Schweizer and Things

The App Store is chockablock with task managers, but Things sets itself apart from other to-do list apps with its flexibility and ease. Organization systems are hugely personal and Things adapts naturally to your own approach: keep it simple with a single checklist or juggle a sprawling collection of projects, responsibilities, and contexts, staged over time. The app's design is minimal and efficient to the point of being practically invisible. Things follows the Apple rule book scrupulously with an elegantly simple design that relies almost entirely on standard controls and colors. The result puts the focus on tasks and goals instead of the app's own interface.

Jürgen Schweizer is founder and one of the chief developers of Cultured Code, the company behind Things. He shared the philosophy and process that went into planning the app's features and navigation, from concept to paper to iPhone screen. (Sketches by Cultured Code designer Christian Krämer.)

Organizing the App

Jürgen Schweizer: We do a lot of work before we even start thinking about an interface. We start out by having lots of conversations, really talking through what we want the app to be. The most important thing is to understand what you're trying to achieve at the conceptual level: what problem do you want to solve, what kind of users do you expect to have, and what are their expectations? Many designers jump ahead and start working with interface controls before they even figure out the user's mental model—what problem they need the app to address.

Once we know what we want an app to do, we move to paper to start working on interface sketches and mockups. We build flow diagrams of every screen, with arrows drawn between them so that we can see exactly how people

The desk of Christian Krämer, who crafted the visual design of Things and its paper prototypes.

will move through the app (see page 123). You can really do a lot on paper, but you never know for sure whether it will work until you build it and try it with actual users. Still, we start building only after we've planned the whole thing because you can't give people a half-finished app to test. You have to have a full implementation for them to try out, and that means coding an entire app before you can give it to testers. That's why it's so important to do these paper sketches first, to have a solid plan in place because you really don't want to recode the whole thing over and over again.

Choosing the Navigation Style

Jürgen: We originally liked the idea of using a tab bar for navigation to allow fast browsing of all your tasks from different perspectives—projects, tags, due date, search, and so on. But we soon found that we would need more than five tabs, which meant some would have been hidden inside the More tab. Tab-bar navigation didn't scale well enough for the features we wanted to include. We also realized that we needed a toolbar in order to provide tools to create, move, and edit list items. We decided to go without the tab bar and use tree navigation with a toolbar. The built-in navigation controls really take you a long way. The tree navigation is a powerful metaphor, and it got us really far right out of the gate.

Early sketches for Things contemplated tab-bar navigation.

An early sketch (left) for the main screen of Things used a grouped list, but the final version (right) evolved to better group its to-do lists into logical clusters.

Using table views for navigation also let us use groups to communicate which lists are alike and order them to reflect workflow. When you start off with Things, the main screen shows four groups: Inbox, Today/Next/Scheduled/Someday, Projects, and Logbook. Inbox is where you collect ideas that have not yet been assigned a place in your system. That means you haven't yet decided when you want to start the to-do. When you make that decision, the task lands in a list somewhere in the second group: today, next (as soon as possible), on a certain date, or someday in the hazy future. Projects lets you organize your tasks into separate goal-focused lists and Logbook is the archive where completed tasks wind up. So the standard table view lets us group and order lists based on when you want to start a task, and then organize those lists in a way that suggests a typical workflow.

Minimal Graphics

Things uses graphics sparingly, using a limited number of simple icons in carefully chosen locations to guide the eye and suggest meaning. Icons are used to label primary lists on the Home screen, for example, but not for individual to-do items themselves. This gives lists visual weight as top-level containers.

Jürgen: If you overuse icons, users will stop paying attention to them, and you've only added visual clutter. On the other hand, if you use icons in specific places while omitting them in others, you can use them to communicate the difference of certain parts of your interface. It's important not to use icons just to add visual candy. You should use them only to communicate meaning. (Of course, as long as you succeed at that, it doesn't hurt to make them beautiful as well!)

When you navigate to the detail screen for a to-do, for example, you'll see items both with and without icons. All the items that show secondary information

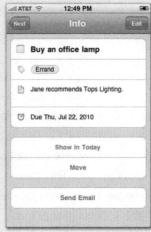

An early sketch (left) for the task detail screen included icons to differentiate descriptive data for the task, and the final design (right) further distinguished the buttons at screen bottom.

about the to-do—notes, tags, and so on—have icons describing each type of info. The action buttons below the info fields, however, have no icons. This has two advantages: first, the title and notes fields both use text and the icons help the user distinguish them from one another. Second, by using centered blue text instead in the buttons instead of icons, we tell the user that they are fundamentally different from the info fields. It's easy to figure out which elements are part of the to-do item and which parts are buttons for action.

What Makes the Feature List?

Things started life as desktop software for Mac OS X. When Cultured Code started developing the iPhone version, they considered how the two versions should relate to each other. The team began with the assumption that the iPhone version of Things would be a light version of the desktop app, but they surprised themselves.

Jürgen: The first thing we thought about was how would people use Things differently on a mobile device instead of the desktop application. It turns out that for a to-do list app, people didn't just want a satellite companion to the desktop app that would offer only a subset of features, like maybe only capturing new to-dos or showing some simplified version of your to-do lists. We found that we needed to build the full functionality of the desktop version into the iPhone app. It was the only way to give people everything they needed, and we couldn't go with half measures. This surprised us at first, and it's not true for all applications. The Photos app is very different from iPhoto on the desktop, for example. But for a to-do list app, we learned that we really did have to build all these features—users expected it. We were challenged with trying to figure out a way to put everything on the iPhone.

One place where we said no, however, was using the location sensor. At first, we dreamt that Things would figure out where you are and then be smart enough to tell you all the tasks you have to do at a certain location. It would just give you a fresh to-do list, like magic. But as we started thinking about it, it turned out that it's not so obvious or easy to get that magic into the app.

People would have to do a lot of setup just to associate tasks with places to teach the iPhone how to manage these location-based tasks. And then, after all that work, it wouldn't be clear exactly how the app should suggest the tasks to do at the location. You have to be careful how much you impose the app's logic on what people want to do at any given time. At best you can give small hints about available tasks, but then are small hints really worth all the work users would have to invest? In the end, we decided that we couldn't really solve it in a way that resulted in a satisfying experience.

For developers it's not easy to *not* do things. Apple gives you this great technology, and they want you to use it, and your users want you to use it. But unless you can really make it work in a satisfying way, you have to resist that temptation. It's hard to say no, but it's important.

Rhyme with Apple's Design Language

Jürgen: Before we started to design, we analyzed literally every screen in all of Apple's apps for the iPhone. It was important for us to understand every nuance of Apple's user-interface "language." The amazing thing about Apple's own apps is the level of design consistency they achieved. They all speak the same language. This is so different from other platforms, and it means that your app can be a seamless part of the overall platform experience, too. When your app follows Apple's design conventions, users feel immediately at ease when they tap your app icon. It's a huge motivation to try to deeply understand Apple's design decisions down to every detail so you're able to do it the same way and create the same kind of experience.

One of the reasons the iPhone is so successful is that Apple really tried to make the technology behind it invisible. You don't have to think about how it works. I think that's the thing to aim for as a developer—make the interface essentially invisible, too. You take it out of your pocket and you just tap somewhere. You really don't want to make people think about where to tap or what's the next step. For users, the focus should be on the task and the goal, not the interface.

In iPhone design, beauty and elegance comes from a sense of simplicity. There are always many, many different ways that an application can approach a certain task, but only a few of those options will actually be simple and clear, something that people can easily understand and figure out. As developers, our first tries are often more complex than they should be. When you're finally able to do something in the simplest, clearest way, it clicks. It feels like the fog has lifted, and there's a sense of beauty in both the code and the interface.

Eye candy isn't as important to the beauty of an interface as a lot of designers think. That's not what sets you apart. If you figure out the right way to solve a user's problem and do it right, the eye candy is secondary. You can add some nice visual touches later, but it shouldn't be where you start. Even if you use only standard controls, the application will develop a personality and spirit of its own. If you put the right controls at the right place at the right time, then you have an application that's easy for people to use and accomplish what they want to do.

You don't need fancy graphics for that. We use standard iPhone controls whenever possible. Developers should think hard before reinventing the wheel and creating their own controls. People feel right at home with what Apple provides, and that's a great starting point.

5

The Standard Controls

USING THE BUILT-IN INTERFACE ELEMENTS

VANILLA NEEDS A PRESS AGENT. Somewhere along the way, the flavor got a bad rap. The word is trotted out to suggest bland conformity, a drab lack of imagination, color, and flavor. Seriously, what happened here? Vanilla is a subtle, complex, vivid, and bright flavor. When it comes to dessert, a scoop of vanilla ice cream goes with nearly everything. It's versatile *and* delicious.

The standard iPhone controls are vanilla. They're the buttons, text fields, list views, keyboards, and icons that commonly and comfortingly appear in app after app. The standard controls provide a rich and varied set of options for manipulating an app, but because they're commonplace, they're often taken for granted and are sometimes dismissed as visually dull. Don't underestimate just how delicious they can be. Commonplace means familiar, and for your audience, familiarity leads to efficiency and ease—exactly what most folks want from an app. In usability testing sessions, people are routinely most successful at completing iPhone tasks when they're able to use behaviors learned from other apps. Novices in particular benefit from interfaces that use icons and controls they've seen elsewhere. Nobody wants to spend brain power figuring out how your app works; standard controls make for intuitive apps.

Photo: Peter Gorges

In this chapter you'll roll up your sleeves with a thorough review of the toolbars, buttons, and other controls cooked into the iPhone operating system. There's lots of detail here to supplement the iPhone Human Interface Guidelines (page 99), all of it aimed at making you fluent in every user-experience aspect of the standard controls. You'll learn the do's and don'ts for all of these elements, exploring the opportunities, pitfalls, and potential usability gotchas of each one.

Some designers bridle at relying on these pre-packaged interface elements, understandably concerned that leaning on built-in controls will lead to a humdrum design, perhaps even a humdrum app. Because the standard interface elements are generic building blocks, they can make designs feel generic, too. But as you'll see in the coming pages, generic has its benefits, and following conventions doesn't have to make you conventional.

No matter what language you speak or what country you're in, the familiarity of standardized road signs give drivers clear and unambiguous instructions. Standard controls in iPhone interfaces lend similar authority to the apps shown here. From left to right: Now Playing, Bento, and the built-in Settings app.

The Power of Standard Visuals

Familiarity and consistency lend designs authority. That's why road signs around the world are standardized. Drivers hurtling down the freeway shouldn't have to do double takes to figure out what a sign means. When instant and effortless communication is critical, conventions are a designer's best friend. Buttons, icons, and toolbars are the road signs for your app, and iPhone screens that use standard controls have a no-nonsense seriousness that lends them a similar authority and don't-make-me-think understanding.

But eesh, that's a lot of blue and white, and the gray orthodoxy of so many pin-stripe backgrounds is enough to nudge anyone into an interface coma. Different isn't always better, but neither is heedless homogeneity. There's room to take some license with your interface design as long as you do it thoughtfully and keep the interface intuitively second nature. Even standard controls can be dressed up to give your app its own unique visual stamp, for example, a trick Apple itself deploys in some of its own apps.

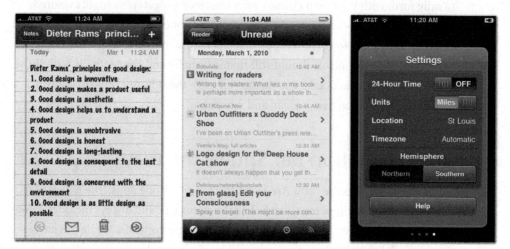

Standard interface elements don't have to be bland. Even relatively small tweaks of color and style let you give an app its own personality. The built-in Notes app (left) takes the look of a legal pad by putting colors and fonts to work in its navigation bar and text area; sketched versions of standard toolbar icons complete the sketchpad look. Reeder, a Google Reader app (middle), creates a rich look by adding a subtle gray texture to its navigation bar and toolbar and styling its list headings as torn paper. Phases (right) colors familiar iPhone controls to create an intuitive but altogether individual look.

As usual, it's a matter of degree. Don't be like those restaurants that get a bit too clever with men's and women's restroom signs, turning your bathroom break into a head-scratching riddle to figure out which door is yours. Give your app a personality suited to its function, but don't stray too far from the familiar norms of the iPhone environment. "Efficient" is a personality, too. For productivity apps in particular, your interface chrome shouldn't be too distracting; unadorned standard controls recede into the background, becoming almost invisible, to allow the content to become the main event. As designers, we naturally want to be daring and adventurous, to try something new, and it's true that iPhone fans appreciate app aesthetics. Even more, though, they appreciate getting stuff done. The true test of creativity is to find opportunities for expression within the helpful constraints of real-world use. Apply a light hand, and be careful not to allow your design whimsy to interfere with your audience's ability to actually use your app. Vanilla often trumps more exotic flavors.

It's cheaper, too. Relying on Apple's stock controls gets you lots of code for free; no need for you or your developer to build it on your own. Even when you decide to sally forth with your own custom-built interface gadgetry—a topic explored in the next chapter—understanding the standard controls and usage metaphors is the starting point for making apps that feel natural in the iPhone environment. Your own custom controls should still rhyme visually and conceptually with those provided by Apple. Let's take a look, starting with the iPhone's built-in control panels: the navigation bar, toolbar, and search bar.

The Navigation Bar Shows the Way

The *navigation bar* is the "You Are Here" beacon of iPhone apps. The navigation bar hugs the top of the screen, just below the status bar, and always includes some combination of screen title, back button, or other app controls. While the navigation bar isn't limited only to tree-structure apps—it can display the screen title and tools for any type of app—it's especially essential in drill-down apps because it lets you drill back *up,* too, thanks to the all-important back button. The navigation bar helps users keep their bearings as they move up and down your app's tree of information and features.

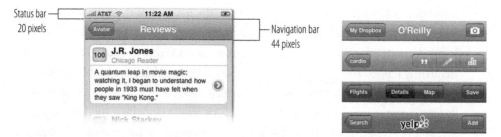

Status bar — 20 pixels

Navigation bar 44 pixels

The standard arrangement of the navigation bar (left) displays a back button at left and the screen title at center, but you can customize the navigation bar with your own colors, controls, labels, or graphics, as shown in the examples at right. As shown here, the navigation bar is 44 pixels tall in portrait orientation, but when you flip to landscape, it shrinks to 32 pixels. (For more on this and other considerations of landscape layouts, see page 262; Chapter 9 is all about working in landscape orientation.)

Behind the scenes, the navigation bar is divided into three regions—left, center, and right—where you can pour in text or buttons. In the standard setup, the left displays a *back button*, the center announces the *screen title*, and the right is blank. You can override that arrangement to fill those regions with your own controls or display elements, but go cautiously before you start making replacements. The screen title, for example, is a helpful way to cue your audience where they are in the app. In fact, at the top level of a tree-structure app, the screen name is often the *only* thing in the navigation bar. That's logical enough: since you haven't yet drilled down into the app when you arrive at the main screen, there's no back button to show. That changes when you venture at least one level down, where the navigation bar automatically sprouts a standard back button on the left. Tapping it takes you to the previous screen, one more level up toward the app's main screen.

In the to-do list app Things, the navigation bar in the app's top-level screen says simply, "Lists," the screen title shown at left. Tap a list to view, and the navigation bar updates to show the title of the new screen, with a back button to return to the Lists screen.

Honor thy back button. Treat its home at the left side of the navigation as sacred ground, and avoid planting any other controls in that spot, a space that should be used only to return to the previous screen. On the Home screen, where there is no back button, it's a good practice to leave the left side of the navigation bar empty; don't be tempted to fill it with another control just because you've suddenly got unused space. Because the back button always stakes out such familiar and frequently tapped real estate, putting a different button there inevitably invites a mistap. That's especially true when you're deep inside a tree-structure app, busily tapping your way back up to the surface. An empty slot at the top level signals that you've arrived at the main screen—there's meaning in the button's absence—but if you put some other control there instead, an eager over-tapper will eventually keep on going, tapping right through your button switcheroo. In particular, avoid putting an Edit, Logout, or other similar button that could change the state of the app (or its data) in some significant and surprising way. Don't make 'em think: be consistent with your placement of controls and, whenever possible, reserve the left side of the navigation bar for the back button or nothing at all. (In modal views, for example, this is a good place for a Cancel button, which is functionally the same as a back button in that context.)

The right side of the navigation bar, however, is all yours. Add any button or control that you like: a labeled text button, your own custom icon, or one of the many standard icons that come bundled with the iPhone coding toolkit (page 145). As you saw in Chapter 3, the right corner of the screen is, ergonomically, one of the most out-of-the-way locations for wandering thumbs, a good place to plant controls that are infrequently needed or that you don't want users tapping accidentally—actions that add or delete data, for example. The Edit button makes frequent appearances in this slot; you'll learn more about the Edit button on page 148.

If the left side is sacrosanct and the right is anything-goes, the navigation bar's center is, yes, somewhere in the middle. Be cautious about commandeering the center of the navigation bar for something other than the screen title. It's common to slap an app's logo in that space, for example, but it's best to limit that usage to the app's top-level screen. Chances are, your app's branding is more important to you than it is to your audience. They already bought your app, and they're actively using it—they know who you are. No need to bludgeon them with your logo branding on screen after screen. Go ahead and slap your logo on the first screen's navigation bar if you must, but then switch back to using the traditional screen title on other screens. Except in cases where the content of the screen is bluntly self-explanatory, avoid losing that title. It performs an important no-nonsense usability role by telling users where they are, fending off navigation vertigo as they spin deeper into your app. The iPhone's tiny screen reveals only a sliver of your overall app at any one time, and a titled screen helps people stay oriented.

 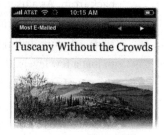

The New York Times app drops the screen title from the navigation bar on many screens. Top-level sections (left) instead show the Times logo, compensating by including the screen title (the name of the content section) in the content area below. That means less room for headline content, though. Space could be saved by putting the screen title in the navigation bar instead. On article pages (right) where most headlines won't fit in the navigation bar, the app wisely keeps the title in the content area. The extra space is used for previous/next buttons to step through the articles of the current section.

For screens that require more explanation than a meager title, the navigation bar also accommodates *prompt text*. This is especially handy on modal views where you're manipulating content in a way that might require a hint about what to do, like moving an email message to a new folder in Mail. When moving an email message to a new folder in Mail, for example, the app displays the prompt text, "Move this message to a new mailbox."

Like the screen title and prompt text, back buttons also provide grounding context, albeit more subtly. In addition to helping you get around, the back button normally shows the title of the previous screen, a reminder of where you came from and of what lies on the other side of the back button. Some apps replace that title with the blandly unhelpful label "Back." Avoid watering down the content of the back button, except where tight space causes the previous screen's title to be lopped off so much as to be meaningless. The back button is a road sign, and taking

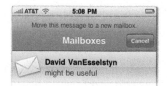

Prompt text appears above the navigation bar's usual collection of controls, extending the navigation bar's height by 30 pixels to an overall height of 74 pixels in portrait view.

that contextual information away removes one of the locators that keeps your audience grounded in the app.

An even better way to keep people from getting lost is to limit how far they can wander in the first place. Try to limit the depth of tree-structure apps so that your users don't disappear down a rabbit hole that takes them forever to climb back from. As a user, if you find yourself deep inside one category but want to switch to another primary category, you first have to tap all the way back to the surface before drilling down again. If you can't limit your app's navigation depth to just a few levels, then consider some creative shortcuts for jumping back to the top of a deep stack of screens. The standard iPhone toolkit doesn't provide a way to instantly teleport back to the start, but a few apps have pioneered some workarounds by adding custom swipe or tap gestures on the navigation bar. The Twitter app (formerly known as Tweetie) lets you leap back to the main screen by swiping left-to-right across the navigation bar. Facebook lets you do the same by tapping the screen title. (You'll learn all about working with gestures in Chapter 8.) Any app with significant content depth should consider rigging a similar escape hatch.

The navigation bar can stage its own escape, too. You're not obliged to include the navigation bar on every page, and you can send it packing when you want to devote the full screen to your content, useful for photos and long-form content, for example. When you take away the navigation bar and its back button, of course, you have to provide some other way to leave the current screen. For tree-structure apps, which *need* a navigation bar, the standard way to do this is to toggle the display of the navigation bar with a tap of the screen. When you do that, it's often

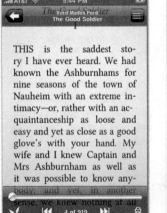

Ebook reader Eucalyptus (left) and the built-in Photos app (right) both perform the disappearing chrome trick: tap the screen to toggle the display of both navigation bar and bottom toolbar. Even when visible, the toolbars in both apps are translucent to allow the underlying content to remain visible.

appropriate to make the navigation bar partly transparent, too; even when the interface chrome is visible, the full-screen content still shines through. For more about handling transparency and color for navigation bars and toolbars, see page 186.

While the navigation bar can accommodate tools to work with a screen's content, you should let its primary role remain, well, navigation. Leave the navigation bar as uncluttered by controls as possible so that it can clearly announce the current location and offer a way back to previous screens. The main home for screen controls should instead be the *toolbar* at screen bottom.

The Toolbar

Where would Batman be without his utility belt, Martha Stewart without her glue guns, or MacGyver without his paperclips and chewing gum? Getting stuff done requires tools, and the toolbar is the onscreen toolbox for providing gadgets for editing, manipulating, or sharing content. If you need to give people controls for working the current view, give 'em a toolbar. The toolbar anchors the bottom edge of the screen, displaying a collection of text buttons or unlabeled icons. Don't confuse the roles of the toolbar and the tab bar (page 106). Tab-bar buttons are for *navigation,* for moving about your app's main features, but toolbar buttons work on the current screen of content. Put another way, tab bars think globally, and toolbars act locally. The toolbar's gadgets and gizmos are for doing stuff with what you're looking at right now, providing the commands to manage the immediate content.

Toolbar: 44 pixels —

The toolbar glues itself to screen bottom, as shown here in Mail (left) and Calendar. In portrait orientation, the toolbar is 44 pixels tall as labeled above, but it compresses to 32 pixels when you flip to landscape. (See Chapter 9 for more about managing landscape layouts.)

When viewing a message in Mail, for example, the toolbar offers options to check for new mail, move the message to a folder, delete the message, reply or forward, or create a new message. Safari's toolbar provides similarly action-oriented options to work with the content in the main browser view. In many cases, a toolbar button triggers the display of a modal view (page 117) or action sheet (page 169), but you can use them to kick off a background process (refresh your email list in Mail), filter the displayed content (direct messages in Twitter), or display the content in a new way (event list versus calendar view in Calendar).

Database app Bento (left) stacks a toolbar on top of a tab bar. Add the navigation bar to the mix, and you've got three stripes of controls, lots of real estate dedicated to interface chrome. Cocktails+ (below) has a better solution. The app provides a tab bar to navigate its collection of cocktail recipes, but hides the tab bar on the actual recipe page to make room for the toolbar.

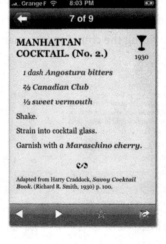

Load up your toolbars with any combination of controls, icons, and text. You can design your own icons, or dip into the collection supplied by Apple, which you'll explore on page 145. Just don't let too many controls elbow their way into the toolbar. An app's main controls need breathing room for both visual clarity and easy tap targets. *Apple recommends limiting the number of icons to five.* You can adjust the toolbar's transparency, or choose any color for it, just like the navigation bar. Be sure to coordinate the toolbar's appearance with the navigation bar so that the two are a matched pair. (For more about treating colors and transparency of these controls, see page 186.)

Avoid stacking a toolbar and tab bar on the same screen. Jamming so many controls in such close proximity at the screen's bottom edge is a recipe for tap mistakes, and all that stacked interface chrome also squeezes available space for the main event—your app's content. If you have a tab-bar app, and you'd like to include a toolbar on detail views, consider hiding the tab bar on that screen.

"So an Icon Goes into a Bar . . ."

Tab bars, navigation bars, and toolbars: that's a hoppin' bar scene, and one you should populate with a cast of one-of-a-kind characters. The icons and controls that fill your app's crucial control panels have to be visually distinct, easily identifiable and, wherever possible, consistent with those of other apps. Don't be obscure. Designing your iPhone app will provide lots of opportunities for cute and clever design, but the form of your toolbar icons isn't one of them. Icons should be direct, efficient, and familiar, leaving little room for doubt about their meaning. It's a tough thing to do in just 20 or 30 pixels. Good icon design is hard.

That's all the more reason to rely on the iPhone's collection of standard signage. Apple bundles a sleek set of icon buttons into the iPhone OS for a broad set of common tasks. Before trudging off to design your own buttons, check Apple's icon pantry to see if you've already got what you need. Using a standard button saves you effort, sure, but it saves your users some head scratching, too. When people encounter an icon they've seen over and over again in other apps, they understand its meaning immediately—no thinking required. That's exactly what you want for your app's primary controls.

The catch in this bargain is that you have to use the standard buttons the right way. Each has a very specific intended use, reinforced by their consistent appearance in other apps. The standard icon set isn't a place to take creative license. Even if an icon's shape suggests an alternative meaning, don't go there. Just because the Reply button is a left-pointing arrow, for example, doesn't mean you can use it as a back button. Don't get distracted by what standard icons look like: pay attention only to what they *mean*.

Apple gives you two separate sets of icons—one for tab bars and another for navigation bars and toolbars. Don't be confused by this double duty for navigation

Standard Tab Bar Icons

Bookmarks. Show a list of the app's bookmarks.

Contacts. Show the users contact list.

Downloads. Show a list of downloads.

Favorites. Show a list of user-determined favorites.

Featured. Show content specially selected by the app.

History. Show a rundown of user actions.

More. Show additional tab bar items (see page 109).

Most Recent. Show the latest content.

Most Viewed. Show the content most popular among all users.

Recents. Show items accessed recently by the user.

Search. Enter a search mode.

Top Rated. Show the highest-rated items, based on the user's own ratings.

bars and toolbars; as you've seen, the toolbar is the main home for button controls, but the navigation bar can hold buttons, too, particularly in its left and right regions. It just happens that both bars accommodate the same style of icons. Any icon that you can use in a toolbar, in other words, you can also use in a navigation bar. Just don't try the same wardrobe swap with the tab bar. The tab bar is larger than the other bars in both role and dimension, and that means the tab bar gets dressed in its own icon set.

Although you can use the same icon set in either navigation bars or toolbars, buttons get a subtle makeover depending on where you use them. Buttons in navigation bars always have a shaded 3-D effect, and this *bordered style* is added automatically to any control you add to the navigation bar. Toolbars can likewise

Standard Icons for Toolbars and Navigation Bars

	Action. Show an action sheet (page 169) with a menu of options.
	Bookmarks. Show a list of the app's bookmarks.
	Camera. Show an action sheet (page 169) to choose a photo.
	Compose. Show a new-message view in editing mode.
	Reply. Send response to item.
	Add. Create a new item.
	Delete. Delete current item.
	Organize. Move an item to a folder or other destination.
	Search. Show a search field.
	Refresh. Refresh contents of current screen.
	Stop. Cancel the current process or task.
	Play. Start media playback or slideshow.
	Rewind. Move backwards through media playback or slideshow.
	Pause. Pause media playback or slideshow.
	Fast Forward. Fast-forward through media playback or slideshow.

use bordered buttons, but it's more common for them to go in the buff in the *borderless style,* flat icons resting flat on the toolbar. Whatever style you choose to use for the toolbar, be consistent: don't mix bordered and borderless controls in the same toolbar. (Hint: If your toolbar includes only icons, without any text-based buttons or other controls, go with the flat borderless style.)

Navigation bars (left) always display bordered buttons with a rectangular outline. Toolbars (right) can use either bordered or unbordered buttons. Here, the buttons of the top right toolbar are unbordered, and the ones at bottom right are bordered.

Navigation Bar **Toolbar**

As you might expect, Apple's standard icons are a sturdy and reliable lot, but one of them is a little squirrelly—the Action toolbar icon. This odd little guy shows an arrow slinging out of a tray, which may or may not be an outbox (or an inbox? or a litter box?). The icon seems to suggest sending or forwarding content, appropriate for actions related to sharing perhaps, but not to all-purpose "action." Use this icon for actions related to sharing content—that's how users understand it—but seek out alternatives when you want to offer a set of more general or varied actions. (The designers of Twitterrific did exactly that, creating their own custom Action icon to present several varied options for working with a tweet; see the case study on page 205.)

When the standard icon sets don't cover an action you need to represent, you can always design your own icon, a topic you'll explore in the next chapter (page 194). An alternative, however, is to use a text-based control. Rectangle buttons (page 172) and segmented controls (page 174) make frequent appearances in toolbars and offer the bland but important usability advantage of descriptive labeling. When you tap List, Day, or Month in Calendar's toolbar, the app shows you a list, day, or month view. No ambiguity there, and hey, it pays to be direct. You'll dig into these and other controls later in this chapter.

A handful of those text-based controls gets special treatment in toolbars and navigation bars. The Edit, Done, Save, and Cancel buttons don't look especially remarkable—just run-of-the-mill rectangular buttons—but they play such a frequent and important role that they're cooked into the iPhone OS to ensure that they have the same appearance and verbiage across all apps. Use the Edit and Done buttons as the flip sides of a single button in a navigation bar or toolbar. When you tap Edit to switch to edit mode, the button should morph into a highlighted Done button, which you then tap when you're ready to save and return to the regular view—and the button morphs back into the Edit button. This Edit/Done two-step should take place on the same screen, making just small changes to the display to indicate the switch back and forth from edit mode. When you edit a list, for example, delete and drag controls typically materialize without flipping you to a new view. This is good practice, keeping you visually anchored as you switch modes so that it's obvious you're still working with the same collection of content. By contrast, the Save and Cancel buttons are typically used when editing content in a separate view—updating contact details in the built-in Contacts app, for example. In that case, tapping Save or Cancel should return you to the previous screen.

In Things (right), tapping the Edit button summons controls for deleting and moving items in a list.

In Contacts (below), tapping Edit likewise changes the screen to edit mode (middle); from there, tapping a phone number calls up a new edit screen (right) with Cancel and Save buttons in the navigation bar.

The Search Bar

The final ribbon of standard interface chrome is the seek-and-you-shall-find *search bar*. If your app manages or accesses big collections of info, your audience will clamor for a way to search it. The search bar provides a standard interface for doing just that, offering a special text field with a magnifying glass icon to advertise its search savvy. The search field can include placeholder text ("Search" is a good choice) and a cancel button to clear text, and the optional bookmarks button can display user-saved content or search results. When you tap a search bar, the keyboard automatically slides into view. (For more details on these standard bits of text-field anatomy and behavior, see page 163.)

The search bar fits right in with its cousins, the toolbar and navigation bar. All three are 44 pixels tall in portrait mode (but unlike the others, the search bar doesn't resize in landscape orientation). You can adjust the color and transparency for any or all of these toolbars (page 186). If you decide to go with something other than standard blue, be sure to color-coordinate all these toolbars so that they're at least in similar team colors.

While these options let you make your toolbars look good together, piling more than two of these toolbars (or a tab bar) into the same screen all at once turns into an interface traffic jam, as you've seen. When it comes to iPhone toolbars, three's a crowd. If your layout already has controls anchored to the top *and* bottom of the screen, don't keep the search bar permanently fixed onscreen, too. Instead, let it scroll with the rest of your content, and consider whether you even need to display it when you first land on a screen. You already saw this sleight of hand in the discussion of hidden panels in Chapter 3 (page 85): add the scroll bar to the top of your scrolling content area, but nudge it out of view when you first land on

Mail includes a search bar at the top of the mailbox. Tap the search bar (left), and it conjures the keyboard, a Cancel button, and in this case, a scope bar (circled) to choose which email field to search.

a screen, so that users have to scroll back up to see it. That keeps the search bar handy in the wings but lets your content take center stage.

Beyond just a text field, the standard search bar comes with a few optional accessories. If your search requires some explanation, the standard search bar comes with options to add *prompt text* above the search field (just like a navigation bar, page 141). The search bar also has an optional *scope bar* that you can add immediately below the search field. The scope bar is the standard way to let people choose how to focus their search; it shows up along with the keyboard *after* you tap the search bar. In the Mail app, for example, the scope bar lets you choose which field to search (To, From, Subject, or entire messages).

Of course, giving people a search bar is only half the job; you also have to give 'em search results. The heavy lifting for your search is done behind the scenes by your code. If it's practical—and that's a big if—your app should offer *live search*, updating the list of search results every time you change the search term, letter by letter. This feature is a boon for slow-tapping typists, because it shows the search results as you go, often revealing your search result after typing just a few characters instead of waiting to tap out the whole word. Thing is, all those searches can be demanding if you're searching a big, big collection or a complex data structure, and it's almost always an incredibly slow crawl if the search goes out across the network for web searches. If you decide to go for it, test your live search on an actual device to make sure it holds up to stress testing. Better to drop live search altogether than to drag the app to a standstill. If you go without, never fear: most people won't give it a second thought and are content to type the full search phrase.

As for how to display the results, the standard route is to display them as a simple list, and you do that with a table view—hands down the iPhone's most versatile display element. The last chapter's discussion of tree-structure navigation whispered admiringly about table views a few times already. Time for a proper introduction.

Table Views Are Lists on Steroids

Despite its name, a *table view* isn't really much of a table. You know tables as collections of rows and columns—grids for organizing all kinds of information from spreadsheets to racing sheets. Table views organize information, too, but unlike traditional tables, they have just one column—and friends, where I'm from, we have a name for a single column of items: a list.

When you boil it down, the standard iPhone table view is just that, a list, but it also has several superpowers that let it do things a handwritten laundry list never

These table views show the range of roles that even simple, unstyled lists can play. Top left: A table view presents the main content categories in the Instapaper app. Top right: A table view presents a set of checklist options; tap an item to select it. Bottom left: Long lists, like artists in the iPod app, can display an index on the right edge, providing a one-tap jump to the corresponding heading in the list. Bottom right: Table views can organize content into visually distinct groups, little islands of lists each labeled with its own heading.

could. In particular, table views have a sense of touch; tap an item in a list to do something with it—check it off, navigate to a new screen, delete the item, or move it. The versatility of table views lets them tackle a wide range of roles, and iPhone apps use them to manage lists of pretty much everything, whether they're long scrolling lists or blocks of just one or two items. Table views come with lots of options for switching up their display, but even at their most basic and unstyled, they're an essential display element for any app that uses Apple's standard interface elements.

Table views' most common missions include:

- Navigating the categories and content of tree-structure apps

- Presenting a selectable list of options

- Indexing a long list of items for rapid browsing

- Listing and grouping content details

While naked table views don't have much panache, you can dress them up with accessories that are both functional and visually engaging. First, the functional: table views have three standard icons that apps can add to any *cell*, the proper name in iPhone lingo for an item in the list. In the standard layout, these icons always appear at the cell's right edge, and just like the standard toolbar icons, they have very specific meanings:

Standard Icons for Table Views

>	Disclosure indicator. Labels cells that lead to another screen: "There's more stuff this way." Tapping anywhere inside a row with a disclosure indicator should take you to the next view.
⊙	Detail disclosure button. Similar to a disclosure indicator, but specifically intended for cells that lead to a detail view.
✓	Check mark. Indicates a selected cell. The standard iPhone controls don't include familiar checkboxes; instead, you tap to toggle these check marks in a table row, or use switch controls (page 173).

In addition to these standard table-view icons, you can also place a standard control (or your own custom-built gizmo) into a cell's right-hand slot. The Settings app does this frequently to add on/off switches to cells to let people enable or disable individual settings, for example, or text fields to enter email account info. All of this makes the right side of table cells an important action area, providing indicators and controls that give instant visual clues about what tapping a cell will do.

The standard icons, while appropriately efficient, aren't exactly visually stunning. In addition to those functional accessories, you can also add images for graphical oomph. The standard table cell layout provided by the iPhone toolkit can display a single custom image at the left edge. This is especially helpful in tree-structure navigation to help distinguish items among long lists of options. News apps often display a photo alongside each headline in a story list, for example, and productivity apps trot out icons to make menu items more distinctive. When you do this, though, it's important to make the images or icons truly distinct. This is generally true of all icon design, but it's especially true in a list format: if icons are too similar, they'll just blend together without providing helpful direction to your audience. The primary goal for these visuals should be to make the list items easier to scan and to provide additional meaning, not just to "add graphics." When in doubt, keep it simple and elegant. If your images feel like window dressing instead of actual content, leave them out. (You can also add colors and background images to table cells to give them a completely new look; find out more on page 186.)

Only add graphics to table cells when they add value to the content and make the list easier to scan, like the three food-focused examples here. Cocktails+ (left) shows a silhouette of the proper glass for each of its drink recipes, which also suggests its style of drink. The Lose It calorie counter (middle) illustrates foods with detailed icons that are faster to identify than their sometimes lengthy text descriptions. Gowalla (right) uses artful icons to illustrate the style of cuisine for each restaurant.

In addition to displaying item content as a simple title and optional image, standard table-view cells comes in three other styles, all of which include an additional chunk of detail text. This secondary text appears in different locations for each cell style, with each style best suited to specific roles. You can mix and match cell styles from item to item within the same list according to your needs. Here are the three standard styles for subtitles:

Table-View Cells: Subtitle Styles

Subtitle. This cell layout is ideal for longer text descriptions, useful in content-rich apps for giving a preview of the content on the next screen—a helpful time-saver. The subtitle appears in small gray text.

Blue text. The main title appears at left with the detail text hugging the cell's right side in blue text. This treatment is ideal for settings or other contexts where the main title acts as a bold label for the svelte detail text. Space is limited here; keep the text short, and don't use images in this cell style.

Labeled value. As in the blue text style, the main title again acts as a label for the detail text, but the visual weights are reversed. Here, the main title is a small label at left in blue, and the detail text is visually the primary value, left aligned to the right of the main title. Stacking cells of this style on top of each other creates a neat column display for labeling field values, a technique put to good use in the Contacts app, for example. (Sorry, no images allowed in this cell style, either.)

All of the standard cell styles are a fixed height—the magic 44 pixels—and if your text doesn't fit, it gets lopped off automatically. Keep your titles and detail text short to avoid getting chopped. Short text is also easier to scan quickly, requiring less concentration from your hard-workin' audience. Truncated text isn't such a big deal in the subtitle cell style—there, the detail text is presented as an excerpt or supplemental info—but it's difficult to make sense of truncated text in the two-column layouts of the blue text and labeled value styles. Do your best to make text fit the available space. Edit, edit, edit.

If none of the standard cell styles fit *your* style, you (or your developer) can create your own. Table cells can accommodate all kinds of layouts, but as usual, custom layouts mean custom code. When it comes to displaying basic lists, the standard styles should have you covered, but more complex layouts or multiline text snippets, like news headlines and descriptions, require extra programming attention. The layout and display of your app's content, however, is what your app is all about. If you find that it needs a precise, just-so layout, make sure you give your table cells the coding love they deserve.

Setting the Table: Indexes and Grouped Lists

The design of individual list items is important, but only if you can actually find the items you're looking for. Flicking through enormous lists can be frustrating for both thumb and eye. Categorizing the list can be a big help, providing visual landmarks to help locate content. The table view provides two methods of adding headings to a list: *indexed lists* and *grouped lists*.

An indexed list embeds headings directly into the flow of the list as bold strips introducing each new category. As you scroll through the list, these headings "stick" to the top of the screen while their subitems scroll past, ensuring that you can always see what category you're in. Indexed lists are ideal for very long lists with many category headings. A big list of US cities might be organized by headings for each of the 50 states, for example, or countries by continent. You can optionally display these headings along the right side of the screen as a tappable table of contents, the *index*. Tap an item in the index and you leap straight to its corresponding heading in the list. This is a huge time-saver for long lists. Do your users' thumbs a favor and consider an index for lists that spill into more than two screenfuls of items.

A Contacts-style alphabetical index is by far the most popular use for this style of list exploration, with an A–Z index letting you skip through an alphabetized list.

The Contacts app uses indexed lists to select a country when adding a new contact address (left). When you scroll the list, the continent headings stay glued to the top until all of their subitems have rolled off the screen. When browsing contacts (right), the app adds an index to the right edge, and you can tap a letter to jump to that section of your Rolodex (or tap the magnifying glass at the top of the index, circled here, to jump to the search bar at the top of the list).

The index doesn't have to hew to the alphabet, though; you can use any headings you like. State abbreviations, airport codes, whatever. If you plan to use this right-edge index, though, it's best to keep your headings short and sweet so that they don't jut too far into your cells. Even when they're single-character A–Z headings, though, the index already takes up a precious slot; when you display the index, you don't have room for right-side icons or controls, and you should leave them out of your table cells. The index should always have sole occupancy of the cell's right side.

Grouped lists (shown on page 158) are simpler than indexed lists, and they're designed for relatively smaller collections of items, ideal for displaying settings, feature menus, or distinct groups of content. Grouped lists visually cluster the table view list into blocks, an archipelago of list islands sprinkling down the screen. Unlike plain lists, grouped lists are inset from the edge of the screen with a rounded border. Because each group is separated by a physical gap along with an optional headline, the visual distinction between groups is much stronger in a grouped list than an indexed list. Although you can further subdivide each group into headings just like an indexed list, grouped lists can't display those headings along the right edge like an indexed list can. That means a grouped list offers no single-tap navigation shortcut for skimming its headings, another reason grouped lists aren't as well-suited to very long collections as their indexed cousins.

In addition to adding a headline, or *header*, to each cluster of a grouped list, you can also add a *footer*—small text that appears immediately below the group. Footer text is useful for explanatory text or fine-print caveats about the info or controls above. You can also add a header or footer to the overall table, not just individual groups, and you can do that for plain and indexed lists, too. It's worth noting that headers don't have to be traditional descriptive headlines. The Phone app, for example, displays your phone number as the header introducing its Contacts table view, a convenient but non-obtrusive place to tuck a reminder in case you forget.

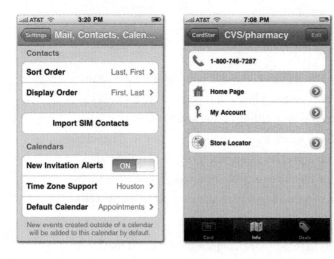

Grouped lists subdivide a table view into islands of sublists. Each of these groups can optionally display a header or footer, like the table view in the Settings app at left, or you can leave them completely unlabeled, like the table view in the CardStar app at right. If a group includes just one item, it looks like a wide button, a useful effect that can replace the need for a regular rectangle button (page 172).

Table View Editing Tools

Your app's ever-flexible table views can bend to your audience's will, too. The standard table view has an optional *editing mode* to allow people to add, delete, or shuffle list items. Flip this option on when you want to let people manage or reorder a collection of personal content, like emails, to-do tasks, or other fleeting data that's just passing through. Most apps advertise this editing option with the familiar Edit button (page 148). Tapping the button reveals the standard deletion control and/or reordering control for each cell. (Behind the scenes, you decide which items you'll allow users to delete or move, and the controls appear only for those cells.)

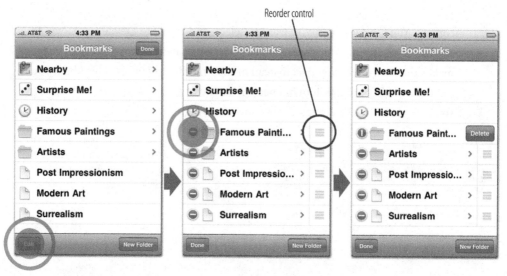

Reorder control

The Articles app for browsing Wikipedia uses standard editing controls in the table view for its Bookmarks screen. Tapping the Edit button (left) reveals the deletion and reordering controls (middle). Here, users may edit only some of the items in the list, while "Nearby," "Surprise Me!" and "History" are permanent fixtures with no edit controls. To delete an item, tap the red deletion control at left to reveal the cell's Delete button (right). To move an item instead, tap and drag the reorder control, the gripped handle located at the cell's right edge.

In this common setup, deleting a list item is a three-tap process: Edit button, deletion control, Delete button. This combo of standard controls makes for some clever *defensive design* by Apple, with enough taps to make accidental deletion unlikely, but not so many that it's a huge chore either. For even more flexibility, table views can also turn on the swipe-to-delete gesture for cells, letting users swipe from left to right across a list item to reveal its Delete button. While this requires just two steps instead of the tap-tap-tap dance of the Edit button, the swipe gesture is likewise difficult to do accidentally, another good example of defensive design. You'll learn more about this kind of gestural jujitsu for preventing mistaps on page 255.

These built-in controls are tuned for letting people remove just one item at a time. That's swell for the occasional deletion, but if your app has people frequently striking batches of items at once, all that defensive design soon swamps people in repetitive swipe-and-tap combos. In that case, it's a good idea to develop custom controls to select multiple items at once, and then delete them all in one fell swoop. When you tap the Edit button in the Mail app, for example, a set of custom controls—round checkboxes—appear in place of the standard deletion control. You tap each item you want to select, and then tap Delete (or Move) to send all of them on their way. To make selection as easy as possible, Mail also makes the entire cell tappable; instead of tapping directly on the checkbox, you can tap anywhere in the item to check or uncheck it, a good practice. Wherever you can, always make tap targets big and forgiving.

In the Mail app, tapping the Edit button (left) reveals custom checkboxes (right) for selecting multiple messages to delete or move.

Text Me

While table views are the go-to design containers for collecting brief snippets of content, the text itself is managed under the hood by one of the iPhone's text-savvy interface elements. When designing custom cells—or drawing text any-where in an app, for that matter—developers use one of these four text containers. We'll explore these options over the next few pages, but here's the quick roundup:

- **Labels** are built for displaying really short text (for labeling a field, displaying a brief explanation, or listing a Twitter message, for example).

- **Text views** are suited for managing longer text—and letting people edit it, too, as you'll see.

- **Web views** are browser windows that you embed right into your screen. You can use them to display a web page, but also to display your app's own elabo-rately formatted text.

- **Text fields** are input areas that let your audience enter brief snippets of text or data.

To display longish, multiline text, iPhone developers use either text views or web views. Like table views, both of these elements have a built-in talent for scrolling. When the text to be displayed runs longer than the available space, swiping scrolls the text inside the boundaries of the text view's frame. Pour the chapter of a book into a text view, and you're all done, right? Bam, instant ebook! Well, not exactly. Text views aren't as useful as you might wish for long documents, because their text is completely uniform—the same for labels. You can set the color, font, and alignment of these text elements, but that change applies to all of the text inside. You can't italicize individual words, include a bold heading alongside regular text, or mix centered and left-aligned text—all you can have is just a single, uniform plain-text presentation.

For truly long-form text, where you typically need to offer more subtle formatting, you can instead turn to a *web view.* Web views are little web browsers embedded right into your interface but without the back button, location bar, or other controls we typically associate with a browser. Instead, a web view is just the viewport itself, an unadorned window to a web page—Safari without the toolbar. As you might expect, you can use web views to display website content inside your app (a topic you'll explore briefly on page 300), but you can also use them to display formatted text. Instead of pointing your web view at the Internet, your app can feed it an internally generated "web page" with the formatted text. That means you can display headings, tables, and any type-addled mix of fonts you might dream up—anything a web page can show, a web view can show, too. In fact, some designers prefer to use web views not only to display formatted text, but to draw most or all of the app's interface using plain old HTML and CSS. (The techniques for coding apps this way are outside the scope of this book, but another book has you covered. Check out *Building iPhone Apps with HTML, CSS, and JavaScript* by Jonathan Stark for details about using this web-based technique.)

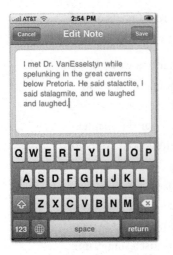

Text views (left) let you display and edit multiline text, as shown here in the Notes field of the Contacts app. Text fields (right) are suited to editing shorter snippets. Here, the Shopper app uses text fields to accept quantity and price info.

Editing Text

So why bother with text views at all when you can have the fancy web view option? Easy: You can make text views editable, but not web views (at least not without spinning lots of your own custom code). When you want to allow people to edit multiple lines of text, give them a text view with its edit switch turned on. Tap an editable text view, and a keyboard automatically slides up from screen bottom to take your input. In practice, this is most useful for brief notes, like the Notes field of the Contacts app, where formatting is rarely needed but editing most definitely is.

Wikipanion, a Wikipedia browser, includes the Bookmarks button at the right side of its search bar (top), and tapping that button displays a list of bookmarked Wikipedia articles to choose from. Once you start typing, the Bookmarks button is replaced by the Cancel button (bottom), which you can tap to clear the text.

Text view's scrappy little brother is the *text field*, a rectangular field which accepts only a single line of text. Like its multiline sibling, a text field summons a keyboard when you tap it to edit, but it also sports a few decorative features that text views do not. The standard text field lets developers add an image, button, or text inside the field at the far left or right. The basic rule is to use the left side for identifying text or icons (insert the word "Search," or a magnifying glass icon for a search field) and the right side for buttons to trigger an action. The button that most makes the most common appearance in this right-side slot is the X-shaped Cancel button, which comes as a built-in option for text fields. The

Cancel button clears the field's text, then disappears while the field remains empty and reappears when you type some text. Text fields inside search bars (page 149) get special treatment with one other optional built-in button: the Bookmarks button. Add this button to a search bar to signal the availability of saved search terms, like street addresses in the Maps app.

Text fields offer a few features that can help folks better understand the purpose of each field and enter appropriate values. A field's *placeholder text* appears in faint gray inside the field before someone enters their own text. As soon as you start typing, the placeholder disappears to make way for the "real" text. The placeholder can act as a label for the field ("Search Wikipedia") or it can hint at the type of entry or data format to type ("1234 Main St."). In either case, it's an effortless and subtle way to clue in your audience about how the field should be used, and a method you should embrace in all text fields.

Fixing Typoz

Text fields and text views have a built-in typo safety net to help people dodge fat-finger typing mistakes. You can flip the switch in any text view of text field to turn on the iPhone's *auto-correction* feature to fix misspelled words. This is almost always the right thing to do for text views, which are typically used for the kind of plain-language prose that benefits from this kind of dictionary check. But don't assume every text view or field should have auto-correction. Fields for proper names, addresses, URLs, or other terms that don't show up in dictionaries soon become maddening when auto-correction is enabled, like when the urbane Dr. Hauser "corrects" to Dr. Hayseed, for example.

Give each field a similar once over before turning on the optional *auto-capitalization* feature for text fields and views. Turn it on for fields where your audience is likely to tap out prose sentences or other values where capitalization is important, but leave it off where it's not appropriate, like password fields, for example. Think carefully about the content you expect for each text field and how the iPhone's editing tools can help or hinder typing the expected values and formats in each. (Providing the proper keyboard layout for a text field is another big piece of this, a topic you'll explore in a moment.)

Is That for Here or to Go?

There are two especially common strategies for managing the layout of screens of several text fields, and Apple's own apps use both. One approach lets you edit all of the fields in place, and the other lists all the current values but takes you to a separate screen to edit each value individually. The Settings app, for example, uses the first approach to add and edit email account info. The borderless text fields are all embedded in a table view with labels at left and placeholder text indicating the expected info. You tap

In the Settings app (left), you edit the text fields directly in the table view to set up an email account; tapping Return takes you to the next field in the series. In Contacts (below), a table view lists all the fields, and tapping one takes you to a separate screen dedicated to editing that field.

in one field, type its value, and then press Return to skip to the next field, an efficient process for moving quickly through a set of required fields. This is a good pattern to follow when you have a brief list of fields and you would like the user to provide values for all of them.

The Contacts app follows the second approach. When adding or editing a contact, a table view lists all of the current values for that contact. Instead of editing those values on the same screen, tapping a value takes you to a new screen with an editable text field or text view. This method works best when you don't expect people to enter the values as a series, or when you have many fields that your audience might not enter all at once.

Don't Make 'Em Keybored

Most of us get by just fine tapping away on the iPhone keyboard, but few would describe it as a pleasure. The experience is about as good as it can get for a touch-screen keyboard of this size, but flipping through the various layouts to swap among letters, numbers, and punctuation is a tedious hassle, slowing us down and inviting mistakes. Help users stave off keyboard boredom by providing a keyboard tuned to the type of input you're asking for in each text field. There are eight different keyboard layouts bundled in the iPhone OS, each designed for a particular flavor of content, and you can associate individual text fields with any of them. Details like this matter: be sure each of your fields conjures the best keyboard for the data you want.

Unless you specifically choose a different keyboard for your text fields and views, the iPhone will give you the *default keyboard,* which varies according to the user's language preferences, dishing the Cyrillic alphabet for Russian or kana script for Japanese, for example. The default keyboard is just right for general-purpose text entry, but you can specify any of these targeted keyboards to ease entering particular types of info:

- *ASCII.* This is the default keyboard for English-language users, offering the alphabet on its main keyboard, with options to switch to other layouts for numbers and punctuation. (ASCII is the name of the original set of letters, numbers, and punctuation characters used by modern computers; it doesn't include any fancy characters or non-Western script, for example.)

- *Numbers and punctuation.* This is the same as the ASCII keyboard, but with the keyboard pre-selected to start on the numbers and punctuation layout instead of the alphabet layout.

- *URL.* Aimed at entering web addresses, this layout includes dot, slash, and .com keys on the main keyboard, replacing the space bar. The punctuation on the keyboard's second layout is likewise tuned for characters that commonly appear in URLs (#, +, %, and so on).

- *Email address.* The familiar @ character takes center stage on this keyboard, with common email punctuation staking out the keyboard's secondary punctuation layout.

- *Number pad.* Zero through nine, that's all. (No Return key, so the keyboard has to be dismissed with a separate Done button elsewhere in the interface—a good idea anyway.)

- *Phone pad.* This one's identical to the number pad, but with an additional layout for the +, #, *, and Pause keys.

- *Name phone pad.* The main keyboard offers letters—the same as the ASCII keyboard—but the secondary layout is a modified number pad, no punctuation options.

ASCII

Numbers and punctuation

URL

Email address

Number pad

Phone pad

Name phone pad

In addition to choosing the appropriate keyboard style, you can also customize the Return key label for each input field's keyboard. "Return" is the standard setting for the key, but where appropriate, you can use the text of the key to signal exactly what will happen next, yet another way to orient your audience about the purpose of the text field. There are several standard label alternatives to choose from, and all except "Next" shift the button color to blue to signal that something special will happen when tapped:

Multiple Choice: Pickers, Lists, and Action Sheets

Even better in some cases than choosing the right keyboard is getting rid of the keyboard completely. Remember the dreaded high-school pop quiz? And how much easier it was when it was multiple choice instead of short answer? A limited set of options, all displayed in front of you, made for a better shot at dodging wrong answers. You didn't even have to strain your delicate adolescent wrist to write anything out; you just picked your answer and moved on. The same considerations apply to iPhone apps: picking from a menu of options is faster and less error prone than pecking out the full text on the keyboard. Wherever appropriate, put the keyboard away and give your grateful users a quick-tap menu of options to choose from. The standard iPhone controls include a few different tools to do exactly that.

The *picker* control installs slot-machine dials in your app to let people "spin to win," choosing from a set of options. The picker can consist of a single wheel, or you can squeeze several wheels side by side to ask your audience for several values at once. Pickers can (and should) include an optional *selection bar,* a translucent strip that hovers above the dials to make it completely clear which option is selected, and which can also display the units you're working with. Apps typically

The timer screen of the Clock app (left) features a two-dial picker to choose the hours and minutes for your countdown. Note that labels for hour and minutes are fixed to the selection bar so there's no confusion about which dial is for what. Lose It!, the diet log at right, uses a picker to choose food portions. (Mmm, bacon...)

either fix pickers onscreen as a primary interface element, like the timer function in the Clock app, or keep it tucked away until summoned like a keyboard, skittering up from screen bottom when you tap a button or table cell to enter a value.

Urbanspoon's three dials let you browse restaurants across three categories. You call it dinner, but information designers call it multidimensional data. That's an enormous number of combinations that would be inconvenient to display in a single table view list, and the picker is also more compact than drilling down through several levels of a tree structure to browse the categories as lists.

Pickers are especially handy for entering dates, and the standard toolkit includes a prefab *date picker* designed to do just that, with three dials for month, date, and year. This highlights the main advantage pickers have over displaying options in a table-view list: they can provide *multidimensional options*, a high-falutin' term for choosing several settings (like month, date, and year) all at once in a single control, providing a more compact interface than a straight list every could.

Pickers aren't great for everything, though. Because only a few of a picker's options are visible at any one time, pickers are best for displaying either very familiar sets of options (dates, times, numbers) or very small sets, where only a few options are ever tucked out of view. For the same reason, the order of picker items should be very obvious—alphabetical or numeric—so that people don't spin back and forth through the list like some manic version of the Showcase Showdown, trying to find that elusive value.

For longer or less familiar collections of options, it's best to send the picker packing and instead use a table view, letting people tap an option from a plain scrolling list of options. The Settings app, for example, uses table views throughout to let people choose setting preferences. These full-screen lists have several advantages over pickers: they're easier to scan than a picker's tiny window; they provide built-in editing tools if you want users to customize the list; and where appropriate, table views also let you choose multiple items, marking each selection with a check mark in the cell's right side.

For very long lists, try to surface likely selections based on the user's history or, where appropriate, by community popularity. In Foursquare, for example, users "check in" to announce their arrival at a physical location; the app lists all the nearby restaurants, bars, and venues, but at the top it features "favorites," places you've checked in before. By highlighting these likely spots, the app saves you from searching through all the options. This is something lists can do much better than pickers, especially since lists can display headings to call out and explain these special option categories.

Surface favorite or recent picks in your selection lists. Foursquare's Places screen (left) floats personal favorites to the top of its list of places to speed selection. The PCalc scientific calculator app (right) provides a categorized list of constants to plug into your calculations but makes it easy to grab the last constant you selected (here, the Avogadro Constant).

Pickers or lists are the way to go for offering multiple-choice options for data entry or choosing preference settings, but when it comes to choosing among possible *actions,* Apple provides a very specific tool: the *action sheet.* Think of action sheets like flipped versions of the familiar pull-down menus of desktop software. There, menus drop down from a screen-topping menu bar to offer a selection of commands to choose from. Action sheets do the same thing but spring up from the bottom of the screen—often from the toolbar or tab bar—to present a sliding sheet of buttons. You most commonly trigger an action sheet by tapping a toolbar button, like the Reply button in Mail or the Add button in Safari. Conceptually, these toolbar buttons work the same as menu headings in a desktop menu bar: Tap to reveal the action sheet's spring-loaded collection of related commands.

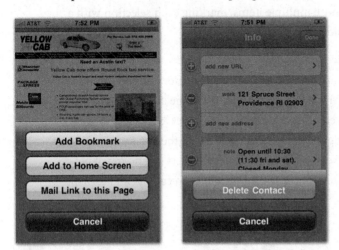

In Safari (left), the Add button triggers an action sheet to file or share the web page. In Contacts (right), an action sheet is used to confirm the deletion of a contact, a last-chance fail-safe against accidental deletion.

Action sheets are another example of the hidden-door approach of tucking secondary controls offscreen until needed (page 85). They allow you to offer buttons and options that won't physically or cognitively fit on the iPhone's toolbar. Action sheets' text-based buttons may look different than elegant little toolbar icons, but their behavior is effectively the same as a toolbar button. Action-sheet buttons present options for editing, manipulating, or sharing the current screen of content. Like toolbar buttons, they often trigger a modal view (page 117) to handle the details of the selected action. The action sheet behind Safari's Add button leads to three different modal views for bookmarking, saving, or sharing a web page; the various reply options in Mail likewise call up a screen to compose a new message.

The main exception to triggering a modal dialog happens when you use an action sheet to confirm a potentially regrettable action. It's the "Seriously, you're really gonna wear that top with that skirt?" reality check for the iPhone interface. Confirmation action sheets are typically used to protect against destructive actions by throwing in a speed bump on the way to deleting content. Tap the Delete button in the Mail, Notes, or Photos toolbar, for example, and an action sheet slides up with Delete and Cancel options, forcing a second tap to complete the deletion. Well-intentioned as it is, this double-tap two-step sometimes creates more irritation than relief, slowing people down by putting their goal one more step away. (Mail even offers an option to turn these confirmations off.) Their utility fades over time, too. As we become accustomed to these confirmations, we tend to tap right through them without thinking; they become part of an action's muscle memory and their gatekeeper protection starts to fade. Cushioning people from accidental mistaps, particularly destructive mistaps, is a delicate and imperfect art, a topic that you'll explore further on page 255.

Action sheets are themselves modal views: they temporarily pause the action and dim the main screen underneath until you choose an option. Because you must tap a button to move on, action sheets should always have a Cancel button to let people get out of there if they've changed their mind. The standard Cancel button is shaded slightly darker than other buttons and goes at the bottom of the action sheet, a good practice for both logical and ergonomic reasons. This bottom placement not only encourages people to read the other options first, but it also puts the button in the thumb's most comfortable tap zone.

Be consistent on this. By making the Cancel button subtly easier to tap than the others and by always anchoring it in the same place, the "whoops, never mind" option is reliably easy to find, an understated protection against accidental taps.

Destructive actions should always get similarly special treatment, with red-means-danger coloring and placement at the top of the sheet. This top placement makes a Delete button more visible while also putting it furthest from the thumb's hot zone to make a mistap less likely. Delete is the most common use of this red destruction button, particularly in confirmation action sheets, but it's appropriate to use it for other actions of similar permanence. Instapaper, for example, uses the red button to archive an article you're reading. Archiving doesn't actually delete the article from your Instapaper account, but it takes the article out of your

In Instapaper's action sheet, the Archive action appropriately gets the red-button treatment even though it's not strictly a destructive action.

reading flow by stashing it in a big bucket of already-read-it articles, a suitably major action to flag with the red button.

The text buttons of action sheets have the benefit of being explicitly descriptive—none of the guesswork that so often accompanies icon buttons—but the trade-off is that they present a slew of words to read at once. As you add more buttons, it's no longer a quick scan of options, and you ask more and more of your audience's neurons. Practically, of course, there's only so many buttons you can add anyway. It's wise to cap action sheets to five buttons, including the Cancel button, for both space and scannability. Even five buttons makes for a busy visual, though, presenting yet another opportunity to ask yourself: does this app really need all these features? As always, focus on primary activities and be ruthless about trimming unnecessary actions. If you still wind up with a list of five or more buttons, consider developing a custom alternative that's more compact and graphical than an action sheet (see page 207 for how Twitterrific tackled this).

On the Button

With all the buttons that come built into standard action sheets, toolbars, navigation bars, and tab bars, you're already awash in interface controls to trigger your app's features, but of course you're not limited to using only the buttons that come bundled in those containers. The iPhone toolkit gives developers the basic code

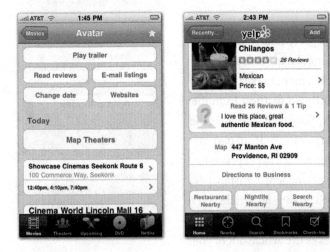

Now Playing (left) uses lots of rounded rectangle buttons for finding out more about movies playing in your area. Yelp (right) uses the same basic buttons, shown here at screen bottom, to launch searches for nearby businesses.

to draw a button anywhere on the screen. Buttons can be styled however you like, from a plain text button to a richly graphical icon. The most basic style is the *rounded rectangle button,* a just-the-facts control with a text label inside.

These basic buttons get the job done, but let's face it: rounded rectangles are a little, um, square. Most apps use custom graphics to spiff up their buttons, at the very least adding a background image to give the button some texture or gloss. (You'll find pointers for creating some of these effects on page 191.) No matter what style of button you use, you should create at least two looks for each button to reflect its *control state.* Buttons are in the *normal* state when they're just minding their own business, waiting for something to happen. Buttons are in the *highlighted* state when tapped—that is, while your finger is pressed down. Visual feedback to taps and touches are critically important for touchscreen gadgets, and your buttons should signal that they've been pressed by changing their look, even subtly, in the highlighted state. The standard settings for a rounded rectangle button, for example, light up the normally white button with a blue background when tapped. For custom buttons, swapping out the background image or changing the icon image when pressed provides similar feedback.

Depending on how you're using your button, you might have two additional states to design for, too. The *disabled* state applies when a button is inactive and can't be used. The *selected* state applies when a button is "on," appropriate for a toggle button.

Yes and No: Switches

Did someone say toggle button? A toggle of course is a control that is either on or off—think light switches, power buttons, and checkboxes. On the iPhone, the only toggle that comes built in is the *switch* control, a left-right slider that looks like a light switch turned on its side. Just like that light switch, it has two settings: on and off.

In traditional web and desktop interfaces, this on/off job would typically be handled by a checkbox, but there's no such thing in the standard kit of iPhone controls. This

Switches are commonly used as the right-hand control in standard table cells, as shown here.

switch control is the closest thing on offer, alongside the option to add check marks to list items in table cells (page 153). If those options just won't fit your needs like a checkbox, the alternative is to build your own—a custom button that shows the image of an empty box in its *normal* state and the image of a checked box in its *selected* state.

Segmented Controls Are Radio Buttons

Like a switch, a *segmented control* also asks you to choose among a prefab set of options, except that a segmented control can offer several options instead of a switch's measly two. While switches work the light-switch metaphor, segmented controls work more like a car radio, the kind you would've found in dashboards in the 1970s. Back then, when you weren't listening to your eight-track tapes, you pushed the radio's heavy mechanical buttons to hop through your favorite stations, each button tuned to a different frequency. Only one button could be pushed in at a time; pressing one popped out the rest.

Photo: Sean Russ

A segmented control works the same way, a band of unified controls where only one button can be selected at a time. Interface geeks call this style of control, you guessed it, *radio buttons*. (The tab bar is likewise a set of radio buttons.) On the Web, you know radio buttons as the round checkbox alternatives that let you choose just one option among several. The shape might differ, but the concept is the same.

Like the original old-school radio buttons, you typically use segmented controls to tune into different content, each button corresponding to a different way to sort, filter, or display a screen. In the Facebook app, for example, you tap a segmented control to flip between wall posts, profile info, and photos. In the Local

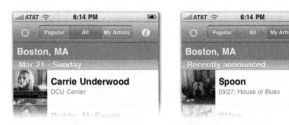

A segmented control appears in the navigation bar of the Local Concerts app to choose which shows to display. Here, the All and My Artists buttons show different results in the main view.

Concerts app, a segmented control filters upcoming concerts to show all shows, popular bands, or artists that you follow. Segmented controls, in other words, are useful for secondary navigation, changing how content is displayed in a single screen or category of an app.

When you limit segmented controls to just two buttons, they become handy for two alternative uses, too. First, in a screen of preferences, a two-button control is good for offering a choice between two settings: miles or kilometers, Fahrenheit or Celsius, Conan or Leno, and so on. Second, in a navigation bar, a two-segment control is a natural for next and previous buttons, a gimmick used in the Mail app and lots of news apps to move from message to message or article to article. For that navigation use, the buttons typically sport icons instead of text labels. If you decide to go this graphical route for one or more buttons of a segmented control, be sure to do it for all of them. All of the options should have equal significance in a segmented control, and that means giving them the same visual weight, too, with consistent graphic or text treatment.

The settings screen of the Umbrella app (left) uses a segmented control to let you choose temperature units. The New York Times app (right) uses a segmented control in its top navigation bar to offer next and previous buttons.

The standard segmented control comes in two sizes—one to squeeze inside toolbars and navigation bars, and the other for elsewhere in your interface. The toolbar version is 30-pixels tall, while the other is 44-pixels tall, the same height as toolbars, navigation bars, and search bars, presenting a tap-friendly target. Although you can technically add as many buttons as you like to a segmented control, the practical limit is five in order to give the buttons enough breathing room to make them easy to scan and tap. The buttons space out in equal width across the span of the segmented control; be sure that the graphic or text label for each button is small enough to fit.

Sliders Stay on Track

A *slider* is a useful way to offer fine-tuned control over a setting that has minimum and maximum values, or to navigate quickly through a lengthy document. The slider is a track with a little knob that you drag left or right, and you can dress it with icons on either side to represent the minimum and maximum settings—a little speaker and a big speaker in a volume control, for example. In the standard settings, the track is blue to the left of the knob and white to the right, but you can customize those colors to suit your app's palette. (For that matter, you can even customize the knob itself, supplying your own image replacement. As usual, don't stray too far from the standard look, but there's some fun to be had here.)

Last.fm (left) uses a slider to control music volume. Stanza (right) uses a slider to skip quickly to a new location in an ebook.

Settings: A Matter of Preference

The last several pages have focused on controls which, when piled all together, become especially handy on settings pages to toggle, slide, and select values for your app's preferences. That raises the question: just where should your app's settings go? Apple recommends that you carve certain types of settings out of your app and stow them away in the built-in Settings app, which includes app-specific settings in addition to general-purpose system settings. That's what you should do if you play it by the book, but seriously: don't play it by the book.

Apple's HIG makes a distinction between "settings" and "configuration options." *Settings* affect nitty-gritty foundational aspects of how your app works. They're preferences that rarely change but determine the basic operation of the app: account login info, alert sounds, screen rotation preferences, notification settings, theme colors, font size, and so on. Apple says these settings belong in the Settings app. By contrast, *configuration options* are less about the app machinery and more about the app's content, choices that are likely to be changed more frequently, even from session to session: content categories, weather locations to monitor, volume controls, and anything that affects the type and manner of content display. If settings determine how the car fundamentally works, configuration options let you drive it. Apple says configuration options should be included inside the app.

Alas, elegant though it is, this distinction is lost on your audience and it only makes people guess where to look for your app's settings. The difference between settings and configuration options is useful when planning what preferences to offer, a topic you'll explore in a moment. But giving that distinction a physical form by shanghaiing some preferences out of your app and into the Settings app doesn't help your audience. In usability testing, I routinely find that most users don't even know the Settings app hosts app-specific preferences; if they can't find preferences in the app itself, most assume they don't exist. Even for those who do know the Settings app offers preferences for individual apps, it's the last place they check when sorting out how to configure the app. The separation is a departure from one of the iPhone's most effective interface principles: tap the thing you want to work with. Instead of tapping your app to change its settings, Apple tells you to tap the Settings app. It's a rare and nonintuitive bit of indirection in the iPhone ecosystem. If you're going to offer preferences—settings, configuration options, call them what you like—put them all inside the app.

Photo: Shahram Sharif

The iPhone OS includes a standard icon to use for a settings button: the "i" button. Outside the iPhone interface, the italic "i" logo has international meaning as a symbol for information, and iPhone newcomers often assume the button will lead only to background info about the app and its developer. Still, the button is used often enough on the iPhone for settings that most users eventually grow accustomed to the notion that preferences are typically tucked away behind it.

Apple provides the standard "i" info button to reveal configuration options; at left, the built-in Stocks app uses the icon in its toolbar. Because the logo's ambiguous meaning doesn't say "settings" to most users, many apps use a custom gear-shaped button (like Momento, middle) or a simple text button (Twitter, right). As these examples show, there's also no standard location for a settings button, but the navigation bar or toolbar are good choices. Avoid putting a settings tab on the tab bar; elevating those options to the same level as your app's primary features gives them too much weight.

To avoid confusion, consider using your own custom button with a gear-shaped icon, a commonly understood symbol for settings.

Whatever style of button you use to conjure your settings, consolidate them all into a single modal view. A common convention, especially for flat-pages utility apps, is to put settings on the "back" of the app, bringing the settings into view with a flip animation. This creates a clear visual distinction between the app's normal operation and its configuration—like you're cracking open the case of a device to change a battery. However, for apps with lots of preferences—more than a screenful—the flip is less effective, since the scroll undermines the card-like effect. In that case, a different animation is appropriate, usually sliding up from the bottom of the screen.

But do you really need all those preference settings in the first place? Designers and developers tend to be control freaks. We're at our best when we're meticulously crafting our creations, considering all the possibilities, designing for every contingency. That fastidious nature often leads us to create more customization options than we should, providing settings to let people tweak and change the interface and app behavior according to their whim. Steer your control-freak sensibility in a different direction: make interface decisions and stand by them. Yep, some people will want to use your app in some different way than you've chosen, but you don't have to accommodate each and every user. Figure out how most people will want to use your app, and make that the way the app works, period. Not everyone will agree with your choices, but optimize for the usual. There's always a "usual way" that any tool, device, or software gets used, and that's how you should design your app.

As you sort out which preferences to include, it's useful to revisit Apple's distinction between settings and configuration options. Configuration options—the preferences that determine which content gets displayed and how—typically make the cut, provided that they fit common needs and use cases. Meanwhile, settings that determine more fundamental application behaviors are typically places where you can make the decision on behalf of the masses. Be the benevolent philosopher king of your app community, and take ownership of your own interface. That doesn't mean that all preferences go out the window, though, and a big-three set of categories typically pass muster:

- *Content settings.* Expense trackers should offer an option to choose what currency you normally use. Weather apps should let you choose cities to track. Apps for sports scores should let you choose the teams to follow.

- *Account settings.* If your app requires an account with an online service, you should have settings that let you sign in, sign out, or update account credentials.

- *Privacy settings.* If your app shares people's info or activities online, it should also provide options to keep that info private.

Even though you should bypass the Settings app as the location for your app's preferences, do look to that app for guidance in how to organize and lay out the controls for a preferences screen. Thanks to the system used by the iPhone OS to plug app-specific preferences into the Settings app, those preference screens have an efficient uniformity that is familiar and compact. No need for reinvention there; following Apple's lead for laying out preference options will serve you well.

Is There More?

This chapter covered lots of ground, and you've now toured nearly all the standard gadgets supplied out of the box by the iPhone code toolkit. A handful remain, though, and you'll dig into these later in the book:

- **Activity indicators and progress bars.** See page 284 and page 287.

- **Alerts and push notifications.** See page 276 and page 280.

- **Map views.** See page 300.

Touchpoints

✓ Favor standard controls. Consistency lends authority.

✓ Limit screens to two bars—a navigation bar at top and a tab bar or toolbar at bottom. Let search bars scroll instead of anchoring them onscreen.

✓ Get friendly with table views, the most versatile element of the standard iPhone interface.

✓ Carefully consider which keyboard and auto-correction options to offer for every text field.

✓ Limit preference settings and sidestep the Settings app.

6

Stand Out

CREATING A UNIQUE VISUAL IDENTITY

HENRY FORD FAMOUSLY PROMISED that his company would paint a car any color "so long as it is black." For 12 years between 1914 and 1926, his Model T fleet was a monochrome monolith—just one color, just one style. To Ford, color choice was an unimportant personal whim—a stylistic nicety that had nothing to do with producing cars that were cheap to make and easy to drive. "I thought it was up to me as the designer to make the car so completely simple that no one could fail to understand it," he said, color choice included. Most folks went along: by 1918, the Model T accounted for more than half the cars on the road, a giant swarm of identical black buggies.

Ford was an autocrat (pun intended), and it's hard to imagine his my-way-or-the-highway philosophy going over well with today's car consumer. Yet his design dictates aren't all that different from Apple's vision of a world awash in identical black iPhones, iPads, and iPods (with the concession of the occasional white iPhone). The difference is the software. Our iPhones might look the same, and the hardware might be standard, but the contents are not. We personalize our iPhones with carefully curated app collections. Just as most drivers think of their choice of car (and its color) as  a form of self-expression, so it goes with iPhone users and their apps. We feel a personal attachment to our iPhones that's almost unseemly for a techno-gadget. The apps we download somehow say as much about us as the cars we drive or the decorations in our homes. (There's even a website, *www. firstand20. com,* to showcase the iPhone Home screens of various designers and developers—"MTV Cribs" for the geek set.)

An emotional attachment to software? Because we carry our phones everywhere and use them anywhere, iPhone apps are personal in a way that software has never been before. As an app designer, your interface choices affect not only what your customers can *do* with their iPhones, but how they *feel* about them, too. For all of this book's talk about the importance of efficiency and focus in iPhone app design, there's also the elusive matter of style. Granted, your audience expects your app first and foremost to get something done (inform, work, entertain), but you'll win hearts if your app gets it done with style, too. A well-designed interface has the power to charm and beguile.

Obviously, though, Ford was onto something with his relentless focus on standardization. As you saw in the last chapter, relying on familiar design conventions eliminates head scratching and ambiguity for the user. It also makes for easier design and production, whether your assembly line produces Model Ts or iPhone apps. It's not a sin to make an app that uses only standard controls and colors. It might seem bland, but it's also efficient, and "efficient" is often exactly the right personality. Productivity apps like Mail, Things, or Instapaper benefit from their buttoned-down, all-business manner.

Even for productivity apps, though, textural flourishes or sparks of color lend a subtle sense of luxury to standard controls without adding interface chrome or distracting from the task at hand. If you choose to go even further, you can fashion your own bespoke interface that imbues your app with rich atmosphere, charming whimsy, retro nostalgia, high-tech gloss, or hipster savvy. Just be realistic: when you depart from the standard controls and interface metaphors, you've gotta be good. Creating a unique visual identity for an app takes taste and skill, the work of a talented designer. If you want to venture beyond the standard controls and you're not a designer yourself, you should find one or work hard to become one.

This chapter can't do that hard work for you, but it does explore practical strategies for crafting a visual personality for your app. You'll learn techniques for adding color and texture to standard controls, crafting toolbar icons, and creating a sense of luxury by conjuring real-world materials. With those basic skills in hand, you'll go on to discover the dark art of crafting entirely new interface metaphors and controls. Send Mr. Ford's penchant for standardization to the back seat, and let's go for a little ride.

What's Your App's Personality?

Your design choices—whether conservative or zany—give your app a personality. Just like people, apps are irresistible when their personalities are in tune with both audience and context. An efficient, just-the-facts design lends an air of confidence to a productivity app. Warm wood textures, meanwhile, give other apps an organic feeling that is both homey and luxurious. Don't let your app's personality emerge by accident. Before you start tinkering with color schemes, graphics, and navigation models, consider how you'd like people to perceive your app. Businesslike and authoritative? Comforting and familiar? Sunny and upbeat? Sleek and poised? Homespun and crafty? Gritty and edgy? Fun and toylike? Opulent and plush?

By choosing a personality for your app *before* you start crafting its visual identity, you give yourself a framework for making consistent decisions based on the emotional vibe you're after. Don't dismiss this as touchy-feely hokum: an emotional vibe is the basis for all marketing and storytelling, and make no mistake, your app

Some app designs create outspoken personalities by conjuring very specific atmospheres tailored to context and audience. Voices (left) has a Vaudeville personality appropriate to a funny-voices novelty app. iShots Irish Edition (right) creates a gritty dive-bar ambience for its collection of let's-get-loaded drink recipes.

is in fact a story. In the very personal context of the iPhone, people think about an app as content more than "software," an experience more than a tool, and entertainment more than a task. Your app's personality sets the mood of that experience and it has to suit its audience as well as the job at hand. When you marry the aesthetics of a thing to both its function and its owner, you get something that is beautiful, functional, and distinct. This feng shui alchemy evaporates when those elements go out of sync, so go carefully as you make your design decisions.

Gussying Up Familiar Pixels

Great, so you've decided that your app is going to be charming and gregarious. As you translate this broad personality statement into actual pixels, one route is to build a completely custom interface from top to bottom, like the Voices and iShots examples shown on page 185, an approach you'll learn more about later. The easier road is to dress up standard iPhone elements, giving them a facelift with colors and images that match the personality you're after. By tinting toolbars or outlining table cells and buttons with specially crafted graphics, you can transform the iPhone's stodgy blue and gray standbys into something dramatically different.

This makeover approach gives your interface a fresh identity that, so long as you're only tinkering with color and adding background images, still offers your

Wine Steward uses good old table views, but creates a vintage ambience by draping a backdrop image across the screen, with a parchment graphic in the background of each table cell that makes each entry appear to be written on an aged wine label. The burgundy-tinted navigation bar maintains the app's wine flavor.

audience the easy familiarity of standard controls—nothing new to learn. Even so, there are a few conventions to observe and gotchas to tiptoe around:

- **The carpet should match the drapes.** If you tint one toolbar, tint them all. The navigation bar, toolbar, and search bar should all get the exact same color treatment, giving your content a consistent frame in the identical color. (Tab bars, however, should always remain black, a convention that gives them a sturdy authority across all apps.) Ditto for transparency; if you choose to make any of the toolbars translucent, follow through for the rest. The status bar figures in here, too. The iPhone OS allows apps to have a black or white status bar, or you can make it translucent to let a background color shine through. If you choose a dark color for your navigation bar, make the status bar black; for light colors, make the status bar white. (Otherwise, your app looks like it's growing out its roots after a bad dye job.)

- **Don't be garish.** Be tasteful and understated in your toolbar color choices. Brassy bright colors create a distracting glare, drawing the eye away from the main event. It's a mortal sin in interface design to let your app's interface chrome upstage the content. It's fine to use bright colors in toolbars when they blend with similarly bright colors in the rest of the app; just remember that the operative word here is "blend."

- **Go into the light.** The standard toolbars have that signature Apple gloss, painted with a color gradient that gives them a rounded, top-lit appearance. When you add a custom color to toolbars, the gradient effect sticks around, now tinted with the new color—no muss, no fuss. With a little custom code behind the scenes, however, your app can replace that gradient with a graphic, perfect for adding some subtle texture to your toolbars. If you do that, just be sure that your brand new toolbar maintains the original gradient's illusion of a top-down light source. Details like this seem small but work quietly to maintain the visual consistency of the standard controls across apps. You'll find more tips for managing realistic light and texture on page 191.

- **Clever adaptation is charming; too clever is confusing.** Making slight tweaks to familiar icons or controls can give your interface a jaunty, playful independence. These interventions should be small, though—a wink more than a broad overhaul. The Meebo instant messaging app replaces the dots of the standard page control with tiny speech bubbles, a clever hint that you're paging through different chat conversations. The built-in Notes app replaces standard toolbar icons with its own hand-sketched versions. In both of these examples, the essential form of the controls remains intact and immediately recognizable. But if you stray just a few degrees too far, you risk making a standard control unrecognizable. Color and form are important: the standard blue arrow of the detail disclosure button, for example, tends to lose its significance if you drain it of color or remove its outer border. (Henry Ford swoops in again with an admonition from 1922: "There is a tendency to keep monkeying with styles and to spoil a good thing by changing it.")

The blue arrow (the *detail disclosure button*) signals that tapping will take you to a detail screen for the selected content. For better or worse, many apps set up this button to take you to a different view than tapping elsewhere in the same cell, so it's important that it stand out as a separate button. Things (left) uses the standard blue button to good effect, but Reeder, an excellent app for reading news feeds, uses a custom version. Without the signature outline and blue color, Reeder's custom button blends in too much. It's not clear that tapping the button will take you to a different view than tapping elsewhere in the table cell (which it does).

- **Contrast is your friend.** Designers love gray text—we just can't help it. Gray is pretty. It's subtle and has an elegance that brutal black does not. But friends, it's not easy to read. If your audience has to squint to read the screen, your gray text isn't doing its job. The iPhone's small screen and frequently distracting environment put a premium on effortless reading and scanning, the crucial core of the glance test. Ebony and ivory, baby: favor black and white for text, and go with high contrast colors for other important interface elements. (After choosing your color scheme, test early designs with the "White on Black" setting turned on in the General→Accessibility screen of the built-in Settings app. This option for the visually impaired inverts colors for higher contrast, like a photo negative. Your app should be easy to read with this setting both on and off.)

- **Be frugal with fonts.** Standard iPhone Helvetica fits the bill in nearly every case; stifle the instinct to stray to other typefaces. The navigation bar in particular is sacrosanct: with the exception of logo graphics, always use Helvetica for screen titles. The navigation bar is such a fundamental part of the interface that it feels like part of the overall iPhone system; consistent use of the Helvetica system font is always the right thing to do there. Elsewhere, using a different sans-serif font (Arial, Verdana, or Trebuchet) in place of Helvetica just feels weird on the iPhone; a lateral shift that succeeds only in making your app seem like it's not a proper iPhone citizen. Changes to more boldly different typefaces, however, can be appropriate under specific circumstances. Serif fonts (Georgia or Times) work well for displaying long-form text like news articles or ebooks, giving apps a stately, traditional feel. Marker Felt, the iPhone's faux handwriting font, is just fine for notepad and grocery-list apps when you want to display users' personal notes in a casual scrawl. Just know that Marker Felt, like most script typefaces, can give your app a kindergarten feel that might not fit the personality you're after. That didn't stop Apple from using it in the built-in Notes app, though, and the font does have an unabashedly personal feel. Proceed with caution and taste.

You Stay Classy

People trust luxury. Right or wrong, if it looks good—if it looks *expensive*—it must be valuable. No matter what's going on under the hood of your app, its *perceived value* goes up when it looks opulent. Luxury brands have a perceived value that outstrips the cost of their basic materials, construction, or function. So it goes with iPhone apps: make it swank, make a customer. This isn't cynical marketing (well, maybe a little bit). It goes back to making the emotional connection that's so important for iPhone apps. The same sumptuous materials of beloved personal totems—a leather-bound notebook, a glossy gadget, a retro timepiece—can likewise be put to good use in your interface to conjure the same attachment. Of course, the luxury materials in this case are just pixels, and the cost of adding that coveted texture and gloss to your app is simply the talent of a good designer.

Organic textures add a sense of luxury to the design. Top: Bills on Your Table, iHandy Carpenter, and Cross Fingers. Bottom: Trip Journal, Cinder, and Jumsoft Money.

The warmth of wood or cork, the flat sheen of glass, the organic appeal of paper or fabric, the cold sophistication of metal—all of these real-world textures have associations that can bolster your app's visual identity. But your textures have to be good, and the light and shading have to be just so, or the luxury spell is broken. Unconvincing textures backfire with a cheap appearance, like pressboard imitating mahogany or plastic masquerading as metal. To work the luxury angle, your design sleight of hand has to be convincingly real.

Keep It Real

Luxury or not, the lifelike use of light, shadow, and texture creates a sense of realism in your interface that invites touch. As you saw in Chapter 3, designing a tapworthy touchscreen interface involves many of the same considerations as designing a physical device. When your design supports the illusion of an actual physical object, you create a sense of solidity, reliability, and even affection. The iPhone OS does half the work for you by providing the lifelike physics that makes your lists bounce, your screens flick, or your keyboards clatter. Your own carefully crafted graphics complete the experience. There's more at work here than simple aesthetics though: touch is a powerfully personal ingredient of how we experience the world. Interfaces that invite and respond to touch forge a direct connection that screens mediated by keyboard and mouse do not. Lifelike interface elements on a web page are simply pretty, but on the iPhone they say, "touch me." On a practical level, that realism provides guidance on how to use your app, but emotionally it creates an appealingly personal realism that draws people into your interface.

These nods to realistic light and physics reflect how digital devices are merging with the physical world though certainly not replacing it. At best, iPhone interfaces that strive for "realism" can provide only miniature replicas of real-world objects. You're not going to fool people into believing that they're playing a real piano, holding a hefty book, or scribbling on an actual legal pad. Those are tricks the iPad is better equipped to pull off, thanks to its expansive screen. Simulating a physical object can still be effective and endearing on the iPhone (page 197), but more modest interventions with standard controls can add similarly inviting realism without creating an entirely new interface. Subtle lighting effects on table views and buttons add tapworthy textures even for interfaces that don't directly crib the look of a physical object:

- **That's *subtle* lighting effects.** Nature has a softer touch than most Photoshop filters, and the most realistic color gradients are the ones you barely notice. Use a gentle radial or linear gradient on elements to suggest top lighting, or simply add a light and a dark line between table cells to create a beveled border. Textures should be similarly subtle, toned-down visual suggestions that

MoneyBook adds a rich leather texture to both its navigation bar and tab bar, but keeps the texture low contrast so that it whispers more than shouts. The fabric texture in the background is similarly subtle.

seem to catch the light without creating high-contrast creases and bumps. (Pro tip: pull back the opacity of texture graphics to soften their impact.)

- **Light casts a shadow.** When you add a top lighting effect to an interface element, don't forget its shadow below. A 1px–3px shadow is enough to suggest depth without drawing undue attention. Again, subtlety: shadows are never pure black but should be a darker shade of the background color below. (Do this by turning down the opacity of your shadows.) If your background is black, use a lighter color for the drop shadow to give a glow or reflection effect.

Adding a color gradient to the top half of table cells gives them a convex rounded appearance. In the Bills on Your Table app, the gradient starts as a darker shade at the bottom edge of each cell and fades to the lighter shade at the center. The app fashions a fold effect between rows by adding 1px white and gray lines respectively to the top and bottom of each cell. The final effect is an undulating sheet of creased paper.

- **Etch or raise button text.** The drop-shadow rule goes for text, too. Instead of painting flat text on your buttons and controls, make labels seem raised or embossed by adding a 1px drop shadow to the text. A dark drop shadow makes a button label look raised, while a light-colored "shadow" creates a highlight that makes it look etched into the button.

- **Nothing's perfect.** The world is full of imperfections, rough surfaces, and blemishes, and the mind naturally rejects fields of flatly uniform color as too good to be true. Even when you're after flat matte buttons, for example, consider adding a light mottled texture (Photoshop's Add Noise filter is a quick and dirty tool for this). If you're after a high-gloss plastic or glass appearance for an element, no texture is necessary, but a slightly textured background helps put your glossy creation in relief. Likewise, take the edge off perfectly square corners and make them rounded.

- **Crisp borders.** Even the "nothing's perfect" rule isn't perfect, and immaculately crisp borders are the exception. Pristinely straight lines are vanishingly rare in nature, true, but sharp borders create clear definition for buttons, table cells, and other elements. The eye catches on jagged lines and slips on blurry borders, so keep borders clean with sharp 1px outlines.

Two-dimensional graphics have their place in iPhone apps, too. Sit-up training app CrunchFu (left) adds a translucent background to each list item so that the overall background shows through with a glassy effect. The flat graphics of the Flickr app (middle) combines with lots of white space to create a sleek modern look. TouchOSC (right), a remote control for musicians, uses colorful graphics to create the look of a sci-fi soundboard.

Pause for a quick *unreality* check: borrowing the look of physical objects and textures can yield a warmly intimate interface, as you've seen, but not every app is after something so cuddly. Unambiguously artificial visuals have a place, too, particularly when you're after a sleek, high-tech look. After all, Apple's own standard iPhone table views and buttons are simple flat sheets that don't resemble physical objects at all, but they're plenty serviceable as we spin through email messages or tap through our contacts. The stuff of science fiction rarely looks commonplace (that's how you know you're looking at the future), and clean, almost sterile screens of two-dimensional graphics and translucent overlays can lend technical luster to an interface design.

Designing Custom Toolbar Icons

Custom graphics aren't just about personality and visual moxie. Your app's visuals give users important cues for how to drive the thing, and that's especially true for its toolbar icons. The iPhone comes stocked with a set of standard button icons (page 145), but of course no icon set can keep up with the fertile imaginations of app developers and designers. When you've got a feature that has no standard icon—

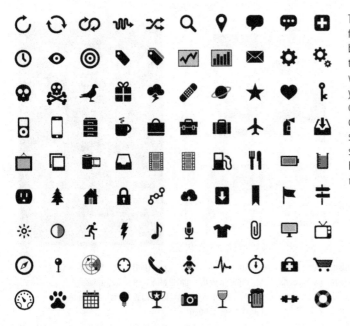

Tab-bar and toolbar icons are always flat, two-dimensional stencils that blend well with the standard set. (The tab-bar icons shown here are black on white for readability on the page, but you should draw your own as white on a transparent background.) If you don't have the chops to build your own, several sites provide free or paid icon sets for download. The icons shown here, for example, are from a free set at *www.glyphish.com*.

or when you want your icons to have their own non-standard style—you've got to design your own. Here are a few pointers.

First, the vital stats: tab bar icons should be 30 x 30 pixels, and icons for the toolbar and navigation bar should be 20 x 20 pixels. Don't fret over the colors for these images; the iPhone OS handles that for you, automatically managing the appearance of the pressed, selected, and idle states of all toolbar icons. Just draw your icon in pure white on a transparent background, and save it as a PNG image. Nothing fancy here: no drop shadows, no zany effects, just simple white, with alpha transparency for gradients or shading. When designing icons to complement the standard set, think stencil. Simple silhouettes make for crisp, legible icons. Every icon in your toolbar should be distinct not only from one another but also distinct from the built-in icons, which already have an established meaning for your audience.

Don't get too abstract or clever with your icons; aim for no-guesswork images that clearly suggest the action behind the button. Establishing a clear meaning is a tall order in just 20 or 30 pixels, and developing a good icon requires more effort and try-try-again revisions than most civilians might guess. Even Apple doesn't always get this right in its own apps. The built-in Maps app, for example, includes an inscrutable page-flip icon that consistently causes head scratching among first-time users. People tap it out of curiosity or trial and error, not because it's clear what it does. Tapping the button makes the screen curl back to reveal additional

The page-flip icon at the bottom right of the built-in Maps app doesn't describe the features you'll find when you tap it.

options like changing the style of map display. The icon illustrates the wrong thing—the nifty page-flip animation—instead of describing the actual actions the button reveals. When you watch people use this app in observation sessions, they often can't recall how to change the style of map even after they've accidentally stumbled on the feature once. The feature is hidden behind an icon whose meaning isn't clear.

In the tab bar, text labels ease the designer's work by helping to explain the icon's meaning, but the role of the icon shifts. There, icons give additional context and personality to terse tab-bar text. When Mercury Intermedia designed the USA Today app (page 90), the team went through several versions of the app's Scores

icon to get it right. Early attempts featured numbers and pixellated scoreboard treatments, but they didn't do enough to suggest the sports context. In the end, they moved away from a literal scoreboard image—the Scores label already said that—and used a pointing hand instead. With this wink to the giant foam fingers so ubiquitous at American sporting events, the result is an icon that suggests "sports fan," complementing and extending the meaning of the Scores text label without simply echoing it. (It's worth noting that the big foam finger has little meaning to sports fans outside the US. The USA Today app targets a primarily American audience, but when your app goes global, look out for imagery that might not translate.)

From top to bottom, the Scores icon of the USA Today app evolved from a literal scoreboard theme to a fan finger.

Metaphorically Speaking

Just as spoken metaphors provide expressive shortcuts in language (your husband is a peach, my computer is a dog, our boss is a monster), graphical interfaces use *visual metaphors* to quickly explain the software's complex inner workings. When you put a document into a folder on your desktop computer, there is, of course, no actual document, folder, or filesystem hierarchy. What you're really doing is stirring a soup of magnetic fields on your hard drive to represent your data's bits and bytes. The filesystem is a metaphor—a visual shorthand for something that would otherwise be impossible for most of us to understand. Interface metaphors empower mere mortals to make computers go.

Waving off the iPhone's prefab controls to craft your own interface metaphor from scratch gives your app an undeniably unique identity, but it's important to make it understood at a glance. The most intuitive interfaces lean on metaphors that we instantly recognize from day-to-day life. The card decks, spinning dials, push buttons, sliders, and light switches of the iPhone's standard toolkit require no learning; we already know how to use them thanks to our experience with their real-world counterparts. Interface design geeks call these things *affordances*, visual cues for what you can do with the app and how. The more directly an app's interface borrows from the real world, the more obvious an affordance becomes.

Besides these practical benefits, using an everyday object as an interface metaphor imbues an app with the same associations that folks might have with the real McCoy. A shelf of books, a retro alarm clock, a much-used chessboard, a toy robot—iPhone developers have used all of these objects as custom interface metaphors for their apps, lending their apps the personal connotations of the original. These physical look-alikes are most effortless when the interface is the same size as the gadget that inspired it. When iPhone apps mimic a real-world handheld device, for example, the iPhone actually seems to *become* that device. When

When apps clone physical objects in both size and appearance, their operation is immediately obvious. Here, PCalc, Guitar Toolkit, and Rowmote create intuitive interfaces by mimicking a calculator, guitar tuner, and Apple remote control.

well-executed, using the app is precisely as easy as using the original. Tapworthy apps that take this approach often use realistic sounds and animations to reinforce the illusion that you're using a real-world gizmo. (As you saw in Chapter 3, gadget clones like these also benefit from the original device's proven ergonomics.)

Other apps depict real-world objects as miniatures, reduced to fit the small screen. This approach can't match the "I can't believe it's not butter" realism of exact-replica interfaces: you're always aware that you're working with a miniature illustration, an abstraction. All the same, when well-done, it's still immediately obvious how these little facsimiles work. By relying on the direct manipulation of miniature chess pieces, air hockey paddles, guitar strings, or other real-world affordances, these apps invite touch and encourage their audiences to explore. Like all miniatures, these interfaces often create a sense of whimsy, and here again, appropriate sound and animation enhance the effect.

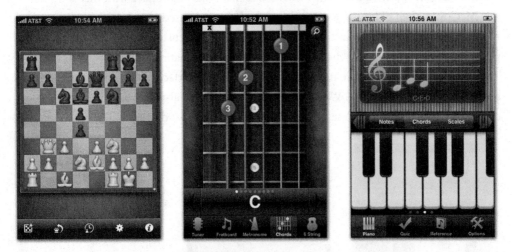

From left: Deep Green, Guitar Toolkit, and Nota.

Just be careful not to go too far, or you'll accidentally stray into kitsch. Your interface is there to support the task at hand, not the reverse. Don't become so enamored of your design that you obscure the very information you're trying to convey, an affront that information design guru Edward Tufte calls "the sin of pridefully obvious presentation." When using animation effects, for example, don't let them last too long or distract from the main content. A playful effect might make you smile the first few times, but beware the ones that start to feel precious, then annoying, and then you're filled with Hulk-like rage. Page flips are a warmly personal addition to an ebook or magazine app, for example, as long as they don't slow you down. Animations should occur quickly and effortlessly.

Be biased toward a relentless focus on accomplishing the user's goal with no fuss, but also know that efficiency doesn't *always* trump style. Some apps manage a toy-like charm that encourages fiddling with the interface in ways that delight and never frustrate. This is a delicate path to follow, but Weightbot and Convertbot, two bestselling apps by the company Tapbots, get this just right. It takes a few seconds longer to enter your info than other apps in the same category, yet working Convertbot's dial, for example, is satisfyingly playful. "Our apps are designed more like a game," explains Tapbots designer Mark Jardine. "Our primary goal for Convertbot wasn't for it to be the most efficient unit conversion app there is. If that's what you are looking for, there are plenty of nice conversion apps that get you from point A to point B in the shortest amount of clicks. Our goal was to make unit conversions fun and enjoyable. Once you get used to it, there's a sense of satisfaction and rhythm to the process." Most iPhone users eventually find themselves distractedly tugging at a list to see it snap back into place again and again—it's the same satisfaction. There's a certain charm to interfaces that encourage absentminded play, part of the very personal nature of the device.

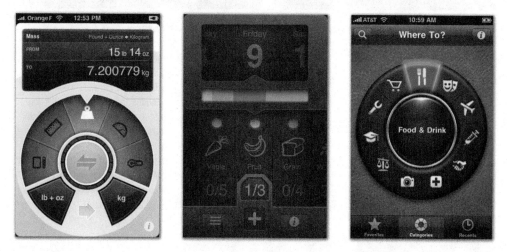

Imagined gadgets brought to life by iPhone apps. From left: Convertbot, Foobi, and Where To?

Classics and Cookmate use a shelf metaphor to browse books, cooking ingredients, and music.

Stanza (left) and iPod (right) present your ebook and music collections using coverflow.

The big pile of stuff: Albums (left) and Mover (right) scatter your belongings across a table top and encourages you to nudge and explore your collection by dragging or flinging items around the screen. Albums is an alternative to iPod, letting you browse and play albums more graphically. Mover collects contacts and photos and lets you share them with nearby iPhone users by flinging them off the table.

Other interface metaphors are effective at building a similar connection through the natural affection we have for personal collections. Photos, friends, music, books, even the contents of our kitchen cupboards define who we are and the spaces in which we live. By gathering and displaying this type of intimate info and media with a trophy case's pride of place, an app can flatter the collector inside us while also inviting the browsing behavior triggered by our physical-world collections. Popular and effective metaphors for presenting collections include book shelves, "the big pile of stuff," and the *coverflow* browsing style popularized by iTunes for browsing album covers. Any of these, when well-executed, can be effective replacements for a traditional table view display while encouraging more browsing and exploration than a plain list might.

I Call My New Invention "The Wheel"

New interfaces always demand extra thought and attention of your audience, and you shouldn't take that lightly. Don't be different just to be different; be different when you believe you can be *better*. Before you shake free of the standard iPhone interface metaphors to create your own, know the warning signs for when you're inventing something that looks an awful lot like a wheel:

- **Are you trying to solve a problem you could solve with built-in tools?** Favor the standard controls instead of creating something new to perform exactly the same function. (Don't craft web-style tab navigation, for example, when a tab bar, table index, or segmented control will do the job.)

- **Are you being too clever?** A great interface makes the app easy and evident to use. Avoid abstract metaphors, and rely on proven, real-world affordances. Tapworthy apps encourage direct, unmediated manipulation of content: tap a content element to read it (or view it or listen to it), drag it to move it, poke it in the belly to make it giggle. This "be direct" mantra applies to the words and icons of your interface, too. Bank of Mom, for example, is a great little app to help parents manage kids' allowances, but it's tarnished by a puzzling gardening metaphor. The app refers to kids as "saplings" and uses a leaf icon for financial interest and a fluorescent lightbulb for activities. Huh? Weed out those tangled metaphors.

- **Is your interface metaphor appropriate to the device?** Your app should feel like an iPhone app. Your new-to-the-world interface should blend in with the visuals and metaphors of the apps around it. In particular, be cautious about importing interface elements from other platforms, particularly desktop computers. For example, limited screen space means that the windows of desktop platforms don't work well on the iPhone; but even more important, they don't jibe with the sliding screens that iPhone users are accustomed to. Don't use windows or other metaphors that go against the grain of established iPhone conventions.

- **Got more interface than you need?** As you create new controls and interface elements, constantly pare them down to the simplest possible presentation. That doesn't mean you should strip out the personality or take the bot out of Convertbot, but rather that you should remove unnecessary steps, distracting animations, and extra buttons to keep the flow as easy and obvious as possible. In the early designs for image enlargement in the USA Today app, for example, the image included an X button to close it and return to the article. An artifact of desktop software windows, the button was unnecessary on the iPhone, creating the expectation that you had to tap the button directly to dismiss the image. The designers removed the button to allow users to tap anywhere to get rid of the image, a faster and equally intuitive solution.

An early design of the USA Today app (left) included the X button to dismiss enlarged images. The final version removed the button.

And Now for Something Completely Different

None of the stuff you just read should dissuade you from being inventive with your app's design. When it comes to the possibilities of personal touchscreen devices like the iPhone, we're still babes in the woods. Designers and developers are still hatching fresh iPhone magic every day, and there's still much to explore and invent. While you should look hard at whether you might accomplish what you need to do with the standard controls, it's also worth asking, *Am I going far enough?*

By using a physical object as your interface metaphor, for example, you might ensure your user's instant familiarity, but you're also limited by the expected form and function of the original real-world artifact. The curling page flip animation of an ebook app, for example, is a cozy gesture for book lovers, but what does a page even *mean* on an iPhone, where text could swoop, scroll, and scatter in any way you might imagine? A page flip requires computing power, coding effort, and lots of swipe-swipe-swiping, all for a relatively quaint retro effect. Could your energy be better spent trying to investigate new ways to interact with a book, discovering how an ebook might enable readers to do things the paper version could not? New devices create opportunities for new interfaces, even for old media. Sometimes the right thing to do is leapfrog familiar metaphors instead of reinventing them.

Allow yourself to explore the possibilities, and don't be afraid to experiment with offbeat concepts. How about a singing robot? When developer Russell Black and designer Lily McDonnell created a sophisticated sound synthesizer for the iPhone, the predictable thing would have been to use a keyboard for the interface. Instead, they created Bebot, a crooning cartoon robot. You tap or slide your finger around the screen and Bebot sings and warbles. Under this sweet exterior lurks

Tap and slide across Bebot's screen to make the animated robot perform your synthesized tune.

enough sound-engineer nerdery to engage serious musicians and sound enthusiasts. Yet the adorable interface makes the app accessible to mere mortals, and the touchscreen operation results in a unique-to-the-iPhone musical instrument. It's almost enough to persuade you that every app should have a robot mascot—as long as it's painted black.

Touchpoints

✓ Tapworthy designs have the power to charm and beguile. Choose a personality for your app before you start to design.

✓ Use custom colors and graphics to give fresh identity to standard controls. Luxurious textures increase your app's perceived value, and realistic interface elements invite touch.

✓ Icons should emphasize clarity over personality. Favor clean silhouettes over finicky details.

✓ Borrow interface metaphors from the physical world, but make sure they're appropriate to the device and favor standard controls.

✓ Don't be afraid to take risks.

First Person: Craig Hockenberry, Gedeon Maheux, and Twitterrific

Twitter apps have been popular projects for app developers since the App Store's get-go, but Twitterrific found a perch at the top of this crowded category right from the start. Twitterrific captures the essential ease of Twitter itself—great for casual Twitter fans—but its clever filtering tools and a flock of carefully chosen features make it easy for power users to sift and act on vast volumes of tweets, too. The features that aren't included are nearly as important as those that are. Twitterrific emphasizes simplicity, eschewing the feature creep that complicate so many Twitter apps whether on the desktop or on the iPhone.

Twitterrific was created by the crew at The Iconfactory, led by principals **Craig Hockenberry** and **Gedeon Maheux.** The app began when Twitter itself was simple (post and read 140-character updates—that's it). By the time the team started work on Twitterrific 2.0, Twitter had developed a complex ecosystem of third-party services, cultural conventions, and intertwined conversations that went well beyond posting standalone tweets. To keep up with this headlong surge of changes, Twitterrific gained several carefully considered custom controls to access advanced features while keeping the main interface clean and simple. Craig and Gedeon explained the challenges of designing for Twitter's overwhelming feature set and shared the insights that led them to create controls for Twitterrific that could do things better than (not just different from) the standard controls.

Craig Hockenberry (left) and Gedeon
Maheux (right)

Gedeon Maheux: Twitter is such a moving target. They keep adding things, and the environment changes so frequently that it's difficult to design for it. It's difficult to make the app future-proof, in other words—to make it simple but also give those additional features to people who need them without making them jump through hoops. The more things you support in a single application, the more complex the user interface has to get; things start getting out of hand. So you have to focus and choose your features carefully.

Craig Hockenberry: Simplicity is important in a mobile device. You're often using it in chaotic situations. You're on a bus, or you're late for an appointment, or you're in other situations where there are lots of stimuli around you. So, less is actually more in those situations. It's actually harder to make a simple interface on the iPhone than it is to make a complex interface. One of the problems with Twitter is that there's such a rich data set, and there are so many things you can do. You've got to leave stuff out. A lot of other Twitter clients try to do it all without staying focused on what you *really* need to do and how to keep it as simple as possible.

You get some power users who want every new feature immediately. They want the feature just because it exists, not because it provides some actual use to their lives on Twitter. For us, choosing a feature is always about the use case. Twitter always has new features coming down the pipeline, but we don't jump on them right away, because we don't know how people will use them yet. Our focus is always on figuring out, "Why would you want to use a feature? Why do you need geotagging in Twitter? What's the best way to use Twitter lists?" Until we figure it out, we don't put it in. We always start with "why," with the use case. Say somebody tweets, "Where's the best place to get a hamburger in San Francisco?" You want to know how people respond, so you want to see recent messages directed to that person. That's a common use case that other Twitter clients don't make very easy, and we decided to make that something simple to do. You just hit the asterisk button in the toolbar, hit the @author button, and there it is.

Twitterrific gives you fast access to the replies to a tweet's author. Select the tweet and tap the asterisk icon in the toolbar to summon the action buttons (left). Tap the @author button (middle), and Twitterrific shows the latest replies and mentions for the author (right).

Taming a Dense Thicket of Options

Even with the design team exercising heroic self-restraint, the feature list for Twitterrific 2 still added a slew of options for manipulating individual tweets. At the same time, they wanted to make it faster to get at those tools. Twitterrific's first version required you to tap to a separate detail screen to work with a tweet. One goal for Twitterrific 2 was to let you do more directly from the main list of tweets. The challenge was where to stash all the controls for those actions. The standard approach would be to add the action icon to the toolbar and display an action sheet listing the options.

Craig: We found the action sheet to be really frustrating for this, because the list would change for different tweets. You can't delete somebody else's tweet, for example, so the delete button goes away for those tweets. Having buttons appear and disappear from the list gave you no positional stability. Buttons appeared in different locations on the screen, so you had to hunt through this long list of options every time. Designer **Louie Mantia** came up with the idea of doing a kind of custom keyboard, a collection of buttons for actions. The difference is that you can actually disable those buttons, so the Delete button stays where it is but is just disabled, which was a good solution to that problem.

Gedeon: There was a lot of debate and back and forth about the order of the buttons, how many buttons to have, and what position they would be in. Is it two rows of four? Is it a row of three, a row of five? Which ones are on top, which ones are on bottom? We went around on that through so many revisions, changing the actions available and their layout, until we finally arrived at what we have now.

Craig: A subtle thing about the placement of the buttons is that they're oriented towards one-handed use. The Delete button is off to the right, the hardest location to tap for right-handed users, and we put other options where your thumb has to work less in order to get to more commonly used actions. We think a lot about where things get placed based upon ergonomics.

Through the early design stages of Twitterrific 2, the action buttons evolved from a standard action sheet to a row of action buttons, and finally became two rows with buttons carefully placed according to thumb-tapping ease.

Asterisk = Action

With the presentation problem for actions solved, the focus turned to how to advertise those buttons. When Twitterrific's designers considered Apple's standard

Action icon (page 148), it didn't seem to match up with the app's broad range of options.

Gedeon: What *is* that Action icon? It's not immediately clear what it stands for. The icon suggests sending or forwarding something, but that's not what you're doing in the actions we present. Some of the actions apply to the tweet, some of them apply to the author, and there's no one type of action under there. We just didn't feel that Apple's preexisting Action icon addressed all of those different features. We considered using the "More" (…) icon, but that didn't really do or suggest anything either. So we decided to design our own. We have a whole page of things we tried for that icon, but we finally arrived at the asterisk. I don't think the asterisk is the best solution—a lot of people don't immediately know what it is— but given the alternatives, it was the least of 300 evils.

Icons are really important, and being the Iconfactory—we do icons for a living—we probably anguish over icons more than we should. It's one of those things that people take for granted when they use an app. For us, though, it was especially important that they be clear for this app, because we made the conscious decision that we weren't going to label the icons. Even if you don't figure out what they are right away, though, our thought was that you learn quickly enough that you don't need to take up that extra space with labels.

Tapping the funnel icon (left) summons Twitterrific's filter bar (right) to display only specific types of tweets. These icons get a different style and highlighting effect to distinguish the filter bar from the main toolbar. From left to right on the filter bar, tap an icon to filter by: replies and mentions, direct messages, favorites, your own tweets, or those you've marked.

Color Me Unique

Craig: We've always been people who like to customize our workspaces, and part of the reason we added themes is that we like to make things look pretty. But on a more basic level, we thought about the use cases for when you might need dark or light backgrounds. Are you using it during the day or at night? A lot of people tweet in bed in the middle of the night. They can't sleep, and they get on Twitter, and at night, the dark theme is easier on the eyes.

Gedeon: When I'm sitting in a movie theater, about to watch a movie, I hate it when you've got someone next to you and their phone is really, really bright. I always use the dark theme unless I'm out in direct sunlight. We also considered the use cases for when you might need to change the formatting of tweets. If you're in a moving vehicle or something, you want the font to be as big and as easy to read as possible. If you want to try to get as much information in the view as possible, then you go and you switch to the smallest font. So we added options to choose the formatting. Of course, you can't please everybody. Some people will say, "Why didn't you include the avatar in the small view?" Or, "Why doesn't the large view have the geolocation stuff?" You give

Twitterrific offers three color schemes. The dark "Raven" theme (middle) is the app's standard setting, but you can change to two light-colored themes, like "Snowy" (right)

an inch, and they want a mile, but we try to take the most widely used or most generic kinds of applications for those things.

Testing the Bare Bones

Craig: We don't do this with every application, but Twitterrific was complex enough that we started by putting together an interaction prototype. It was ugly. It used only standard buttons, no customized look or design. It just showed fake tweets, and it didn't show any real data, but we could find out how the app would feel. One of the things that's important for me in designing an iPhone app is how my fingers interact with the interface, and you can't really get that from a Photoshop mockup. There's a lot to be said for watching the transitions while you actually tap through the app. You have to experience the app enough so that you can base your designs on what you're feeling.

Twitterrific 2 went through several design revisions, starting with a no-frills working prototype. Here, the profile screen evolves from prototype to final design.

7

First Impressions

INTRODUCING YOUR APP

GOOD CHEMISTRY with an app works a lot like it does with a person: much is decided in the first few moments. To draw people in and put them at ease, your app should be attractive, trustworthy, and approachable from the get-go. Elements that you might consider mere accessories—the app icon, launch image, and introductory screen—turn out to be essential to the first impression. When you don't get those things right, it's like showing up on a first date with dirty fingernails. It might not put you out of the running, but it doesn't exactly make you irresistible. A bad icon can dissuade people from even trying your app, and an unhelpful welcome for first-timers can leave them frustrated and nonplussed. Run a comb through your hair, and put on something pretty: this chapter describes how to design your app for love at first sight.

Your Icon Is Your Business Card

Business cards create expectations. When you hand someone a card, you give them information that goes beyond simple contact details. Heavy card stock? Printed on the inkjet at home? Flashy design? Color? Conservative font? Groovy image on the back? All these presentation decisions create an impression not only of the card's design but of the person handing it out. Your card has to be crisply informational while communicating your professional personality (or at

Photo: L. Broadwell

least your company's). For people meeting you for the first time, that flimsy scrap of paper is one of the few things they use to form an opinion. The same goes for your app's icon in the App Store and on the iPhone Home screen.

Your icon is the first thing people see when they encounter your app. It's the primary element of your listing in App Store search results, pulling even more visual weight than the app's name. (When you browse App Store listings, the only info you get is the icon, name, and price. Even when you visit an app's detail screen, the icon is featured well above the screenshots that show what your app does.) Quality and polish in an icon suggest the same in the app itself and reassures customers considering a download. For such a tiny collection of pixels, the icon has disproportionate weight in the marketing and perception of your app. Give it disproportionate design attention. If you're not a designer yourself, consider hiring one for at least this one aspect of your app. It's important.

Icons are constantly shoulder to shoulder with other icons, and your icon design has to stand out in a lineup—it should have a look of its own. Color is a good

Borrow color, style, and texture directly from an app interface to create recognition and fidelity. Clockwise from top left: Cellar, Deep Green, and Canabalt.

place to start: fields of blue or green are all too common for icons, and choosing something different is immediately helpful. Draw from your app's interface for inspiration. If your app has an unusual design metaphor, color scheme, or personality, consider how those might be reflected in the icon, too. When the app delivers on the expectation created by your icon, you create trust and confidence, and making your app borrow directly from the interface is one way to do that.

Make your icon colorful, make it memorable, make it fun, but whatever you do, don't make it *mysterious*. The app icon is fundamentally an advertisement, and like any good ad, it has to be clear what it's selling. The icon should picture, in a very direct way, something tapworthy and intimately related to your app. This can be a visual description of its function, its interface, its name, or its brand. As always in the mobile environment, don't make people think too hard or take a second look. Think of the icon as a packaging label—it's great if it's pretty, but it's even more important that it be descriptive and identifiable at a glance, for both branding and usability. Avoid cryptic or inscrutable imagery, and don't be overly clever with the visual metaphors. More commerce, less art.

The Iconfactory learned this lesson the hard way with Ramp Champ, the company's gorgeously atmospheric Skee-Ball-style iPhone game. A handsome but obscure icon combined with an ambiguous name to confuse App Store shoppers. In hindsight, the developers believe the icon reduced sales. "While the icon itself is unique and stands out in the App Store, it's still cryptic, and people didn't understand it," says Iconfactory principal Craig Hockenberry. "They didn't get it, and they weren't enticed to click beyond it. One of the things we learned from Ramp Champ is that icons need to be more literal even when that's not always the best looking design."

The Ramp Champ icon (left) has a bold and unique design, but the blandly descriptive icon for a similar game, Skee-Ball from Freeverse (right), is more effective.

There are several ways for well-designed icons to be descriptively literal. As you've already seen, icons for apps with distinctive designs can visually quote that design, creating a kind of preview of the app itself. While that approach might hint at the function of the app, the focus is on emphasizing the app's look and feel, a good approach when the app's design merits it. A more direct route focuses on the function of the app and what it does for you. Like a reliable road sign, this style of icon uses an explanatory symbol to show you where you're headed. The challenge here is to be descriptive without being generic so that the icon maintains a unique personality. Beware of crowded categories and iconography by herd: with few exceptions, nearly all of the iPhone's jillion to-do list apps use a checkmark for their icon, and developers of photography apps can't seem to resist the image of a camera lens. Be descriptive, not duplicative. Some successful examples:

Some icons focus on function. From left: Cha-Ching, an expense tracker; Kineo, a flipbook app; cab4me, a taxi locator; Cocktails+, a cocktail recipe app; Lose It!, a calorie tracker; and Delivery Status Touch, a package tracker.

Some apps tackle jobs that are too abstract to be easily described by a simple pictogram. A fallback in that case is to make an icon that instead illustrates the app's name, in effect building a visual brand around the title itself. This route can be risky since the icon offers little clue about what the app does or what it looks like, making it even more important that the icon bear enough interest, design quality, or personality to reassure (or at least intrigue) potential customers. The advantage, though, is that this approach often yields icons that stand out from those around them:

Some icons focus on name. From left: Aardvark Mobile, RedLaser, Birdhouse, MoneyBook, Ego, and Cellar Rat.

This self-referential approach is particularly effective when your app is for a brand that's already well-established with your audience. In that case, lean on your logo, since it's already loaded with instant meaning for your customers:

Logo-inspired icons from left: Yellow Pages, FedEx, Twitterrific, myStarbucks, Flickr, and NASA.

For brands that are *exceptionally* well-established with their audience, a simple logotype of just a letter or two cuts a clean, easily identified profile. You might've already heard, though: there's just a limited number of letters in the alphabet. That means the letter gambit can collide with other icons. The approach is most effective for brands with an established text logo and a readily recognized typeface:

Logotype icons from left: New York Times, Facebook, GQ, PayPal, Skype, and Wall Street Journal.

Don't go overboard with text in your icon. One or two letters look great, and if you have a well-known logotype (like FedEx, Yelp, or NPR), that works, too. Apart from those examples, avoid stamping your app's name on your icon or, worse, adding several words of descriptive text. The best icons rely on visual descriptions; if you're resorting to a text label, you probably haven't explored all the options. Remember, too, that your icon is always accompanied by a text label—the app's name—in the App Store and on the iPhone Home screen, and there's no need to spray it across the icon itself. More crucially, text adds too much visual detail to the icon and doesn't reduce well for the tiny version displayed in the iPhone's Spotlight search results and Settings app: when quickly scanning a screenful of icons, the eye already reads icon text as noise; in the miniature search version, it's just an illegible scribble.

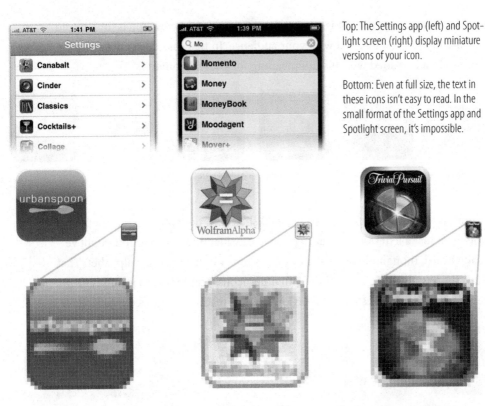

Top: The Settings app (left) and Spotlight screen (right) display miniature versions of your icon.

Bottom: Even at full size, the text in these icons isn't easy to read. In the small format of the Settings app and Spotlight screen, it's impossible.

See, text muddies the overall silhouette of the icon. The best icons emphasize a single overall shape. You can and should use subtle detail to create lustrous light effects, rich textures, and 3-D realism, but it's the *outline* of the primary image that's most important. The foundation of your design should be a simple shape that can be identified at a glance. You know you're off to a good start if you can flip on your desk lamp and reproduce your icon's shape as a shadow puppet. Avoid making the image too busy or complicating it with multiple figures. If your icon absolutely has to juggle more than one shape, handle them carefully, making sure that they're all visually distinct and their interaction is clear. Although you can afford more artistic license in app icons than toolbar icons (page 194), the fundamental rule is the same: clarity of meaning is the priority.

The importance of a clean silhouette has always been a staple of good logo design, and your app's icon is exactly that: a logo for your app. In concert with the interface design, your icon creates your app's visual brand. Thinking more broadly, if you have a suite of apps, it's worth considering how you might build a coherent brand around all of them. Tapbots and App Cubby are two development shops with apps featuring a complementary interface style (retro machinery for Tapbots, a wood-grain theme for App Cubby), and their icons are similarly consistent across all their apps. App developer iTrans likewise uses nearly identical icons for its city transit apps, mixing it up by changing the city name and skyline reflected in the icon's windshield.

From left to right: App Cubby, Tapbots, and iTrans all make good use of cross-app branding.

Building Your App's Icons

Don't look now, but your app actually has multiple versions of its app icon, a Goldilocks ensemble of big, medium, and small. The version your audience sees most is the medium size, the Home-screen icon that they tap to launch the app, but the other two sizes have important roles that deserve attention and, often, their own custom treatment. The App Store uses the large icon as the basis for the big icon you see in an app's detail screen (it gets scaled down), and the small icon appears in the iPhone's spotlight search results and settings screen. To muddy waters a bit more, the iPad uses different sizes for its small and medium icon; if you're creating a single universal app that contains the code to run your app in both iPhone and iPad (and you should), you'll need to add those two additional icon sizes, too. Here's the rundown:

App Icon Pixel Sizes

Small icon for iPhone	29 × 29
Small icon for iPad	48 × 48
Medium icon for iPhone	57 × 57
Medium icon for iPad	72 × 72
Large icon	512 × 512

That's a big variation in icon size—the large icon is nearly 20 times bigger than the iPhone's small icon—which means that the three sizes accommodate very different levels of detail. When designing the icon graphic, start with the large version and take advantage of its big canvas to fill your icon with rich detail and lighting effects. Your goal with this version is to create an effective, eye-catching billboard for your app in the App Store. When iTunes puts your creation on display, though, it won't appear full-size, so before you call it quits, check to make sure that this large icon looks good when scaled down to about 175 × 175.

Build the medium icon next, using the large version as the foundation and stripping out details that turn muddy in the downsize. As always, focus on the main silhouette. This is your app's Home-screen icon, so the primary shape should be crisp and easily recognizable so that people can spot it quickly at a glance. The same goes for the small icon, only more so. There's no room in a 29-pixel square for much detail work; reducing the large icon as-is all the way down to this size will give you little more than a blot of murky color. Depending on your design, you may need to start from scratch to optimize this small version so that the silhouette still remains clear.

The result of all this work is often three subtly varied icon designs, but don't take this as license to create wildly different designs. App Store reviewers sometimes reject apps whose icons mismatch so that they're "confusing to users." To casual observers, the three sizes should all look like identical designs, even though details may vary. Apple does tolerate "Sale" badges and other marketing messages on the large icon for the App Store—the equivalent of hanging a sign in your shop window. (Careful, though—these icon sales gimmicks tend to look cheesy and of course obscure your gorgeous design. Nobody ever said commerce and taste

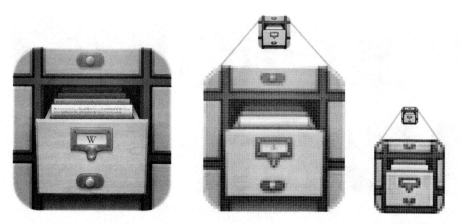

The large, medium, and small icons for Articles, a Wikipedia reader, were each designed from scratch to look their best in their respective sizes.

always go hand in hand, but it doesn't mean you can't try; be thoughtful when you pin a badge on your icon.)

App icons always show up with rounded edges, but that effect gets applied automatically by the App Store and iPhone behind the scenes. Don't chisel off your icon's corners on your own. Instead, submit a simple square graphic—no rounded corners—for your icon images. (Pro tip: the graphic should be a 24-bit PNG image with no transparency; any transparent pixels will be replaced with black, which looks crummy for people with custom wallpaper on their Home screen.)

As for the automatic gloss that gets applied to images, don't let it happen. It's a well-intentioned effort on Apple's part to create a gemlike consistency across all icons. While you should honor that consistency in spirit, don't let an automatic filter apply a lighting effect that you can create yourself with more care and consideration (see examples on page 222). Even Apple passes on the standard gloss for several of its own built-in apps. Instead, add your own lighting effects, glossy or not, to give your icon a luminous glow appropriate to your design. Don't cede control over one of your app's most essential elements. (Nitty-gritty developer note: you can turn off the automatic shine effect by adding the UIPrerenderedIcon key to your app's Info.plist file. For more details, see Apple's *iPhone Application Programming Guide*, available at *http://developer.apple.com/iphone*.)

Icons with the standard gloss (top) have a consistent treatment but lack the custom flavor of icons that apply their own glow or none at all (bottom).

What's In a Name?

What do you call your app for finding waffle houses? Wafflr? iWaffle? Whence the Waffle? Your app's name is less important than you might think—at least from your audience's perspective. Sure, the name is important for *marketing* your app. A memorable name is crucial to word of mouth—it contributes to the brand personality of your app, and it determines how easily your app will be found via search keywords. By all means, have the marketing folks kick the name around for a while and do what they do best. But once an app finally finds a home on an iPhone, people tend to identify it more by its icon and function than by its proper name. People don't scan the screen for the words "iAwesome Game-o-Rama," they go looking for that flashy orange icon. In terms of user experience, both icon and interface carry far more weight than whatever name you might call it. Onscreen, the app's name is simply the caption for the icon.

In that context, perhaps the best thing you can do is *keep the name short.* If the name doesn't squeeze into the space allowed, the iPhone forces it to fit by lopping the name off at the middle. "Local Concerts" becomes "Local…ncerts," and "Whence the Waffle" becomes "Whenc…affle." Huh? Just like that, the name goes from innocuously helpful label to confusing distraction. App Store reviewers typically allow some leeway to use an abbreviated version on the Home screen. That means you can submit a longer name to show up in iTunes and a shorter version for the Home screen. The to-do list app Remember the Milk, for example, shows up with the abbreviation "RTM," Dragon Dictation appears as "Dictation," and package-tracking app Delivery Status Touch uses "Deliveries." Do whatever you need to do, just don't let the name get chopped.

Because the characters of the Home-screen typeface aren't all the same width, there's not a hard and fast rule for how many letters will fit in the name, but Safari gives you a relatively painless way to test names for fit, without constantly rebuilding your app. The web browser lets you save bookmarks as Home-screen icons: Go to any web page, click the + button in the toolbar, and choose Add to Home Screen. Type the name to try out, and an icon materializes on the Home screen with your test name, just as it would look below your own app's icon. If it fits, great. If not, back to the drawing board (or the web browser, in this case).

While You Wait: The Launch Image

So you've coaxed someone to download your app, you've crafted an irresistibly tapworthy icon, and your lucky customer has just tapped it to launch your app. And now . . . they wait. Like all iPhone software, your app takes a second or three to load and start running. That's not exactly an eternity, but it can feel like it in the rushed context of on-the-go computing. No matter how long it takes, *how fast it feels* is really all that matters. You can have a big effect on that impression by carefully crafting what you show onscreen while your app fires up. Some well-timed smoke and carefully placed mirrors can make your app's startup time feel faster than it otherwise might. You'll learn more about the Jedi mind tricks for bending time with good interface design in Chapter 10. For now, consider the effect of your app's *launch image*.

When someone taps your icon, the iPhone OS throws a graphic onto the screen before it even fires up your app's code. This is the launch image—the placeholder screen people see while your app loads. (You bundle the launch image alongside your app's code as a full-screen 320 x 480 PNG graphic, and the iPhone displays it automatically.) It's powerfully tempting to make this image something flashy, a splash screen that dazzles and hypnotizes your audience with your remarkable Photoshop skills or the extraordinary beauty of your corporate logo. Resist that instinct and go the other way: be dull.

Use the launch image to give the impression that the app is already up and running. Apple recommends that the launch image look exactly like the app's first screen, only emptied of its content so that it's just the husk of your interface design. This approach creates the illusion that the app has started immediately—you already see its interface—and that it's already hard at work loading your content even though the code hasn't even started rolling yet. After the app finishes loading for real, it replaces the placeholder launch image with the app's first screen, as if the app has filled in the content of the previously empty screen.

The launch image should depict an empty version of the app's first screen. The launch image for the built-in Weather app (top) includes all the interface details except the content itself.

The Settings app (bottom) includes only a blank navigation bar and the pinstripe background.

Contrast this faux interface strategy with a launch image that shows a lavish splash graphic featuring an illustration or logo. The second approach feels like an ad. While a fake interface image suggests, "I'm working for you," the logo says, "I'm talking about me." The practical result is the same—with either image, it takes the same amount of time to load—but the psychological difference is pronounced. The bland interface image makes the app *feel* like it's loading faster. It also suggests more respect for the user's task than a marketing message, no matter how lively that message or graphic might be.

In fact, liveliness in a launch image is a problem. The more the launch image draws attention to itself, the more it draws attention to the delay while your app launches. It even makes the delay seem intentional, as if you're slowing the start of the app to show off your own logo, like the gratuitous Flash splash screens on websites from 1999. Some apps complete that outmoded effect by displaying an animation immediately after the launch image. The PayPal app shows one or two seconds of bouncing coins before it lets you do anything. The otherwise laudable Flying Without Fear app from Virgin Atlantic starts off with several seconds of title animation before launching its relaxation exercises for overcoming a flying phobia. (When you're hyperventilating at the thought of shoulder rolling through an airplane aisle at 700 mph, the last thing you want to see are production credits.)

The PayPal and Flying Without Fear apps both launch with animations that take several seconds, extending the perceived launch time.

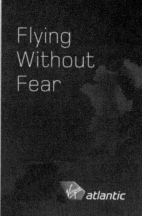

To be fair, these apps may very well be doing some heavy work behind the scenes to get the app ready to go, and they're buying time with animations while the setup completes. As you'll learn in Chapter 10, a simple activity indicator or progress bar would do the job better. Unfortunately, the splash-screen approach makes the apps seem like they're stalling to preen about their brands. Moreover, this kind of visual drumroll underscores that you're *launching* the app, which of course you are, but you should instead cultivate the impression that you're *switching* to an app that's already running, just waiting for you to return. That trick is the topic of the next section.

The Illusion of Suspended Animation

The idea has unmistakable appeal: have yourself frozen and then thawed out years later, fresh as a spring flower and ready for action. Alas, despite the popular myth that Walt Disney's body is awaiting resuscitation in a vault under Disneyland, science hasn't had much luck with suspended animation (Uncle Walt was cremated in 1966). The iPhone has had slightly more success with its own version of the concept, though. Starting with iPhone OS 4.0, the iPhone learned how to "freeze" an app when you quit; when you relaunch it, you pick up exactly when and where you started. As you hop back and forth among apps, you're just switching between screens held in suspended animation, frozen and ready to resume when you are.

Even before this feature was introduced, this freeze/thaw experience was how most people understood the experience of moving between apps. Unlike desktop software that often takes several seconds to quit or launch, an iPhone app quickly makes its entrance and exit, creating the sense that all apps are already loaded and at the ready. It doesn't feel like quitting and relaunching, although that's exactly what's happening. While the iPhone can now sidestep this relaunch by suspending and resuming apps, its cryogenic powers are limited. Not all iPhone or iPod hardware has the horsepower to suspend apps, and even those that do can suspend only so many apps at a time before starting to nudge them out of memory. In both of those cases, returning to an app means launching them all over again. Your audience doesn't care about these technical niceties, though; no matter what's happening under the hood, they just want your app to start up where they left off. When your app launches, it should work hard to give the impression that it's reviving from suspended animation even when it's not.

For developers spinning iPhone code, all of this means that how your app says hello depends on how well it says goodbye. When an app quits, it should hustle to store not only any unsaved data but also information about the state of the app's interface—the view, position, and content currently on display. With that info safely stashed away, the app can restore the interface to its exact state when the app relaunches, giving the impression that it was running behind the scenes all along.

A well-designed launch image is an important piece of this illusion, as you've seen. For apps with several different screen designs, however, a launch image doesn't always help. Apps can have only one launch image, and they can't change them on the fly. Faking the look of your interface during launch works only when the app has a consistent background from view to view. If your app's screens have very different backgrounds or layouts, the launch image may not match up when your app restores the interface, a visually jarring false start. For example, in the scientific calculator app PCalc (page 67), there are several different keyboard layouts, which means it isn't possible to show a satisfying launch image without risking a collision with the wrong layout. Developer James Thomson fell back to displaying the app's icon graphic as the launch image. "Now there was no jarring transition," James says, "but people stared at my splash screen for four seconds before the calculator appeared and it felt like an eternity while they were waiting to start typing. I actually got emails accusing me of having a massive ego because I was making the splash screen stay up for so long."

He developed a clever hybrid solution: before it quits, PCalc takes a snapshot of the current screen and stores the graphic. When the app is launched again, it shows the launch image (the logo splash screen) for less than a second while it quickly fetches the snapshot saved from the last session. Only after planting this accurate place-holder image does PCalc turn to churning through its startup code to get itself up and running, finally replacing the image with the "real" screen when it's done. This sleight of hand gives the effect that the app has started nearly instantly, right where you left off. (Happily, the app even captures the taps that you make on this decoy graphic; nothing happens until the code fully loads, but after it does, the app goes ahead and shows any numbers you tapped in the mean-time.) This would be even more ideal if PCalc didn't show the logo image at all. Unfortunately, an app can't replace its own launch image, so the app always has to use the same original graphic—in this case, the PCalc logo image—before it can display the interface snapshot.

Because the app has several screen variations, PCalc's launch image can't mimic the app's interface and instead displays a logo (left). This image appears only briefly before being replaced by a screenshot image from the last session (right). On slower hardware, a tongue-in-cheek status message appears while the app finishes loading.

Put Out the Welcome Mat

Wading through icons and launch images, your customer has finally made it to your app's first screen. Now what? Ideally, your app is so easy and intuitive that it's immediately obvious to everyone exactly how the thing works. A simple app or a dead-easy interface borrowed directly from the real world (air hockey!) doesn't take much head scratching. For apps with more complex features or tasks, even the most well-designed interface can benefit from a few introductory hints. This is especially true in the first seconds and minutes of your app's debut with a customer. The first date is all about getting comfortable, and your app should be welcoming and courteous. The first screen is responsible for this greeting, and it's helpful to tweak that screen slightly when viewed for the first time. Think of this specialized addition as a *welcome mat*, a layer you roll out to make your app's first screen more inviting and helpful.

This is especially important if the first screen would otherwise start out empty. A blank screen is disorienting—it's helpful to offer some one-time instructions to show people how to start adding content to the app. For example, Articles is a Wikipedia reader that has nothing to display until you search for your first article. Likewise, CardStar is an app that manages chain-store membership cards, but there's nothing to see before you add your first card. In both apps, the first screen is empty, but they add welcome mats with quick notes pointing out how to get started. If your app requires action to start adding content to the first screen, use a welcome mat to hint where to begin.

The first screens of Articles (left) and CardStar (right) are empty on first launch but add quick tips to help you get started.

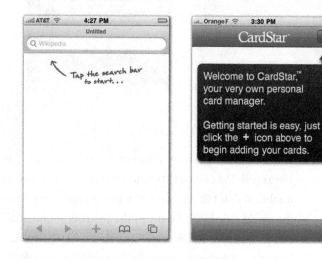

Apps that require an online account also call for a bit of extra politesse at first meeting. When first-timers arrive, don't send them hunting for a settings screen to find where to enter account information. Instead, the first-visit screen should invite people to introduce themselves by signing in or registering a new account. Again, this screen is the very first impression people have of your app; make it attractive, clear, and welcoming. Avoid alert boxes (page 276) or blandly dowdy layouts when inviting people to create an account for the first time.

Note-taking app Evernote (left) offers an attractive welcome screen to invite first-timers to sign in or register. Bills on Your Table (right) nearly does the right thing but takes you to a settings screen with an alert box to explain what's going on. A purpose-built welcome screen would do the job better.

Instructions Can't Make You Super

While the rest of America was glued to *Dallas,* my favorite TV series of the 1980s was *The Greatest American Hero.* In the show, aliens visit awkward school teacher Ralph Hinkley and give him a superhero suit with special powers to save the world. The hitch: he drops the instruction manual. A clumsy crime-fighting career ensues as Ralph tries to work out how to make his superpowers go, tumbling through the sky when he flies and accidentally triggering some new power in each episode. It was deliciously frustrating to watch; you just knew the suit could do *anything,* if only Ralph could figure the thing out. It was the dawn of the personal computer era—the IBM PC debuted during the show's first season—and the show was a prescient parable for the tension between the fabulous possibilities of technology and our frustrating inability to make it work.

If only Ralph hadn't lost the instructions, right? Here's the thing: good instructions aren't always (or even usually) the answer. No offense to the aliens, but Ralph's super suit had some glaring usability problems, with warning signs you should watch for in your own app design. Tapworthy apps give you a super power, too, helping to make you awesome in some way large or small. When an app is easy to use, it melts naturally and effortlessly into your routine, no extra thought required—instant superhero. Everyone's first outing with your app should be smooth and easy (Ralph's first flight crashes him into a wall). Your app's primary tasks should be easy and obvious to complete with only minor exploration and perhaps the help of some welcome-mat hints for first-timers. In the use-it-quick world of mobile apps, the essentials have to be blindingly simple.

If you find yourself pondering the addition of help screens to explain how to do the basics, you should first revisit your design to figure out how to focus your feature set, reduce visual clutter, highlight primary tasks, and make interface labels more clear. Something's wrong when people constantly stumble when they attempt your app's main tasks and features. At that level, bolting on screens of detailed instructions won't help. To the dismay of technical writers everywhere, most people don't read software instructions, and they don't seek them out. That's doubly true for mobile apps, where people expect fast, frictionless experiences that require little thought and certainly no extra reading.

This doesn't mean you should never offer dedicated help screens, only that they shouldn't be *required* in order to get started. For deeper apps and nuanced use cases, extra explanation may be required for advanced features. Tips and pointers can help novice users become experts, and it's fine to add help screens to an app's settings area or offer links to a mobile website where people can find tutorials for becoming power users. A drawback to that approach, however, is that it segregates the instructions into a dusty back corner of your app, and people have to be motivated to find them. Don't expect casual users or beginners to stumble across them.

A more convenient approach integrates help into a well-traveled area of the interface. Evernote, for example, offers a Tips tab on its New Note screen as a way to offer suggestions for creative uses of the note-taking app. That treatment is ideal for providing hey-that's-neat pointers for people to graze on from time to time. But it's not well-suited to more basic help that you're more likely to need just once; don't clutter primary screens with elements that people rarely use, if ever.

Evernote's New Note screen (left) includes a Tips tab at bottom right. Tapping it summons a sheet detailing an unusual use for the app or an advanced feature (right).

Sometimes there's no getting around it: Some apps require more explanation than a simple introductory note can offer. Apps introducing an unfamiliar concept benefit from taking the audience by the hand to lead them through; an extended version of the welcome-mat technique is an effective approach. Backwords is a fun iPhone parlor game that's tough to explain but simple to play after you run through it just once. Here's the gist: one player records a secret phrase on the microphone out of earshot of the second player. When the second player returns, the app plays the word backward, a distorted and unidentifiable sound. The second player then has to mimic that jumbled sound, growling and chirping into the microphone. (This is generally hilarious.) Finally, Backwords plays that attempt backward and, if the second player did a good job, it sounds somewhat like the first player's original phrase. Score a point if you can guess the original phrase.

Whew. The Backwords gameplay is a case where showing is better than telling. "We had these Backwords parties every weekend during development, and nobody ever wanted to read the instructions during a party or when it was their turn to play," says developer Shadi Muklashy. "They just looked around the room: 'All right, what do I do?'" To help, he added an optional overlay that gave instructions at each step. A big, casual handwritten font keeps the vibe friendly, with the effect of a game show emcee taking you through every stage of the game. Once you've got the hang of the game, a setting lets you turn the instructions off.

Backwords includes play-as-you-go instructions on the interface itself. When a player is trying to guess the backward word (left), handwritten instructions show where to tap and why (middle and right).

The First Screen

Clean layout and clear language are important on every screen of your app, but it's especially true of the first screen. Whether they're first-timers or not, people rely on your app's top-level view to get their bearings, get summarized info, or remind themselves of the app's offerings. The specifics of how you design this screen depend on your chosen navigation model (page 100) and interface metaphor (page 196), but these general principles will hold you in good stead:

- **Avoid engineerspeak.** Good copywriting makes everything better. Focus on audience needs instead of developer concerns. Avoid obtuse technical jargon, and aim for accessible prose written in lingo that's familiar to your audience.

- **Think dashboard.** For apps that collect or tabulate data, consider a first screen that offers a summary snapshot of the app's tallies and systems. This is especially useful for financial apps, fitness logs, calorie trackers, and other catalogs of varied personal data. Apps like these juggle lots of discrete entries and a dashboard screen reveals the forest instead of the trees: how much money is in your account, how many calorie you've burned, and so on.

finarXFax is a capable app for sending faxes from your iPhone, but it's marred by engineerspeak. Soften the edges with more accessible phrases like "Fax history" instead of Outputconsole, or "Web Disk" or "Online Account" instead of WebDAV.

Financial apps MoneyBook (left) and Mint.com Personal Finance (right) offer quick-look financial dashboards on their first screens.

- **Embrace the glance test.** Remember the glance-test measure of success for no-scroll utility apps (page 77)? A similar principle applies to the first screen of most apps. The screen should be organized so that people immediately understand the app's offerings. Savvy use of icons can help bring order to table-view lists, while a highly graphical interface metaphor can offer similar instant recognition, particularly for apps with dense offerings. The Facebook app, for example, borrows from the iPhone OS itself, styling itself after the iPhone's Home-screen layout—the *springboard*—to show a grid of icons listing the app's features and content categories. The layout is at once highly

Facebook 3.0 (left) introduced springboard-style navigation for the app's top-level screen. A similar icon-happy approach was later adopted by other apps, including Yelp (middle) and LinkedIn (right).

visual and easy to scan but also underscores that the app itself offers a collection of app-like features. Ready for more Facebook? Flip the page for the inside track on the app's design and development.

Touchpoints

✓ Make your app icon a literal description of your app's function, interface, name, or brand.

✓ Embrace a strong primary silhouette in your icon design.

✓ The best name is a short name.

✓ Disguise the launch image as the app background for a faster perceived launch.

✓ Cultivate the illusion of suspended animation.

✓ Provide simple welcome-mat pointers for first-timers.

✓ The app's first screen should be especially clear. Favor a dashboard view where appropriate.

First Person: Joe Hewitt and Facebook

The world's most popular social network is also the world's most popular iPhone app: Facebook was the most downloaded app in the App Store's first year. The app's vast user base and the sprawling features of the original website created a challenge for Facebook developer **Joe Hewitt,** the one-man show behind the first three generations of Facebook for iPhone. While most iPhone apps focus appropriately on a small feature set, Facebook's users demanded broad access to the service's entire range of features. Although the first version of the app launched with a limited feature set, Facebook 2.0 and 3.0 evolved quickly to embrace nearly all the features available on the full Facebook website. Joe shared the challenges and solutions for squeezing a big feature set into the small screen.

More Than a Lite Version

Joe Hewitt: After I had my iPhone for about six months, I started to feel like I shouldn't need a PC anymore. I should be able to do just about anything on an iPhone that I can do on the desktop. There's so much stuff that is actually better on the small screen because it requires designers to focus on what's really important. I've changed my original opinion that this is a companion device to now thinking that this is the device people should use to start new projects or new companies: develop for this touchscreen experience first and the desktop web second. I think that's where we're headed. So many things work better on a hand-held touchscreen that's with you all the time. We shouldn't think about iPhone apps as lite versions.

For the first version of the Facebook app, I had time to build only the most important features. That was the beginning of the App Store, and none of us knew what user expectations would be. Turns out they were extremely high. I assumed people would be satisfied with a companion app to the website with a limited feature set, and I was really wrong about that. For Facebook, people expected every feature that they had on their desktops. And now I tend to agree with them.

A Collection of "Sub-Apps"

Joe: I definitely agree with the general philosophy that iPhone apps should do one thing well, but it doesn't apply to Facebook overall—people demanded that the app have all the features of the website. To reconcile the need for simplicity with this demand for every feature, I broke the app into sub-apps, and then pared each of those down to make them as focused as they could be. That's what inspired the Home-screen grid in Facebook 3.0.

Three drafts of the top-level screen for Facebook 3.0, inspired by the springboard grid of the iPhone Home screen. The left mockup introduced the concept and overall layout, evolving into the final design at right.

Facebook is really a platform in itself, and I realized that a lot of the core apps that are built into the iPhone are also built into Facebook itself: photos, address book, notes, and so on. The more I thought about it, the more it felt like Facebook was this parallel version of the iPhone itself, and I thought people might understand it that way if I used the same Home-screen approach. At the time, I felt it was a little risky, and I wasn't sure that people would like it, but I was pleasantly surprised by how well people took to it. It's something they're used to from the iPhone Home screen, so there was nothing new to learn there.

Laying out a grid of nine buttons wasn't a big deal, of course, but adding Home-screen editing was a bit of work. Just like the iPhone Home screen, the Facebook app lets you customize and reorder icons: tap and hold an icon, the icons start jiggling, and you can move them around. Apple broke that ground on the Home-screen springboard, so I felt comfortable doing it in the app. As I was working on it, though, I wondered what Apple's designers were thinking about what percentage of users were going to figure out Home screen editing. I'm guessing there are a lot of people with iPhones that haven't figured out that they can do that by holding down an icon.

Physics According to Apple

Joe: Facebook is in a category of being so ubiquitous that I don't feel like it needs to have its own crazy, unique style that a lot of other apps could maybe justify. I thought it was better not to go crazy and reinvent the wheel. It was important to make it feel, not so much that Apple *made* it, but that it was following the same style guidelines that Apple established in its built-in apps.

The photo viewer in Facebook was probably the part that took the most effort in that way. Apple's built-in Photos app is just amazing, and I was very disappointed that more of that code wasn't available in the SDK [the iPhone's code toolkit]. I had to build my own, and I still don't feel like I nailed the physics for it. Getting the photo viewer to work with a similar motion as Apple's took a lot of experimentation. For example, when you zoom in as far as you can go, it lets you zoom just a little bit past the limit, and then when you let go, it bounces back. That takes a lot of time and attention, but those details are really important to get right.

With the touchscreen, you can give users the illusion that they're touching a real thing, but if it doesn't move like the real thing, like it jitters or jumps around, it breaks the illusion. You feel like you're using a computer again and not just moving something physical around with your finger.

The touchscreen makes all the difference in how an interface should be designed. On a PC, it's okay for things to be a little digitized because the whole thing is an abstraction anyway: using a mouse is almost like using a robotic arm where you're controlling this prosthetic. There's a distance between you and the interface. But when the robotic arm is gone and you're really touching the screen, things should feel more realistic. You have to design for that.

Easy on the Chrome

Joe: The news-feed screen was a real challenge because there are a lot of different actions the user can take. It's also the first screen that comes up when you launch the app and there's some risk that people won't explore much beyond that screen. So I wanted to make sure that the top actions were accessible without cluttering up the interface. I went through many versions of that screen; it was definitely the biggest challenge.

The news feed's evolution for Facebook 3.0, from left to right. Early versions included extra interface chrome for filtering news feeds. The final design (right) tucked the filters behind a button at the right side of the navigation bar, freeing space to anchor the status and picture controls in a toolbar at the top of the screen.

You can filter the news screen to show updates from different sublists, and I had to figure out a way to squeeze that in there. In the second generation of the app, the filters were much more prominent. I got the sense that filters weren't being used very much, so I decided to tuck them away behind a button in the navigation bar. That let me get rid of the bottom toolbar and fix a toolbar to the top of the screen for updating your status or uploading a photo. I've seen a lot of apps that have too many rows of fixed navigation, and the part of the app that's actually content is uncomfortably small. You shouldn't have more than one row of controls on the top and a row on the bottom. Otherwise, it's too much chrome. There are just way too many apps that I use that drive me nuts with that.

The Trouble with Notifications

Joe: Apple's solution for notifications on the iPhone is just really crappy; I just can't stand those modal alert boxes [page 276]. When you're using an app and a notification pops up—this happens to me all the time when I get text messages—you go to tap something, and whoops, you just accidentally tapped on a little alert that popped up instead. Even worse, these alerts force you to pay attention to them right away. You can't scan them and then go back to what you're doing. If you get more than one message, it just groups them and says you have two, but you can't read them. There's no way to just easily scan messages—they take over what you're doing and demand your attention. But if you want your app to offer push notifications, you have to do it that way.

Within the app itself, though, I could be more subtle. When you get a notification in Facebook, it appears at the bottom of the screen; it just slides up from the bottom. I actually based that on notifications in Palm's webOS. Palm really nailed it: when you get anything important, it shows up in a very thin line at the bottom of the screen with the content. You can tap it to act on it or you can just swipe it to get rid of it. That's what I tried to recreate in the Facebook app. I like those challenges where I have to go the extra distance. That's the fun of it.

8

Swipe! Pinch! Flick!

WORKING WITH GESTURES

COMPUTING HAS ALWAYS BEEN an arm's length activity. For decades, we've used software from a distance, mediated by screen and mouse and keyboard—work by remote control. The touchscreen collapses this awkward model, closing the distance to make computing at once more immediate and personal. Just touch the content you want to work with: it's a direct and decidedly more humane approach to working with personal gadgets. Because touch interfaces lean on interactions we know from nudging and poking real-world objects, they lend themselves to more naturally intuitive experiences.

The affection of adoring iPhone owners aside, however, it's not all cooing and caresses. Even as this new generation of oh-so-personal computers clears away some dusty conventions of computing, new opportunities create their own dilemmas. Not only can you drag, flick, and pinch the iPhone's virtual objects, but the touchscreen enables a broad range of *gestures*—the onscreen shorthand of taps and swipes that make your iPhone do your bidding. Some of those gestures are immediately evident (tap a button to "push" it), and others are quickly discovered (swipe a screen to move to the next, or pinch to zoom in and out). But other gestures, especially those that don't borrow from familiar physical interactions, aren't as easy to guess, and some multifinger gestures are just plain awkward. A tapworthy interface provides savvy, gesture-based shortcuts

Photo: Chaval Brasil

but also strives to make those gestures easy to discover and use. It's a balance that can be more complex than it sounds.

This chapter explores how tapworthy design provides cues and feedback to reinforce gestures. You'll learn the gestures you can expect your audience to figure out right away and what you can do to help them discover new gestures on their own. You'll even find out how you can make life easier by making certain gestures harder, protecting against accidental mistaps in the bargain.

Finding What You Can't See

Some things are just hard to spot without help. How does Wonder Woman remember where she parked her invisible plane? How do you find the edge on a roll of scotch tape? So it goes with touchscreen gestures. Little more than a flick of the wrist and a smudge on the screen, a gesture is unlabeled and invisible. People rely on visual clues or past experience to figure out when and how gestures might apply.

The most obvious gestures are those that directly manipulate onscreen objects: tapping buttons, dragging objects, or sliding a list up or down. As you learned on page 191, tapworthy design invites touch with clear tap targets that encourage exploration. Obvious visual controls make for obvious gestures. That's the guiding principle for desktop software, too, where buttons, handles, scroll bars, and changing cursor shapes guide both eye and mouse to tell us what to do and what to expect. Unlike desktop interfaces, however, touchscreens create the expectation that you can work not only on individual buttons but also on the screen's canvas itself. Navigating iPhone screens and lists reinforces this expectation through similarity to real-world gestures: flipping through the screens of the Weather app feels like dealing cards one-handed and flicking a picker wheel is just like spinning the numbers of a combination lock.

Gestures become less obvious when they're not specifically focused on selecting or moving a discrete interface element. The less a gesture resembles something you'd do to a physical object, the less likely it is for people to figure it out on their own. The pinch gesture for zooming in and out, for example, is not immediately obvious, but it instantly makes sense once you see it. It's still a gesture that's focused on direct manipulation of the onscreen image—it feels like stretching and squeezing—and it's unforgettable going forward. More abstract gestures, however, tend to go overlooked. Even experienced iPhone users often don't realize they can zoom out in the Maps app by tapping once with two fingers; it's not a gesture that would have any obvious effect on a physical object and so most people never think to try it. They're unlikely to discover it unless they're specifically told about it. (In general, tapping with two fingers is something users rarely try since it feels imprecise to paw the screen with two digits.)

By contrast, most newcomers *do* discover that tapping twice with one finger zooms in on the map. While that gesture doesn't have a real-world equivalent either, our double-click training from desktop computers kicks in. Double-clicking in Google Maps on the full desktop website zooms in, and it's common sense to think that it would work the same way on the iPhone with a double-tap. The most discoverable gestures work from experience: *if it's something you'd do to a physical object or try with a mouse-driven cursor, it's something people will try on the touchscreen, too.*

Pave the Cowpaths

Past experience conditions people to expect certain gestures even when the app designer hasn't anticipated them. A popular yarn among interface designers (and landscapers!) describes a university campus that was built without footpaths. Instead, the founders just let students walk where they might, wearing dirt paths across the lawn, and the university paved sidewalks only after these "cowpaths" emerged. The idea of paving cowpaths is appealingly simple: design according to the patterns people already follow. When you substitute touchscreen fingers for the meandering undergrads in this tale, you get a useful method to discover if your app could put gestures to better use. Watch first-timers use your app and look for two things: unsuccessful gesture attempts and repetitive, time-consuming actions.

- **Unsuccessful gesture attempts.** Experience with other apps creates expectations for how new apps should work. People anticipate that gestures will work in a certain way and become frustrated when they don't deliver. New users of

The only way to switch months in Calendar is to tap the arrow buttons at the top of the screen, but that doesn't stop new users from routinely trying to swipe to a new month. The big calendar spread looks like something you could grab and move, while the small arrow buttons are understated and out of the way.

the built-in Calendar app, for example, routinely try to swipe to change months or days. Alas, the only way to do that is by tapping the arrow buttons at the top of the screen. The arrow controls are clearly labeled and designed to invite touch, but the swipe is even more irresistible. Even these iPhone newcomers already expect that they can swipe to flip through adjacent views. Paving the cowpaths suggests adding a swipe gesture to navigate the calendar.

- **Repetitive, time-consuming actions.** When people constantly repeat the same multitap sequence over and over again, the situation demands a new cowpath—a shortcut to speed through the tedium. The standard left-to-right swipe across a list item, for example, is a shortcut for deleting. Instead of tapping the Edit button, then the list item's delete icon, and then its Delete button, the gesture saves time by simply letting you swipe and tap to delete. There's a similar gesture shortcut in Reeder, an elegant app for browsing Google Reader news feeds: instead of opening each article to mark it as read (like you might do with the built-in Mail app), Reeder lets you slide the item to change its status, letting you skip past articles that don't interest you. (This is also an example of piggybacking on a standard gesture, a topic you'll explore in a moment.)

The swipe-to-delete shortcut lets you delete a list item in a two-step process. Swipe left to right across the item to delete, then tap the Delete button.

Reeder uses a shortcut gesture to let you mark an article as read by sliding it to the right. A pointer appears, and sliding it to the empty disc icon marks it as read. You can mark the article unread by repeating the gesture, and the disc icon changes to solid. Or, slide the item left to move the pointer to the star and mark it as a favorite.

Shortcuts and Backup Plans

Creating shortcuts for time-consuming actions is the motivation behind nearly all custom gestures the finger-tapping innovations that app developers create to save effort. Because custom gestures aren't part of your audience's standard repertoire, however, there's a hitch: you can't count on people figuring them out. When you add non-standard gestures to your app, be sure that you also offer the same options through visible controls. Adding a shortcut, in other words, doesn't mean you should eliminate the long way around. Non-obvious gestures require a sturdy backup plan.

For example, the Twitter app lets you swipe left to right across the navigation bar to go directly to the top level of your Twitter stream—convenient if you've drilled several levels down in the app. Facebook similarly lets you jump back to the app's Home screen by tapping the center of the navigation bar. Neither are standard gestures that you're likely to discover on your own, but you can always go the long way: tap the navigation bar's Back button several times until you arrive at the top level. Similarly, tapping the status bar in most apps takes you immediately to the top of the current screen. You probably won't find it on your own, but that's okay: you can always flick and scroll your way to the top of the screen the old-school way.

Even some common gestures aren't widely known and, in those cases, should be reserved for advanced features or, again, shortcuts for more time-consuming actions. The tap-and-hold gesture is a favorite of power users, for example. It's the right click of the iPhone world and typically triggers extra options for that element. In Safari, tap and hold a link or image to get an action sheet of options. On the keyboard, tap and hold a key to get extra character options; holding down the ".com" button, for example, gives you options for .org, .edu, .net, and other domain extensions. Non-expert iPhone users don't typically know the tap-and-hold gesture, however, and those who do, often discover its uses only through trial and error. Wherever possible, make sure any options you offer here can also be managed in some other way.

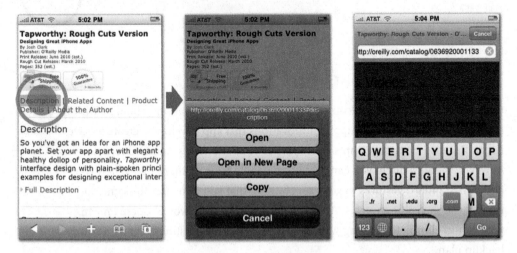

Tapping and holding a link in Safari (left) summons an action sheet of options for the link (middle). Tapping and holding the ".com" key on the keyboard (right) lets you choose additional domain extensions.

When you trap a feature exclusively behind a non-obvious gesture with no long-way-around alternatives, you create invisible features that can only be discovered through instructions and FAQ pages. In the PCalc calculator app, for example, you can flip through your calculation history—the equivalent of undo and redo—by swiping the app's LED display area. It turns out to be a natural, elegant way to handle the feature, but you have to know about it first, and there's no visible button or control to do it otherwise; you have to read the app's help screen to learn the gesture. An alternate design would include an undo button; when tapped, this button would animate the LED screen to flip to the last calculation, a hint that you can nudge the screen yourself. (See the similar animation hints used in the USA Today app on page 93.) Of course, the tradeoff is yet another button in a crowded interface. As always, it's a matter of knowing your audience and understanding which features are most important and should be most accessible. When in doubt, though, always offer a visual alternative to a gesture-based action.

Swiping across PCalc's LED display lets you move through your calculation history, the equivalent of undo and redo. It's a useful gesture but difficult to discover, and there's no other way to do the same action with visible controls. (The app also offers an optional setting to undo/redo by shaking the device; for more on shaking, see page 252.)

Piggybacking Standard Gestures

The best way to help people discover custom gestures is to hide them in plain sight by replacing or extending a related standard gesture. The Twitter app does this in such a natural way for loading new tweets that its custom gesture completely replaces a traditional button, banishing unnecessary interface chrome. Some background: the first version of the app (then called Tweetie), tucked its reload button at the top of the list of tweets, instead of in the app's toolbars. It was a natural location, since new tweets always appear at the top of the list. "As you scrolled up, reading newer tweets, eventually you'd get to the top of the list and, bam, there's a reload button—it just slid into view exactly when you needed it," developer Loren Brichter explained in an interview with designer Joshua Kaufman. The next version of the app built on this approach by replacing the button entirely. When you scroll all the way to the top of the screen, you instead see a message that tells you to tug the screen down to load new tweets (see page 250). Scrolling itself becomes the gesture to fetch new messages. "It's discoverable because you already know how to scroll a list, and as you scroll up, [the interface] reveals itself," Loren said. "It's explanatory because once you start tugging down there is some great feedback, actual text that provides instructions as you interact."

In Twitter, scrolling to the top of the screen reveals a hidden message telling you to pull down to refresh the list (left). When you've pulled it down far enough to trigger the refresh, the message tells you to let go (middle). When you do, the message is replaced by a status message (right) until the new tweets arrive, and then the refresh panel slides back out of view.

This particular innovation is well on its way to becoming a de facto standard, with several apps adopting the gesture. Reeder, for example, uses the technique to move through next and previous articles in your news-feed reading list. This technique works so well because it piggybacks on the standard scroll action. You find the feature by using the app as you normally would, stumbling onto some brief onscreen instructions that complete the education.

On page 247, you saw a different piggyback approach with Reeder's sliding gesture to mark articles as read. The app trades on the familiar swipe-to-delete gesture,

When you're on the detail screen for an article in Reeder (left), you can tug the screen down to see the title of the previous article (middle); releasing takes you there. Similarly, tugging the screen up (right) takes you to the next article.

replacing it with Reeder's own action that's not *quite* deleting but close enough that most folks can guess and remember the gesture. In news-feed readers like this one, there's no such thing as delete. Articles are either read or unread, and read articles eventually get removed from view. Marking an article as read removes it from your to-read list—in other words, an action that's not all that different from deleting. Metaphorically, both actions "cross out" an item—the inspiration behind the swipe-to-delete gesture. Because of the similarity, the alternate use of a standard gesture is okay here.

Just don't let your piggybacking turn into outright hijacking. It's bad form to use a standard gesture for a purpose entirely different than what's generally understood. The Twitter app commits this particular sin by hijacking the swipe-to-delete gesture. Swiping left to right across a tweet reveals a set of icon buttons, a kind of in-place toolbar for actions that you can take on the tweet: send a reply, view the author's profile, and so on. It's at once a clever way to tuck advanced controls behind a hidden panel, but it's also a violation of user expectations for a familiar gesture. Because you can't delete most messages on display (only your own), the delete gesture doesn't have much meaning in a Twitter app. That means that people either don't discover it on their own or are at least initially surprised to find that it has nothing to do with deletion. Continued use of the app smoothes these bumps as people get accustomed to the alternate use, but it creates headaches for new arrivals. Avoid replacing standard gestures in ways that upturn expectations.

Swiping left to right across a tweet in the Twitter app reveals a custom toolbar instead of the standard Delete button.

Here's an exception: it's okay, even desirable, to let individual users choose their preferences for what happens with certain gestures. Not many apps do this, but for relatively complex apps, it's an effective way to give users custom shortcuts to actions they frequently use. (The iPhone itself did this in its own way prior to iPhone OS 4.0; you could customize which screen appeared when you double-clicked the device's Home button: Home screen, search, phone favorites, camera, or iPod.) Twitterrific is one app that offers custom gestures, letting you choose what happens when you tap an avatar icon or when you double- or triple-tap a tweet.

Twitterrific's settings let you customize the action for three gestures: Tapping an avatar, double-tapping a tweet, or triple-tapping (left). For each gesture, you can choose a range of possible actions (right).

Shake, Shake, Shake

When the iPhone first debuted, its built-in motion detector (the *accelerometer*) was a delightful novelty, and it inspired a corresponding number of first-generation novelty apps. Your iPhone could be a light saber, a glass of beer, or a shotgun. Give it a tilt, a shake, a wiggle, and your iPhone responded with animations, sound effects, you name it. The shiny new hardware feature proved irresistible to developers of more staid apps, too, who experimented with using hand waving gestures to trigger some actions—moving the iPhone itself as an alternative to touching the screen. In particular, the *shake* gesture showed up everywhere and for all kinds of uses: Urbanspoon used shake to choose a random restaurant; Facebook used shake to load new content; PCalc used shake to clear the current calculation; and Etch-a-Sketch used shake to erase a drawing.

Even at the time, here's what all of those developers knew: shake is a gimmick, a cute novelty more than a useful gesture. While shake works well for casual entertainment apps—it's great for games and music apps—or to support an interface metaphor like triggering Urbanspoon's slot machine, it's a disruptive and awkward motion for other uses. Shaking draws attention unnecessarily to the hardware and away from the task at hand. When you're tapping away and focused on the screen, shaking the entire device pulls you out of your flow and, afterward, forces you to find your place again onscreen. It's not exactly the most discreet gesture, either: it's tough to keep a low profile in a public place or a board meeting when you're waving your phone vigorously to get something done. While shake is awkward to perform on demand, it's also all too easy to trigger by accident. A quick jog, a speed bump, or an over-caffeinated morning can all yield unintended shake gestures. That means that it's an especially bad idea to use shake for a destructive action like deleting content or clearing a screen.

Exactly when you *should* use shake is a point of confusion. Its inconsistent use across apps means that users don't have a stable expectation of what shake might do from app to app (randomize? delete? reload? undo?). Starting in iPhone OS 3.0, the built-in apps started using shake to conjure the undo/redo dialog box, suggesting a standard use for the gesture, yet many apps continue to use it for lots of other actions. Even as Apple's apps settle on shake to undo, it remains clumsy to pause in the middle of typing to shake your device—and it doesn't scale well at all to larger screens like the iPad, where shaking takes a real windup. Still, this emerging standard for using shake to undo will likely become a first expectation for the gesture. For productivity apps, in particular: if you use shake at all, it's best not to fight this standard; reserve shaking to trigger the undo/redo dialog box.

Apps that continue to use shake for other features should at least consider adding a button or other onscreen action to provide an alternative to the awkward shake gesture. Urbanspoon offers a button to spin its restaurant slot machine, for example, and Facebook, likewise, added buttons to supplement its originally shake-only feature for fetching fresh content. "You still can shake in Facebook—it's still an option—but I personally never use it anymore," says Facebook developer Joe Hewitt, who developed the first three versions of the app. "I might even be inclined to take shaking out of the app at this point."

Displaying the undo/redo dialog box (left) is the emerging standard for the shake gesture. Apps that use shake for another purpose should include an onscreen control as an alternative to shaking; Urbanspoon (right) offers a Shake button to spin its wheels.

Two's a Crowd

Shake isn't the only awkward gesture. In general, multifinger gestures are trickier than their single-digit counterparts, and people have a corresponding reluctance to embrace them. Even the beloved pinch-to-zoom gesture makes for an unwieldy gesture, essentially impossible when holding the device in just one hand. For some with disabilities (or others juggling a latte), two-finger gestures are a challenge.

That doesn't mean you should avoid two-finger gestures entirely. With its ability to track several fingers at once, the iPhone's multitouch screen enables a range of innovative gestures. (The iPhone can support up to five simultaneous touches—for five-finger gestures—but the small screen crowds this full-fisted approach.) Don't be afraid to experiment, but consider offering single-digit alternatives to your finger-splaying custom gestures, particularly for common actions. The built-in Safari and Photos apps, for example, both let you double-tap to zoom in and out as an alternative to using the two-finger pinch gesture. Never underestimate the value of one-handed phone use both for convenience and accessibility.

Awkwardness for Self Defense

Awkward isn't always bad. The ease and sensitivity of touchscreen interfaces can also work against you. When it's *too* easy to trigger an action, mishaps ensue. Unlocked phones fire off surprise calls from handbags and back pockets. We carelessly delete important data by tapping the wrong item. Call it touchscreen self defense: by requiring awkward or challenging gestures at well-placed points of your interface, you can protect against miserable mistaps.

Apple gives you an example of this technique in the very first screen it shows to new iPhone owners. The "slide to unlock" control greets you when you fire up your new toy for the first time. That sliding action requires just enough concentration and precision to make it unlikely to unlock the phone accidentally from a backpack or purse. Ditto for the "slide to power off" and "slide to answer" controls you get when turning off the phone or receiving a call. All of these slider controls demand extra attention, defending against accidental tapping and helping to ensure it's actually a person doing the work, not the phone rattling around in your bag.

The swipe-to-delete gesture uses the same sliding action to offer protection against accidentally deleting items in a table view. By requiring a swipe followed by a tap on an item's Delete button, the operation demands just enough focus to offer protection without being annoyingly onerous. As you've seen, that gesture is a shortcut for a longer triple-tap combination (Edit button, delete icon, then Delete button). Requiring a careful series of taps is also an effective defense, but like a lock-laden door, it can also be a frustrating hassle when you actually want to open the door. Use these multi-tap combination locks sparingly and only for relatively rare actions—or provide a shortcut like Apple did with the swipe-to-delete gesture.

Requiring extra taps or clicks is a time-honored tradition in software interfaces that aim to protect against deleter's remorse. Since the get-go, computers have asked for confirmation when we try to throw things out. "Are you really sure you want to do that?" Apple recommends that you do that, too, by using an action sheet to throw up a confirmation screen (page 170). This nagging approach is rarely effective, however, and is typically annoying more than helpful. Over time, people also develop an immunity to confirmation screens, tapping through them without giving them much thought. They're too easy to dismiss, too annoying to heed. (Even Apple offers the option in the built-in Mail app to turn off the confirmation message when deleting messages.) Still, the underlying idea of confirmation screens is sound: good interfaces make you work just a little bit harder to do something you might otherwise regret later. Using an awkward gesture or a multi-tap combination can do the job just as well as a confirmation screen but without the annoyance.

The ultimate backstop for preventing mistakes is simply to let people take it back: the undo command. As you've seen, there's an emerging standard for triggering undo by shaking, but many iPhone users remain unaware of that option, and the shake gesture has lots of drawbacks of its own. A novel alternative is to offer an undo button temporarily to let people change their mind in the few seconds after they do something. Google popularized this approach on the web with its Gmail service by letting you undo a sent email message. You can't *really* call back an email once it's sent, so Gmail instead hangs onto the message for five seconds, giving you a few beats to scramble for the panic button when you realize you've sent that love letter to the wrong girl.

Instapaper uses a similar limited-time undo button. The app lets you store long articles from the web for later reading and saves your place in an article when you pause midway through. "I got frequent emails from customers who were

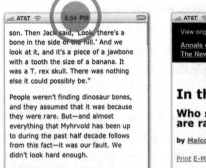

In Instapaper, as in most apps, tapping the status bar (left) takes you to the top of the screen (right). For five seconds afterward, Instapaper replaces its screen-bottom toolbar to offer an option to return to the previous position in the article.

upset that they had inadvertently tapped the status bar, which scrolls to the top of the article and loses their position," says Instapaper developer Marco Arment. "I understood completely, since losing your read position is a form of minor data loss." To address the issue, Instapaper changes its toolbar for five seconds after the scroll, offering a "Restore to position" button to take it back. It's a good example of after-the-fact defensive design.

Phone Physics

With apologies to Isaac Newton, let's call this The First Law of Gesture: for every swipe and tap, there is an equal and opposite reaction. Gestures should be greeted by immediate feedback that not only confirms your input but also sustains the illusion that you're manipulating honest-to-god objects suspended below the iPhone's glass face. The best iPhone apps, including the overall iPhone OS, recreate an environment of real-world physics, complete with momentum, elasticity, friction, and follow through. Things bounce and stretch and spin and squish in response to your touch. The more realistic the response, the more complete the sensation of controlling a tangible interface.

Happily, iPhone developers rarely have to fret over the complex details of Apple's phone physics; the operating system gives it to you for free with the code that manages list scrolling, animations, and the screen's rubber-band elasticity. The same goes for toolbar buttons, which highlight in response to your touch, and other standard controls, which slide and spin without any special coding effort. When you create your own custom controls and gestures, however, you need to bring the same attention to detail to those new creations. A visual response should accompany every touch, reassuring people that their gesture had the intended effect.

Savvy, restrained use of animations is especially useful for linking touch to changes in the app. In the Things to-do list app, for example, tapping the toolbar's star icon switches from checklist mode to a view that lets you mark items you want to tackle today. To underscore the change, the arrow-shaped disclosure buttons on the right side slide offscreen, and the checkboxes dissolve into star-shaped controls. The app could have just made those visual changes instantly with no animation,

In Things, tapping the toolbar's star icon triggers a subtle animation. The disclosure arrows (left) slide off the screen, and the checkboxes dissolve into stars (right) to transform the function of the screen.

but the fluid motion draws attention to the change and gives the impression of a kind of mechanical shift that lends extra weight to the tap.

The Twitter app adds similar grace-note animations throughout. When you swipe left to right across a tweet, for example, you hurl the message offscreen, and the icon buttons that appear underneath bulge briefly, as if affected by the motion like leaves behind a passing car. Again, this animation lends a mechanical effect to the gesture and adds a sense of visual solidity to the interface and your interaction with it.

Twitter further underscores the animation's mechanical illusion with a heavy *tock* sound. Sound is a powerful form of gestural feedback, too, another reassuring confirmation that the app has registered a touch or completed an action. Many find that the click-click-click of the iPhone's keyboard affords a reassuring sense of solidity for its virtual keys, offering the no-look confidence of a button being pushed in the real world. With sound, as with most aspects of interface design, a light touch goes a long way. You're not building a pinball machine; no need to make it bleep and click at every touch. Choose your sound effects carefully and apply them judiciously to your app's most significant gestures and events. As you choose the events for sound, your effects should have a symmetry: if you add a sound effect to open an onscreen panel, for example, be sure you add a corresponding sound to close it. Just remember that a sound effect shouldn't be the only feedback to a gesture or action; anticipate moments when the sound might be off or when the app is used by the hearing disabled. Consider offering options in your app's settings to disable sound effects, too. Some people (and cultures) prefer to be more discreet in public settings—or simply don't share the same taste for audio clatter.

Every touch should have visual feedback, too. But what if you can't see the thing you're touching? When fat fingers obscure the tap target, consider outsized feedback that ripples into the screen around the touch. The standard keyboard is a classic example, popping up a magnified version of the pressed key with every tap. Providing tap feedback near or around the target area is a useful technique in other contexts, too. Brushes, a painting app, lets you switch colors by tapping another color on your screen; to help you see what color you're touching, the app draws a circle in that color around your finger. The Saturday Night Fever Dance game similarly rings your finger in a circle to help you trace lines accurately while you do the hustle. Reliable onscreen feedback gives users confidence—just as surely as a crisp white leisure suit on the dance floor.

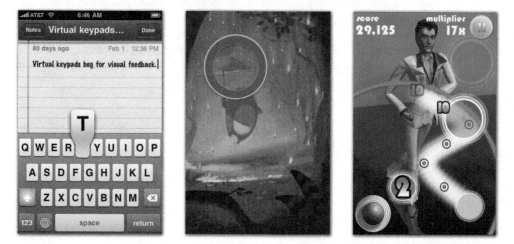

From left to right, the keyboard, Brushes, and Saturday Night Fever Dance apps all provide outsized visual feedback to help track your finger location. The keyboard springs up the letter you press, while Brushes and Saturday Night Fever Dance ring your fingertip to help you pinpoint its location.

Touchpoints

✓ Experience informs gestures. People will try anything on a touchscreen that they'd try on a physical object or with a mouse-driven cursor.

✓ Pave the cowpaths: include gestures by observing how people use your app, including unsuccessful gesture attempts and repetitive, time-consuming actions.

✓ Have a backup plan for people who don't discover your app's gestures. All actions should be possible through visible controls in addition to gestures.

✓ Help users discover custom gestures by piggybacking on standard gestures.

✓ Avoid the shake gesture except to trigger the undo/redo dialog box, or for certain novelty uses.

✓ Provide single-finger alternatives to multi-touch gestures.

✓ Use slightly challenging gestures or tap combinations to protect against accidental mistaps.

✓ Provide visual feedback for every touch and action, supplementing with restrained use of sound effects.

9

Know the Landscape

THE SPIN ON SCREEN ROTATION

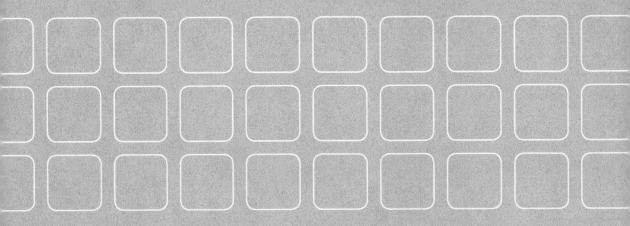

WHICH WAY IS UP? As far as the iPhone's concerned, it's all relative. Spin the device any which way, and it keeps up with you, rotating your app's interface so that it's always upright—provided, that is, that you support rotation in your app. But should you?

You're not *obliged* to offer screen rotation. As you'll see, squeezing your app into a new orientation involves more subtle design considerations than you might at first anticipate. It takes lots of work and careful thinking to show your wares to best effect in both *portrait* (vertical) and *landscape* (horizontal) views. Doing a half-hearted job on screen rotation is worse than not doing it at all. The best advice: make your app the best it can be in one orientation—usually portrait—and once you've nailed that, consider whether you might support the other orientation, too.

What's the big deal—it's just a change in screen dimensions, right? That in itself isn't new territory for software designers. Managing variable window sizes in desktop software or wildly different screen resolutions for the Web are familiar challenges. Some of the same considerations apply here, too—how to reflow the layout to fit the new orientation—but a change in rotation also signals a change in the user's mindset. People flip their iPhones with a purpose, and that motivation can suggest significant interface changes between portrait and landscape views. This chapter explores the opportunities of screen rotation and describes how to cope with the

Photo: Mykl Roventine

pixel-precise practicalities without getting the spins. Pop a Dramamine and let's give your interface a whirl.

Why Do People Flip?

Everything starts with portrait orientation. That's what's most comfortable in the hand, and that's how we're used to holding a phone, but most important the iPhone Home screen itself is always in portrait—no landscape option. When you launch an app, that means you always start off holding the phone upright. So what prompts people to flip? What's so special about landscape? Understanding why people turn the screen informs whether it's a feature that would add value to your app.

First, the obvious: some media is simply formatted for landscape, period. Games are commonly landscape-only apps that launch immediately into landscape orientation. Video-heavy apps could logically do the same, too. If your app relies on media or graphics that are strongly tied to one orientation or the other, embrace that format; no need to wedge it into an orientation that doesn't fit. (By the way, people figure out landscape-only apps on their own. If your app has only a single orientation, don't add an alert or extra chrome to remind people to turn the phone on its side. Just launch directly into landscape orientation; the interface itself makes it clear that you have to turn the device.)

Aside from the physical format of the media, there's also a consideration of the amount of attention the media demands. Landscape orientation is well-suited to games and video because the horizontal layout naturally provides a more immersive experience. In part that's because landscape better fills your vision, but more important, it practically requires a two-handed grip. With both of your user's hands occupied, you can be reasonably sure that you've got their full attention. For immersive apps, landscape's two-handedness subtly pulls people into the screen.

For other content, people flip to landscape largely for two reasons: easier reading and easier typing. In user testing and interviews, people say they expect larger text when they flip to landscape. Specifically, they expect that the app will maintain the same column content, scaling the text to fill the wider space. In Safari

"Jell-O Girl" in its ads, and the pamphlets grew into Jell-O "best-seller" recipe books. In some years Genesee printed as many as 15 million of the free books, and in the company's first twenty-five years it printed and distributed an estimated quarter billion free cookbooks door-to-door, across the country. Noted artists such as Norman Rockwell, Linn Ball, and Angus MacDonald contributed colored illustrations to the cookbooks. Jell-O had become a fixture in the American kitchen and a household name.

"Jell-O Girl" in its ads, and the pamphlets grew into Jell-O "best-seller" recipe books. In some years Genesee printed as many as 15 million of the free books, and in the company's first twenty-five years it printed and distributed an estimated quarter billion free cookbooks door-to-door, across the country. Noted artists such as Norman Rockwell, Linn Ball, and Angus MacDonald contributed colored illustrations to the cookbooks. Jell-O had become a fixture in the American kitchen and a household name.

Portrait (left) and landscape (right) views in Kindle show the exact same text (and in the same font size), but the typography works better in the wider landscape column, with fewer unsightly gaps between words.

(and any other app that uses a web view to display content) that's exactly how it works, and it's very likely the source of this particular expectation. To most people, landscape means big text.

The trouble with automatically scaling up the content for landscape is that you show less content on the screen—bigger text, but less of it. User expectations aside, it's more useful to think of the landscape orientation as a way to display content *differently,* not just bigger. Text-savvy apps like ebook readers Stanza and Kindle, for example, don't resize text when you flip to landscape. Instead, you see the same words, in the same size, but in a wider column. For some people, a wider column means easier reading, too—the type flows better, and the eye doesn't have to jump down to the next line as often.

For apps that trade in words, there's no doubt that offering an option to adjust the size of type is indeed good practice, but it doesn't necessarily require a landscape view to do it. USA Today, for example, decided not to offer a landscape view of its articles. "We believe that when many users request landscape mode, it's because they have been trained by Mobile Safari to expect that rotating makes the text larger," says Rusty Mitchell, creative director for the USA Today app. "Instead, we decided to add an option to adjust the font size in portrait mode."

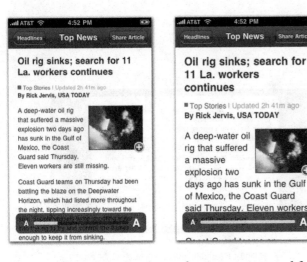

USA Today lets you pinch to change the font size, and a size meter appears onscreen while you make the change. The size can also be changed in the app's settings.

Others flip to landscape for easier typing and find the wider keyboard to be less error prone. Not everyone thinks this way, however, with many users saying that the portrait keyboard's compact layout lets them type faster than landscape does. This one's simply a matter of ergonomic preference. No matter which keyboard someone prefers, though, that preference is almost always strongly held. A landscape typist finds portrait unbearable, and vice versa. For apps that go heavy on writing and messaging, it's good practice to support both landscape and portrait keyboards.

Demographics matter here, too. In my own user interviews, younger people show a greater preference for thumb typing on landscape keyboards. In fact, teens and young adults are typically at ease moving between orientations and are, in general, more comfortable than older people with the landscape view. That's likely, at least in part, because they're more accustomed to using landscape-format gadgets (hello, game consoles). For that matter, they're just as likely to consider the iPhone—and especially the iPod Touch—as a game console, too. Older users meanwhile tend to think of the device more literally as a phone and accordingly hold it upright more often. As always, culture and experience matter here. Know your audience: the landscape option is especially welcomed by the younger set.

A Whole New Landscape

Beyond practical matters of text flow and keyboard size, you can also use landscape orientation to provide a completely different view of your app. Stock and financial apps, for example, commonly display summary info in portrait view but bloom into graphical charts when you turn them on their side. Weightbot takes a similar approach, showing your weight for an individual day in portrait orientation, but revealing a cascade of stats and charts when you switch to landscape. In fact, Weightbot shows different charts depending on which way you turn the device. In all of these examples, the landscape view is used to give enhanced context to the snapshot shown in portrait orientation. This use of landscape orientation gives users a way to *focus the app* and review the content in a more immersive way. As you saw a few pages ago, landscape orientation typically signals increased attention from the user, an opportunity to draw them into the interface. Here, the effect is further enhanced by removing controls and providing a rich visualization to explore.

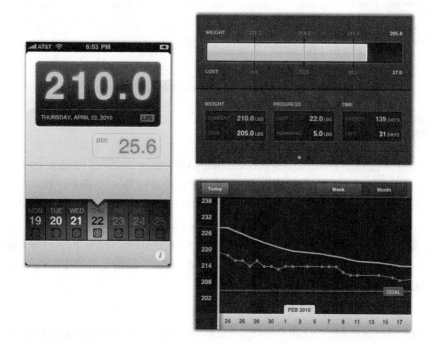

Turn Weightbot on its left side (top) to see stats and a progress bar toward your goal; flip it to its right side (bottom) to see a line graph of your weight over time.

With this approach, you're doing more than just flipping the interface on its side; you're throwing it out and replacing it with a completely new one. In geekspeak, you're *changing modes*, the kind of switcheroo you might see if you select a new tab in your app's tab bar. Landscape modes often sport graphic-laden interfaces, an appropriate choice given the common association with gee-whiz media thanks to landscape's frequent use in games and video. The built-in iPod app and the Stanza ebook reader, for example, both go from staid text-based lists in portrait orientation to a glossy view of album and book covers in landscape view. Similarly, note-taking app Evernote transforms from a text-oriented list view of notes to a denser image-based view in landscape orientation. In all of these examples, it's the same content, but a very different presentation.

Evernote's portrait view (left) offers a thumbnail image with a text description of each note. The landscape view (right) drops the text to offer a dense ribbon of images to browse.

A word of caution about this approach: many will never discover the gorgeous graphical alternative you've tucked around the corner of this 90-degree tilt. If your app works just fine in portrait mode (and of course it does), it won't even occur to some people to try it in landscape— even avid, day-in-day-out users. I met a poker fan who played the Texas Hold 'Em app for *months* before he realized that he could get a bird's eye view of the table—and a much faster game—if he played in landscape.

Like a gesture, screen rotation is invisible. Without visual cues or explicit instructions, these landscape modes can easily remain hidden treasures. That's especially true for Weightbot's approach of showing a different chart depending on which way you turn for the landscape view. It's a novel approach that saves interface chrome, but you can bet lots of people find one chart but never discover the other. Some landscapes simply go unvisited. Plan for that contingency by making sure that any features or info that you show in landscape orientation can also be discovered—albeit in different form—in portrait orientation, too.

Making a Complicated Turn

Depending on the interface you're flipping, the actual code to support screen rotation can actually be quite simple. Under the hood, the operating system essentially lets programmers flip a switch that says, "this screen can rotate." From there, the system handles the rest, animating the screen rotation and reflowing the content to fit the new orientation. For fairly simple layouts like basic lists or a big chunk of text, that may be all that you need to do, case closed. With more complex designs, however, adding a landscape view boils down to creating an entirely new layout and even pruning features.

Consider Twitterrific's screen for composing new messages. It's a carefully composed portrait layout with tabs to switch among different types of tweets, making it easy to choose whether you're tweeting a new update, a reply, or a direct message. Tapping the eyeball-shaped "peek" button slides away the keyboard to show you the tweet you're replying to, handy for checking details. Great, but how do you reformat all that twittery goodness into a landscape view? "It's one of the

Twitterrific's screen for writing new tweets offers more tools than can easily squeeze into a landscape view. Its colored tabs let you choose whether you're posting a new tweet, reply, or direct message. Tapping the eyeball-shaped "peek" button (left) slides away the keyboard to let you refer to your Twitter stream (right).

reasons we haven't done a horizontal layout," says Gedeon Maheux, one of the app's designers. "None of us are willing to sacrifice the ease of those tabs, but if you keep them in a horizontal layout, you'd see only one or two lines of the tweet, and that's no good. You'd also have to lose the peek feature, so it would be a totally different thing—a whole new interface. It's not an easy thing to figure out." Changing orientation in Twitterrific's case, in other words, would mean not only a redesign, but very likely some lost features in that view, too. That kind of trade off isn't unusual, and it's important to consider whether the benefits of a landscape view remain even after some of the bells and whistles fall away.

The question grows more complicated when the features that go missing also affect the user's content. The PCalc scientific calculator app, for example, supports hexadecimal math in some landscape layouts but not some portrait layouts. What to do if someone is merrily doing their fancy hex math and then rotates to a layout that doesn't know about hexadecimal numbers? "What I ended up doing was switching back to regular decimal numbers in the portrait layout, but the app remembers the settings separately for each orientation," says developer James Thomson. "So when the user switched back to landscape again, it would remember and go back to hexidecimal." Supporting different landscape and portrait layouts in this case is almost like supporting two different apps, each with their own parallel settings.

There's often a lot more to it than just tipping your design sideways. Even for relatively simple layouts, there are still a few factors to keep in mind when designing your landscape version.

- **Navigation bars and toolbars get squished.** In landscape orientation, vertical space is at a premium, and the iPhone OS buys you a few extra pixels by squeezing its toolbars. The navigation bar and toolbar both shrink from 44 pixels tall to just 32 pixels (search bars meanwhile hold steady at 44 pixels). Plan ahead to make sure that any custom toolbar icons and buttons fit under these low ceilings. You'll be in good shape if you design buttons according to the specs described back on page 195: toolbar and navigation-bar icons should be 20 × 20 pixels.

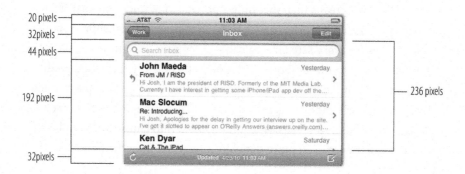

- **Start in portrait.** Your app should always launch itself in portrait orientation. This matches both the iPhone Home-screen orientation and, presumably, your launch image, too. Once your app loads, it should check the device's orientation and rotate to landscape if necessary. (This doesn't apply, of course, to apps that are landscape-only; they should launch directly into landscape.)

- **Mind your animation.** The iPhone handles the fancy rotation effect automatically, and it takes care of you just fine when you're using essentially the same design for both landscape and portrait. For more complex layout changes, though, a little extra help makes the transition go more smoothly. Add a custom animation—a cross-fade, for example—to make one layout dissolve into the other, or use animations to move controls and other interface elements that vary between the two orientations. Don't go too heavy on the razzle dazzle, though. The goal should be to make the mechanical aspect of the rotation itself as inconspicuous as possible, not call attention to it.

- **Go every which way.** Make sure you handle rotation when you go either clockwise and counterclockwise—possibly even upside down, too, if that suits your content and audience. The built-in Voice Memos app, for example, rotates into place when you flip the device on its head, letting you hold the device so that the phone's microphone is more conveniently accessible at the top.

- **All or nothing.** Offering both landscape and portrait orientations is an all-in game. If you add landscape to one screen, add it to all of them. Otherwise, you're asking people to guess through trial and error which screens flip and which don't. Worse, landscape-lovers will have to flip from their preferred orientation for screens that offer only a portrait view and then back again for screens that offer landscape. Go easy on their wrists and support both orientations for every screen. As always, exceptions, exceptions—follow this rule except when you shouldn't. Video and other rigidly formatted media can (and often should) be landscape-only, and it's okay to force people to rotate for that. Similarly, other screens just don't fit landscape orientation in either design or purpose. In those cases, forcing them into landscape complicates the user experience even more than blocking rotation in the first place.

Don't Lose Your Place

Tipping the screen on its side causes a moment of disorientation, and it's your job as a designer to steady that temporary interface vertigo. By choosing a point of gravity for your screen, you can keep the user grounded even as the screen's contents tumble into new locations. It's a good practice to use the screen's top edge as the anchor position. Any text that appears at the top of the portrait screen should likewise appear at the top of the screen's landscape version (instead of anchoring the screen around whatever content is at the center, for example).

Certain screens defy alternate orientations because their precise and persistent layout is itself a usability aid. If Apple let you flip the iPhone Home screen on its side, for example, the icons would scatter into new positions, shifting out of their familiar places and creating a cognitive jumble for you to hunt through. That's the same reason that Facebook's Home-screen grid of icons (page 237) is the app's one portrait-only screen. "I didn't want to change the relative positions of the icons by shifting it from a 3 × 3 grid to 4 × 2 or something like that, but that was the only way it looked good," says developer Joe Hewitt, who created the Facebook app's grid design. "The problem is that your whole layout gets changed. You're used to the buttons being in a certain grid, and in landscape you'd have to go searching for them. It just didn't feel right, so I didn't do it. When you rotate, you always have to make sure everything is lined up in a place where people can easily find it again."

While your app's pixels might be under your control, the person holding it is not. People use their iPhones anywhere and everywhere, and that means all kinds of positions, too. Lying down, leaning over, shifting in your seat—our shimmies in the physical world trigger accidental (and annoying) screen rotations all the time. A comfortable position for bedtime browsing sometimes involves holding the phone in a distinctly awkward way just to keep the orientation steady. Screen rotation is great except when it happens by surprise.

The iPhone's big brother, the iPad, has a physical switch to lock rotation, and beginning with iPhone OS 4.0, there's a software button to do the same on the iPhone. Even with these systemwide switches to keep your baby from rocking, it's not a bad idea for individual apps to add their own rotation lock, too. This is an especially good idea for ebook readers, other long-form reading apps, and any app where someone is likely to spend at least several minutes at a time poring over the screen. Those are the situations that invite reclining, and when you put your feet up and get comfortable that's when the accidental screen tilt inevitably arrives. If your app fits those conditions, consider adding a setting or button that locks your app's orientation in place. The iPhone might not have a fixed idea of "up," but your audience does; give them the ability to point the way.

For a few seconds after the screen rotates, Kindle flashes a lock button (shown here at lower right) to let you freeze the screen's orientation.

Touchpoints

✓ Optimize your app for one orientation before adding landscape support.

✓ Use landscape orientation to display content differently, not just bigger.

✓ Lots of typing in your app? Support both landscape and portrait keyboards.

✓ Use landscape to offer graphical alternatives for organizing content and info.

✓ Not everyone will try tipping your app on its side. Beware of hiding important content and features behind screen rotation.

✓ Some features may not be appropriate (or physically fit) in landscape view. Avoid disorienting your audience when the layout changes.

10

Polite Conversation

ALERTS, INTERRUPTIONS, AND UPDATES

APPS SHOULD BE GOOD LISTENERS. Tapworthy apps pay careful attention to touchscreen instructions and then dutifully deliver the requested info, gameplay, or action. Every so often, though, apps pipe up with commentary of their own: an alert warns something has gone wrong, a push notification announces a news headline, a progress bar says work is underway. There are lots of ways your app can get its message across, and the voice and method you choose has both practical and personal impact. Does your app shout or whisper? Does it interrupt the action or slip a subtle note? Etiquette matters, even to apps, and politesse requires careful thought about both words and manner.

Etiquette maven Emily Post shared her secret for good conversation nearly a century ago, and her lesson turns out to apply as well to apps as it does to people:

"There is a simple rule, by which one can at least refrain from being a pest or a bore. And the rule is merely, to stop and think. Think before you speak. Nearly all the faults or mistakes in conversation are caused by not thinking."

This chapter helps you do that thinking by taking your app to iPhone charm school to review the art of polite conversation. You'll review the iPhone's communication conventions, including the discreet use of alerts, notifications, activity indicators, and progress bars. Most of all, you'll discover how to signal important info to your audience without slowing them down or, worse, getting on their nerves.

Photo: StreetFly

When To Interrupt

An *alert* is an app's emergency brake. It's the blue box that pops up in the middle of the screen, stops the action, and makes an announcement. Like a modal view (page 117) or action sheet (page 169), an alert interrupts the flow and demands attention. That's why they're also called *modal alerts*. Until you specifically dismiss the alert, you can't continue using the app—which means the alert better be worth it.

Three different uses of alert boxes. The app can't go (left): Stitcher is an app for streaming Internet radio and appropriately displays an alert when you request local stations outside of its supported area. Suggest a workaround (middle): the Settings app offers a way around an email problem. Ask permission (right): the iPhone checks to make sure it's okay before sharing your location with an app.

Don't use modal alerts lightly. Alerts are for urgent information and using them for mundane announcements is like calling 911 to ask for the time. Don't cry wolf: trivial messages train people to ignore alerts and tap through them. When something truly important happens, your alert may go unnoticed as a result. Here are some appropriate uses for alerts:

- **The app can't go.** When something is very wrong, or when conditions prevent the app from working at all, show an alert. If your location-based app doesn't work in the current country, for example, or if there's not enough data available to perform an action, an alert is the place to say why. In general, avoid using alerts for more transient issues like a flaky network connection.

Instead, limit alerts to more fundamental problems that prevent the app or feature from working, period.

- **A little help here?** An alert is the right place for an app to ask for assistance if it can't complete a requested task. If airplane mode is turned on when you ask to download data, for example, an alert offers to take you to the Settings app to turn it off. The best alerts suggest a workaround when there's a problem: *this isn't working; want to try another way?* You do this by adding buttons to the alert box, typically just two of them: 1) a default button to dismiss the alert and cancel the action, and 2) a button to trigger the alternate action. Avoid crowding more than two buttons into an alert; if you need additional options, an action sheet is usually more appropriate.

- **Permission please.** Use an alert box to check before doing something the user might not be aware of—and could regret. Protecting privacy is a common example: the iPhone OS, for example, asks for permission before allowing an app to share your location. You should likewise do the same if your app wants to soak up other personal info behind the scenes, like contacts or events. If an action may have a consequence that your user doesn't anticipate, you should also ask for permission. In Safari, for example, clicking the Back button to a page that will resubmit a form triggers an alert to let you know and ask if it's okay to go ahead.

There's a subtle difference between this style of asking for permission and confirmation messages of the "do you really want to delete that?" flavor. Use alerts for events and warnings that your audience probably didn't see coming—conditions that are not a direct result of their own actions. Think of alerts as interruptions that break into the flow of normal events to announce unexpected breaking news. Confirmation messages, on the other hand, are the direct result of a specific request. You should instead handle those with action sheets, as described on page 170.

Alas, alerts are easy for developers to code—easier than coding an entire screen, at least—and we all love easy. The irresistible appeal of the lazy way out makes alerts all too common for relatively unimportant messages. Here are some uses to resist:

- **Don't use an alert as a welcome screen.** As you learned in Chapter 7, it's always great to roll out the welcome wagon for first-timers, but introductory tips and instructions are best accomplished with a purpose-built welcome screen, not an alert. The subtext of an alert is "something's wrong"—not a great vibe to strike on an app's first launch.

- **Don't ask for an App Store rating.** Some apps pop up an alert box at occasional intervals to encourage you to rate the app on the App Store. Hey, we've all gotta make a buck, but interrupting me to ask for some stroking is neither welcome nor polite. Always keep the focus on the user's goals and tasks—don't make it about you. If you're determined to include an App Store link, tuck it away in an "About Us" screen in the app's settings.

- **Don't use alerts for fleeting foibles.** Avoid sounding the alarm for passing problems like flaky network connections or a missing GPS signal. While you shouldn't stay quiet about these issues, alerts aren't the way to go. Instead, find other opportunities in the interface to indicate trouble instead of the full-throated shout of an alert box. The Twitter app, for example, briefly flashes an error message instead of using an alert that would require a tap to dismiss. (Bad networks, cloudy days, and just plain bad luck do occur—and frequently—in the chaotic and variable environments of your mobile app. Be sure to test your app under lousy conditions, including airplane mode, to make sure that it handles problems gracefully.)

Remain Calm and Carry On

Always use your quiet voice. Alerts let people know something's not right, but they should also reassure, and the best way to do that is to use language that is calm, crisp, and descriptive. That goes for all the copywriting in your app, but it's doubly important to keep a cool demeanor in alerts. (You already know, right, that exclamation marks and all-caps text make you seem a little hysterical?) Take a breath. Fashion your alert messages with care, describing the situation clearly, directly, and with just enough information that people understand their options where appropriate.

Alerts are composed of three elements: title, message text, and buttons. Take care not to repeat yourself in those elements or waste space with instructions that are obvious from context ("tap the Settings button to change your settings"). You can often strike the message text completely, relying only on the alert's title to deliver the message, with button labels giving enough context to decide which button to tap. A common approach for that is to make the message title a question, with buttons as the answers. Message text or no, just keep it short. You'll start to lose people with more than a sentence or two—or worse, long messages get clipped and require scrolling. Balance your brevity with clarity, though, and avoid blandly nondescript titles like "Error."

Just because alert messages should themselves be short, that doesn't mean you can't use them to offer a fast track to more information. User experience guru Kathy Sierra often advocates the use of a *WTF?!? button,* a panic button that you offer when things aren't working the way your audience might expect or understand—the same context as an alert box. A WTF button reassures people that they're not dumb, acknowledges that they've entered a trouble zone, and offers a way to get further help or explanation. Our friend Emily Post might question the etiquette of slapping the WTF label on a button, and of course you should, too. WTF describes your audience's state of mind, not the actual text you should use. "Help," "More Info," or "What Now?" are all good options for moments when you anticipate people might have a WTF moment.

The game Eliminate Pro actually *does* include a WTF button on some screens to explain some of the app's more esoteric settings. (The game's developers coyly suggest WTF stands for "where to find it.")

Whatever buttons you include in an alert, be careful choosing not only their text labels, but also their placement and color, which together hint at the app's recommended option—the *default button*. Alert buttons come in two shades, light or dark, and the default button should always be light-colored, appearing at the right side of a two-button alert. For these two-button ditties, favor active verbs like Cancel, View, or Allow. (In single-button alerts, the button typically signals acceptance; OK is the standard label there, and it's always light-colored.)

For an alert warning about a potentially risky or destructive action, the Cancel button should be the default. For an alert suggesting a harmless recommended action, that action's button should be the default, and Cancel should take the back seat, over to the left. Alert messages should be calm and collected, and that means their default buttons should always favor the safest path.

Pushy Notifications

A *notification* is the alert's pushy cousin. With your permission, an app can nudge messages onto your screen even when the app isn't front and center on the device. Text messages, calendar alarms, and voicemail alerts are familiar examples of the boldest form of notification: an alert box that pops up to exclaim its message, interrupting whatever you might be doing on the phone. (Notifications can also take the quieter form of *badges*, a topic you'll explore in a moment.) At their best,

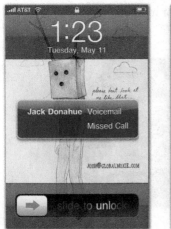

The Phone app (left) triggers a notification when you've missed a call or received a voicemail. At your request, the Umbrella app (right) can notify you when it's going to rain today.

notifications deliver important information in real time—flight changes, news headlines, sports scores, to-do list reminders, instant-message alerts, and so on. If your app deals with personally urgent and time-sensitive information, offering notifications can be a truly helpful way to keep your audience up to date on events that matter most to them.

Thing is, notification alerts always arrive in the same abrupt manner, no matter how urgent or mundane the message. Just like a regular alert box, every notification briefly takes over your phone, blocking your current task until you dismiss the message. If a notification arrives during a phone call, you can't even hang up until you dismiss it. Some notifications come with sound and vibration, too. The effect is like talking to someone who shouts everything they say without discrimination. There's no way for apps to "whisper" a notification; every message arrives as a noisy interruption. It's one of the few false notes in the otherwise elegant iPhone OS.

Since notifications always shout, good etiquette at least requires some discerning choices about when you choose to send them. A potentially useful service becomes irritating and then outright rude when it spams people with more messages than they want. Spew too much, and people will shut you down. Push notifications for individual apps can be turned off in the built-in Settings app, but it's just as common for people to delete a chatty app outright. Software engineer and back-pocket iPhone user Michael "Rands" Lopp summed it up via Twitter:

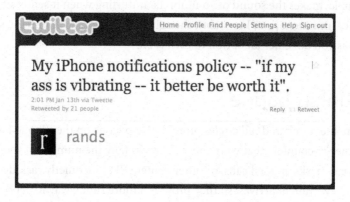

The dilemma is that one person's trickle is another person's fire hose. It's tough, even impossible, to adjust the notification flow to a rate that will please everyone.

You have to leave it up to individual users. If you choose to offer notification alerts, always give people options to fine-tune the timing and content:

- **Offer detailed content control.** Let people specify exactly what kinds of notifications they receive. Social networking apps should let people "subscribe" to notifications from a special few. Sports apps should send scores only for requested teams or even specific games.

FlightTrack Pro (left) tracks flight departures, arrivals, and delays, but lets you turn notifications on for individual flights while tracking others more passively. Similarly, social networking app Gowalla (right) lets you choose the friends whose status updates you want to receive.

- **Establish "quiet hours."** Don't bleep and bloop notifications to your audience in the middle of the night unless they specifically ask for it. Boxcar, for example, is an app that sends notifications about activity in your Twitter, Facebook, and email accounts. To prevent your night-owl pals from waking you up when they tweet, the app lets you turn off alerts during specific hours.

- **Make sound optional.** Notifications can include custom sounds, a clever way to add a little extra personality to the notification. Weather app Umbrella, for example, makes the sound of an umbrella unfurling when it sends a notification of imminent rain. Inevitably, though, not everyone will find the sound as cute as you do. Offer an option to turn it off.

No Stinkin' Badges

Badges are the numbered red circles pinned to app icons on the iPhone Home screen. They're counters that your app displays to tally the number of waiting messages, tasks, missed calls, or other content. Badges quietly rack up their counts as new content arrives, so they provide a more subtle way to get people's attention than notification alerts. Unfortunately, they're also more ambiguous. All those little numbers sprinkled on your apps mean *something*, but what exactly?

A *stinkin' badge* is a badge that misreports its tally of new content, either showing a count for content you've already seen or double-dipping by counting certain content twice. Not all badges stink, but there are enough stinkin' badges in circulation that their overall use is compromised. Apple itself contributes to this problem with its own built-in apps. The badge on the Messages app continues to count messages even after you've read them as notification alerts upon arrival. The Phone app is even worse: when a caller leaves a voicemail message, the app's badge tallies the call twice, once for the missed call and another for the voicemail message. Even after you listen to the voicemail, the badge continues to show the count for the missed call until you specifically visit the app's Recents screen. The result is that you're often left unsure about whether there's anything behind the red-flag badges on your apps. The badges lose meaning.

The Phone app lights up its badge with "2" for a single missed call (left), once for a recent call and another for the voicemail (right). This miscount is not only misleading but obliges you to tap over to the Recents screen to clear the badge even after you've listened to the caller's voicemail message.

Other apps, like Mail, reliably get the count right, and their badges smell like roses. The principle is simple—don't double-count—but the implementation isn't always so easy. Unfortunately, apps that display notifications as alerts can't always be sure that people have seen every alert, and so they increment the badge for every item, just to be safe. The better course of action is simply to offer just one or the other, badges or alerts, but not both at the same time. If you can't offer reliable counts in your badges, don't bother with them at all. We don't need no stinkin' badges.

If you do offer badges, though, offer the option to turn them off. Even when they're trustworthy, badges come with a disquieting cognitive burden: this app has 13 widgets waiting for you, that one has 18 messages, and this other one has 23 whatzits. Instead of being helpful, these tallies sometimes overwhelm, creating the anxious incentive to bring the badges down to zero, even for content that doesn't demand priority attention. The life goal of thinking people typically consists of more than cycling through apps to mark things read, but a bevy of badges sometimes leads us to think otherwise. Let people opt out of the number game; it's not always a service.

Despite the mixed benefits of badges, they do underscore the value of *passive messaging*. Unlike active messages like alerts, badges deliver their message in hushed tones, letting you know that content is accumulating without interrupting you to say so. With apps, as with people, a healthy sense of humility is a big part of good manners, and polite apps do most of their work quietly without drawing undue attention to themselves. To be sure, there's an appropriate role for bold statements through alerts and notifications, but passive messaging tends to be more reliably helpful, providing real-time commentary on the app's status without getting in the way of what your audience is trying to do.

Yep, I'm Working on It

Tapworthy apps make savvy use of passive messaging to provide reassuring feedback. As you saw in Chapter 8, a visual response to every touch gives your audience confidence that their gestures have been registered and that work is underway. This is especially important for tasks that may take a few moments to complete. Simple, understated status indicators stave off the dreaded "Is this thing on?" syndrome, a condition characterized by symptoms of manic thumping on the touchscreen, wild-eyed puzzlement, and frustrated sighs. Things don't always happen as quickly as we'd like, and when an app is working on something, it should say so.

The *spinner* is the all-purpose sign for "I'm working on it." Also called an *activity indicator* in iPhone geekspeak, this spinning gear is the standard way to show that something's humming under the hood. Because give and take over the network is the most frequent cause of delay, there's a special place reserved for the *network spinner* in the status bar to indicate network activity. Behind the scenes, developers flip a simple switch in their code to turn that spinner on and off, and it just shows up automatically. It's easy to implement, and the spinner is understood even by newcomers. When your app communicates online for more than a beat, show that network spinner in the status bar.

The iPhone also provides a larger spinner to use outside the status bar, and you should lean on it for any task that will take a second or more, adding a brief text label where appropriate to say exactly what the app is up to. When your app is working on a task in direct response to a user request, it's worth including the big pinwheel even for network-related tasks that already show the (relatively subtle) network spinner. When someone asks your app to do something, leave no doubt that it's working on delivering. While toolbars and overlays are natural places for spinners to announce work is underway, spinners are also useful placeholders for content that's still loading. Drop a spinner (along with a "Loading" label) into a screen whose content hasn't arrived yet, or show a spinner in place of pictures that are still on the way.

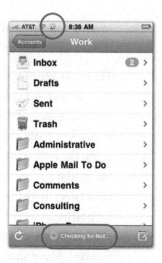

The network spinner should appear in the status bar anytime an app goes online, as shown here in the Mail app. Mail also uses the large spinner in its toolbar when checking mail.

Not only does a spinner say that the app's at work, but it also passively suggests when the app's work is done, too. Make the spinner disappear, and your audience immediately understands that the task is complete, no extra confirmation message required. The Reeder app neatly demonstrates this when you add one of its articles to Instapaper, the online service for saving articles to read later. The app adds an overlay with a spinner during the few moments while it talks to Instapaper. When the spinner disappears, it's clear that the action is complete. Other apps that send content to Instapaper instead display an alert box as confirmation, but that's overkill and also requires an extra tap to dismiss the alert box. Once again: use alerts only when something goes wrong, not when everything is going according to plan. Here, the passive confirmation of a disappearing spinner gets the job done in a more streamlined and effortless way. Other animations can provide similar confirmation in place of an alert. In Mail, for example, deleting a message sucks it into the trash can icon and

When Reeder sends an article to Instapaper it briefly displays a spinner, which disappears when the works is done, no confirmation message required.

moving a message to a folder sends an envelope flying into that folder. The animation says it all, no alert necessary.

The crafty use of toolbar buttons offers another understated way to say that work is underway. A *modal button* is a button that changes its appearance depending on the state of the app and what the user is up to. Twitterrific, for example, changes its toolbar's Refresh button to a Stop button while it's fetching new messages; the button returns to a Refresh button when the work is done. You can also use modal buttons to indicate changing options as people use the app. When you tap a tweet in Twitterrific to select it, for example, the app's speech-bubble button for posting a new tweet changes into a Reply button, and the dimmed asterisk-shaped Action icon lights up to signal that options are available for the selected message. Savvy shape-shifting in the app's controls provides another form of passive messaging to help the app quietly provide feedback and cues.

Twitterrific uses modal buttons in its toolbar to signal changes in the environment and available options. The left screenshot shows the toolbar in its standard state. The right screenshot shows the app loading new tweets (the Refresh button is now a Stop button), and there's also a tweet selected, triggering the appearance of the Reply and asterisk-shaped Action button.

Spinners and modal buttons can satisfy and reassure users that something's happening, but only for a few moments. As those moments stretch into seconds or, heaven forbid, minutes, doubts spring up. You start to wonder if that gear will *ever* stop spinning and, if so . . . how . . . much . . . longer? When something's going to take a while, polite apps let their audience know. To do that, you have to move beyond the spinner.

Bending Time: Progress Bars and Other Distractions

It doesn't take an Einstein to realize that time is relative (file under "time flies when you're having fun.") Stuff happens faster or slower depending on the environment, distractions at hand, and the tedium of the task. As your app's interface designer, you happen to have control over all three. The choices you make and messages you convey affect the perceived time that it takes your app to complete its tasks. No matter how long something might actually take, all that really matters is how fast it *feels*. You've already seen how clever use of your app's launch image can make load times seem shorter (page 223). Other interface sleight-of-hand tricks enable similar illusions for bending time through good communication, misdirection, and outright distraction.

Never underestimate the power of the homely *progress bar*. This tried-and-true interface control displays a bar that fills from left to right as a task proceeds, providing a visual guesstimate for how much time remains. (Many apps supplement a progress bar by counting down the estimated time remaining, too.) You might think that this kind of clock-watching would just make the whole operation seem even longer by drawing undue attention to the remaining time. On the contrary, studies show that people say a process finishes faster when accompanied by a progress bar than without, even when both take exactly the same amount of time. On-hold telephone services, take-a-number deli counters, and package-tracking delivery companies all reveal the same lesson: it's powerfully calming simply to know how much longer you have to wait.

For processes that last more than a few seconds, you should offer a hint, if you can, about how soon the task will finish. Progress bars are ideal for that, and the iPhone's set of standard controls include two styles of progress bars: a skinny one that squeezes into the toolbar, and a fatter one to use elsewhere in your layout. If you're feeling more adventurous, design your own progress indicator, like the filling circle used by Shazam, the song identification app. All of these indicators provide reassurance not only that work is being done but also a visualization of honest-to-god progress being made.

Mail (left) uses a standard progress bar to show how much time remains for sending a message. Shazam (right) uses a custom progress indicator to count down the remaining time it needs to identify a song.

For a very long process, consider whether you might offer your audience something to do or read while they wait. 37signals Highrise is a companion iPhone app to a web service that manages your contacts, conversations, and meetings. Trouble is, when you launch the app for the very first time, it has to sync with your online account; if you have a lot of data to download, it takes a while, not exactly an inspiring welcome to the app. "One of the downsides to the initial download is that it can take some time depending on your connection and the number of contacts you have," admits Alex Bridges of 37signals. "Waiting for anything sucks, but what sucks more is being bored while waiting. So we decided to give you something to do while the initial download is in progress. You can play tic-tac-toe while you wait." And indeed, while a progress bar inches along the bottom of the screen, you can sling Xs and Os to pass the time.

Clever diversions don't have to be games; consider what you have in your arsenal to distract your audience during very long waits. Personal stats, relevant articles, tips for using the app—any of these things can help pass the time. As you learned back in Chapter 2, the best boredom busters give people something to explore (page 37).

Of course, the very best way to make things seem faster is to make them *actually* faster. Stuff takes as long as it takes, sure, but planning ahead lets you stockpile content so that you have it on hand when your audience asks for it. After loading a news-feed screen, for example, the Facebook app goes ahead and fetches

37signals Highrise distracts with a game or three of tic-tac-toe during its initial data download.

the next level of content. "I wanted people to have the satisfaction of being able to act immediately on the items in the feed without having to wait for new things to stream over the network," says Facebook developer Joe Hewitt. "If you want to read the comments on a post, for example, the first few comments are all preloaded, so you can tap right through to them without having to wait at all."

No matter what, you should give people *something* whenever possible—even stale info—instead of serving them a blank screen and making them wait for more. (When you're in the dentist's waiting room, it's better to have last year's *Life* magazine than nothing at all.) As you saw on page 226, saving the content or data from the last session creates an impression of fast app launching; for networked apps, it has the additional benefit of allowing you to show the last batch of downloaded content even if there's no network connection. The illusion of suspended animation isn't just about speed, it's also good manners. Emily Post would tell you that in polite company, one never lets a guest go hungry.

Touchpoints

✓ Use alerts only for urgent events when the app can't go, or when the app needs permission to proceed.

✓ Use calm, descriptive language in alert messages. Consider a WTF button to offer help and information when something's gone wrong.

✓ Default buttons in alert boxes should always favor the safest option.

✓ Notifications always "shout" their message; let people choose exactly when and what to receive.

✓ Avoid stinkin' badges that provide misleading tallies.

✓ Use spinners or modal buttons to reassure your audience that the app is hard at work.

✓ Use progress bars, diversions, and preloaded content to make your app seem faster.

11

Howdy, Neighbor

PLAYING NICE WITH OTHER APPS

"GOOD FENCES MAKE GOOD NEIGHBORS," poet Robert Frost tells us. According to Apple, good fences make good apps, too. The sentiment is baked deep into the iPhone OS, which purposely makes it all but impossible for apps to peek into each other's affairs. Every app is safely walled off in its own plot, where other apps can't touch its data, can't meddle with account information, can't talk back and forth in an intimate way. Every app is more or less isolated.

There are benefits to the iPhone's mind-your-own-business culture: the overall system is more stable, a bad-seed app can't rifle through private info, and the arrangement promotes the useful habit for both developer and consumer to focus on just one task at a time. But fences also make us travel a long way to go what would otherwise be a short distance. Exchanging documents between apps is often a round-about hassle of syncing to a PC or network, and reusing the data you create in one app means a slow slog of copying and pasting into another.

Photo: Peter Morgan

Walls block useful collaboration among apps, and that's hardly neighborly. Even Robert Frost agrees. In the very same "good fences make good neighbors" poem, he writes:

Before I built a wall I'd ask to know
What I was walling in or walling out,
And to whom I was like to give offence.

Something there is that doesn't love a wall,
That wants it down.

Mr. App Designer, tear down this wall. Many of these fences are too sturdy to overcome completely, but tapworthy apps make an effort to be sociable nevertheless. This chapter explores ways to throw information over the walls between apps as well as strategies for making transitions between apps less labored (and sometimes even unnecessary). Before you start vaulting fences, though, first take a look at the places where the fences have already been pulled down.

Public Square: Contacts, Photos, and Events

While the iPhone locks up most information in a private vault for each app, a handful of built-in apps share their info, creating a few public spaces in a neighborhood that's otherwise blocked by walls and fences. Any app has permission to read, add, or edit this shared info: contacts, photos, and (starting in iPhone OS 4.0) calendar events. Apps can also access the user's systemwide preferences, the things you select in the Settings app. Apps that embrace these public archives save headaches for both developers and users.

The iPhone SDK provides prefab screens for browsing contacts and photos, and you can drop those layouts right into your app. Shown here: the standard *people picker* (left) and the two modes of the built-in *image picker,* which lets you take a photo (middle) or choose one from the photo library (right).

For your audience, there's calm confidence in knowing that there's a single master collection of contacts (or photos or events). It creates a trustworthy system: no matter what app you might use to edit contact info, there's comfort knowing that it winds up in "The Master List." People strongly associate those collections with their respective built-in apps—Contacts, Photos, and Calendar—but context makes it immediately obvious when other apps are working with this same familiar content. Apps may provide different windows into this information, but it's reassuring when those windows always look out onto the same view.

By contrast, when information is tucked away into separate pockets, we're burdened with remembering exactly where to find it and how one pocket differs from the rest. Don't keep your own separate stash of contacts, photos, or events. If your app deals even tangentially with people, images, or time, consider how the app might interact with these shared collections instead of keeping the information to itself. A happy side effect is that this approach saves development time, too. Subscribe and contribute to these common data stores, and you don't have to build your own. Some suggestions for putting this shared content to good use:

- **Browsing beats typing.** If your app asks your audience to provide names, addresses, phone numbers, or email, offer the option to grab that info from

Personal journal Momento lets you "tag" entries with people's names by tapping the Contact icon (left). To speed the process, the app pitches in by suggesting names from your contacts as you type (middle), or by letting you browse the whole list (right) by tapping the green + button.

contacts. No matter how much one masters the iPhone keyboard, the swipe-swipe-tap of selecting from a ready list is always faster.

- **Tap into personal info.** People, events, and images together provide a surprisingly complete picture of who we are and what we do. If your app tracks personal information of any kind, consider how you might integrate this shared info, too. Exercise journals might offer the option to stash your workout history in the calendar, for example, or add a photo of the sunset from today's run.

- **Add to the mix.** Help your audience build their collection of personal info by making it easy to save (or optionally export) appropriate data to the address book, calendar, or photo library. If your app spins out drawings, charts, photos, or other images, make it easy to save those to the photo library. If your app manages time-based info, let people hustle that info into their calendar as an event or alarm.

- **Extend existing info.** For apps that brush up against even small tidbits of info about people or events, offer to use that info to create a new record or bolster one that already exists. The Twitter app, for example, assumes many people in your Twitter stream are likely to be friends, family, and colleagues—people you consider contacts—and lets you add Twitter-specific info to the address book. Always consider how your app fits into your audience's larger world and how the app's data can enhance knowledge and info outside the app itself.

With just two taps, the Twitter app lets you add a Twitter contact to your address book or supplement an existing contact. From a Twitter account's profile screen (left), tap the contact-card button, and the next screen (right) shows you the info that will be added (a Twitter URL and a biographical note), letting you decide whether to create a new contact or add the info to an existing entry. Once linked to the address book, you can see the person's complete contact info anytime from their Twitter profile screen.

It would be handy if you could arrange data mixers like this for other kinds of info, too, inviting any and all apps to build mash-ups with your own app's data, for example. Alas, the iPhone is not that kind of party. You can get crazy with contacts, photos, and events, but your exchanges with other apps have to be more limited. Even so, there are opportunities to get at least a little bit cozier with certain apps by sending work their way and letting them know that you'll accept the same.

Tag, You're It: Passing Control to Other Apps

We're accustomed to feature-packed desktop apps—mutant word processors that are also page-layout programs, image editors, and creators of zany "word art." The history of consumer computing is, by and large, a story of ever more complex applications sprouting longer and longer feature lists. Mobile apps present a hard turn in that trend. They work with limited hardware resources, limited screen space, and perhaps most important, limited user attention. As you've seen since the first pages of this book, tapworthy apps necessarily develop an expert focus on a narrow slice of user wants and needs. In place of the all-in-one apps you find on the desktop, iPhones are packed with special-purpose apps that people juggle in various combinations to get stuff done. Friends, it takes a village.

A very smart man named David Weinberger describes the World Wide Web as a set of "small pieces loosely joined," a democratic collection of independent documents strung together by links. The same is true on the iPhone, where we have small *apps* loosely joined. Like web pages, it turns out that apps can also link to each other, passing tiny morsels of information along the way in the same way that web links can include Google search terms or an Amazon product id.

In fact, behind the scenes, apps use special URLs to pass control to other apps, and they happen to look very similar to familiar web URLs. To launch the Phone app and call a number, for example, a programmer tells the iPhone to "go" to a URL like *tel://1-800-555-1212*. The current app quits, the Phone app fires up, and the number gets dialed. iPhone users see this all the time: apps launch web pages in Safari, zoom to a specific location in Maps, or fire up a pre-addressed SMS message. In all of these cases, there are URLs at work under the hood telling the iPhone, "Launch this app and give it this message," where the message is a web link, a street address, or a phone number. It's a limited system, though, and you can't send along lots of info, just a snippet of text. But it's simple and effective, letting you pass control to another app so that people can take advantage of that app's special talents. (URLs can't pass whole documents back and forth, but starting in iPhone OS 4.0, apps have another way to do that. This is done through the built-in document preview system—the *document interaction controller*—used by apps like Mail to let you read received documents. When previewing a document, apps can offer an "Open In…" option to let people open it in another app.)

Be generous. Linking to other apps makes it easy for your audience to take full advantage of your own app by spinning off its data for in-depth exploration elsewhere. Let your app focus on what it does best and make referrals to other apps for the rest. If another app can do something better, or if it handles a task that complements your app, pass the baton. Teaming up is good for everyone.

You're not limited to linking only to Apple's built-in apps, either. Any app can accept links (including yours). To do it, all a developer has to do behind the scenes is claim a URL protocol for an app. Here's a quick overview: a URL protocol is the *http* portion of a web address, for example. When an app requests a URL using that protocol, the iPhone automatically launches the associated app and passes along the URL info. Twitterrific, for example, registered the protocol *twitterrific*, so that any app can launch Twitterrific and start a new tweet by requesting a URL like this: *twitterrific:///post?message=Hello.* (For nitty-gritty details on how custom URL schemes work, developers can check out the iPhone Application Programming Guide at *http://developer.apple.com/iphone.*)

Neat, right? Here's the thing: other app developers have to know about the app and its link format in order to use it. So, speaking of being neighborly, that means you've got to pick up the phone or dash off an email and actually get to know the people who make other apps. Explain how linking to your app can help their own audience and how to do it. Your to-do list app, for example, could accept links that create new tasks, letting other apps specify the task title and due date. Twitter apps, in particular, have been especially industrious about getting the word out about their custom links: lots of apps let you choose a preferred Twitter app and, when you want to tweet a message, send you over with a snippet of suggested text to edit in the comfort of your favorite app.

The Cocktails+ app links to the Twitter app of your choice to announce your potent potable. After choosing your preferred Twitter app (left), you can tap "Share via Twitter" from a recipe page, and the app launches the other app (Twitterrific, right) with some suggested tweet text.

All this linking is great for your audience, unless it takes them by surprise. It's irritating to be dumped out of one app and launched into another when you're not expecting it. A particularly common sin is offering a seemingly innocuous help button that bumps you unannounced to a web page in Safari. (In that case, at the very least, apps should throw up an alert to warn that you're about to leave the app and ask if you really want to do it.) As always, the context sets expectations. Passing control to another app is ideal when an app's primary task is complete and the user is ready to tackle a follow-up task in another app without looking back. Linking out works best as an endpoint.

On the other hand, frequent tasks that always happen in the *middle* of your app's typical workflow are lousy candidates for linking to other apps. Frequent switching with another app during the same session almost certainly highlights a feature that you should build into the app itself. If you don't, you'll slowly melt people's brains as they tediously and repeatedly switch back and forth between apps to get this one thing done. Staying inside your app's fences is sometimes the best option, and that's the topic of the next section.

Roll Your Own: Browsers, Maps, and Email

As you've seen, your app's talents should reflect an undistracted focus on its primary task, and you should bring a jaded eye to feature-creep additions that aren't strictly necessary to that mission. But don't allow tunnel vision to blind you to secondary features that are such natural extensions of your app's main gig that their absence grates. The usual suspects here are browsing the web, exploring maps, and sending email. When roundtrips to Safari, Maps, and Mail begin to pile up, it's best to bring those features in-house.

The main mission of a Twitter app, for example, is to let you read and post status updates, but those tasks don't alone describe the primary *motivation* for using Twitter. People use Twitter to keep up with and share what's happening, and that news often comes in the form of a web link. Browsing the web is an essential secondary task for browsing a Twitter stream, and launching Safari for every link would simply make a Twitter app feel broken. Similarly, the main job for apps that help you find nearby restaurants or drinking holes is to show you their names, addresses, and perhaps some brief descriptions or reviews. But the inevitable follow-on task is to *see* the best candidates on a map, or to email the info to friends you plan to meet there. In all of these scenarios, the secondary tasks are important and frequent enough that you shouldn't link to other apps for them. Instead, trigger a new screen or modal view within your app to handle browsing, mapping, or mailing.

The good news is that the iPhone's code toolkit makes it relatively painless for developers to add lightweight web, map, and email features to your app. Here are the building blocks:

- *Web views* are the web-savvy wonders you met on page 160, windows on the web that allow you to drop a browser right into your app.

- *Map views* let you embed full-featured maps into any screen. Just like the built-in Maps app, map views let your audience zoom and scroll through the world, and you can mark them up with pins, highlighted regions, route directions—the whole shebang.

- *Mail compose views* offer the familiar screen for writing a new email message. Unlike web views and map views, these guys don't let you do anything to dress them up or fidget with the interface. The screen comes as-is, a reassuring standard interface that looks just like the Mail app. The screen is typically displayed as a modal view, sliding up from the bottom of the screen. To save typing, it's good practice to offer some starter text in the subject and body of the message, including the link, address, movie listing, file attachment, or whatever you're helping people share.

The Twitter app includes a simple in-app browser that lets you check out web links without jumping to Safari. The browser includes only limited controls: Back, Forward, Refresh, and Action buttons.

Home brew can be weak broth, though. Web views and map views give developers the raw materials to build a web browser or map feature, but they don't come with the full-blown controls that you get with Safari or Maps. A web view, for example, doesn't include bookmarks, back/forward buttons, search bar, address bar, or any of the familiar controls you expect from a "real" web browser. If you want those, you have to build them yourself, but it's usually just fine to do without. Apart from adding back/forward buttons to a web view to enable very basic navigation, you should typically stick to the basic goal of offering just a quick glimpse at the requested content. Ditto for maps: don't feel obliged to create a full set of tools for search and getting directions—your job here usually stops at showing a simple location.

You certainly *can* do more. The iPhone's WebKit and MapKit frameworks give developers everything they need to build a full-fledged browser or mapping app, and it can be as complex as you like. Adding advanced features may make sense if web and location-based activities are your app's main mission. When it's a secondary add-on, though, keep it very simple. Give your audience the bare minimum to get what they need. For more than that, let your neighborly instinct return: your simple web browser should offer the option to open the page in Safari, and your home-grown map should likewise let people view the location in Maps.

In Gowalla, when you find a "spot" that you want to visit (left), tapping "Details & Map" takes you to a screen with a map view showing the location (middle). For directions and other fancy features, the screen offers a Get Directions button, which passes you over to the Maps app (right).

You naturally focus (perhaps obsessively) on the details of your own app, and you're right to polish and shine every last feature. At the same time, be mindful of neighboring apps that are just a tap away and consider how your app might collaborate with them. Your job as an app designer is to make your audience's lives easier, more fun, more productive—and part of that is understanding how your app might fit in with the other tasks the iPhone handles. Find new ways to fill the cracks other apps don't address, or be bold enough to create an entirely new category of your own. Be creative!

Happy Trails, Neighbor

As an iPhone app designer, you've got a fun and fascinating journey ahead—and make no mistake, you're very much a trailblazer. The iPhone and its smart-phone cousins have introduced an entirely new form of personal computing, and we're in only the earliest days of understanding its possibilities. Fresh magic is minted on the iPhone every day, and your tapworthy app can be part of that new science, too.

Push boundaries and test limits—be bold—but don't leave your audience behind. Lead us by the hand. Strive to create humane designs that are at once effortless and delightful. The goal of this book was to establish common-sense principles for doing just that, and I hope you've found these guidelines useful. Just remember, they're only that—guidelines. Great design is as often about bending rules as following them. Bend away, and have courage in your vision, but always keep your audience's wants and needs in focus.

You have the coolest job in the world: you're designing an iPhone app, inventing the future. Go make something amazing.

Touchpoints

✓ Don't squirrel away your own archive of contacts, events, or images. Use the systemwide address book, calendar, and photo library.

✓ Offer to add or extend existing contact and event records.

✓ Be generous about linking to other apps for secondary tasks, and let your app accept links, too.

✓ Too much app switching melts brains. Linking to other apps works best as an endpoint, not mid-task.

✓ Take a "just enough" approach to web views and map views, letting people jump to Safari and Maps for more advanced features.